Maneuvers with Circles

Teacher Sourcebook

David A. Page
Kathryn Chval

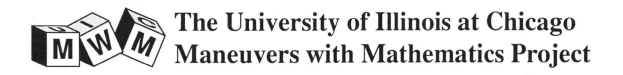

**The University of Illinois at Chicago
Maneuvers with Mathematics Project**

DALE SEYMOUR PUBLICATIONS

Other UIC-MWM Books
Maneuvers with Rectangles
Maneuvers with Angles
Maneuvers with Triangles
Maneuvers with Nickels and Numbers

The Maneuvers with Mathematics Project materials were
prepared with the support of National Science Foundation
Grant Nos. MDR-8850466 and MDR-9154110. Any
opinions, findings, conclusions, or recommendations
expressed in this publication are those of the authors and
do not necessarily represent the views of the National
Science Foundation. These materials shall be subject to a
royalty-free, irrevocable, worldwide, nonexclusive
license in the United States Government to reproduce,
perform, translate, and otherwise use and to authorize
others to use such materials for Government purposes.

Order number DS21330
ISBN 0-86651-821-5

1 2 3 4 5 6 7 8 9 10-MA-98 97 96 95 94

This Book Is Printed
on Recycled Paper

Contents

Essential contributions to UIC-MWM were made by:

John Baldwin
Roberta Dees
Steven Jordan

Janice Banasiak
Marty Gartzman
Olga Granat-Gonzalez
Michael Jankowski
Jennifer Lynná Mundt
Marlynne Nishimura
Pamela Piggeé
Jerome Pohlen
Mary Jo Porn
Mary Ann Schultz
Aimee W. Strawn

Production Assistants:

Lindy M. Chambers
Kimberly Hanus
Tanya Henderson
Tracy Ho
Alex Mak

Stacie McCloud
Erik Merkau
Olga Vega
Wendy Wisneski

Artists:

Lisa Fucarino
Alex Mak

The University of Illinois-Maneuvers with Mathematics (UIC-MWM) project started in July 1989 under the direction of David A. Page and Philip Wagreich of UIC. Earlier versions were tested in the following schools in Illinois:

Louis J. Agassiz Elementary School, Chicago
Albright Middle School, Villa Park
Caroline Bentley School, New Lenox
Daniel Boone Elementary School, Chicago
Carpenter School, Park Ridge
Central Jr. High School, Tinley Park
Christ the King School, Lombard
Walt Disney Magnet School, Chicago
Richard Edwards Elementary School, Chicago
Eugene Field Elementary School, Park Ridge
John Hope Community Academy, Chicago
Andrew Jackson Language Academy, Chicago
John L. Marsh Elementary School, Chicago
Our Lady of Victory School, Chicago
John Palmer School, Chicago
W. C. Petty School, Antioch
Pilsen Community Academy, Chicago
Philip Rogers School, Chicago
St. Germaine School, Oak Lawn
St. Joseph School, Chicago
St. Michael the Archangel School, Chicago
St. Stephen Protomartyr School, Des Plaines
Mark Sheridan Math & Science Academy, Chicago
Wendell Smith Elementary School, Chicago
John M. Smyth Elementary School, Chicago
Washington Elementary School, Park Ridge

Preface

For many years, teachers have been urged to use calculators in their mathematics instruction. Unfortunately, there have been few instructional materials that make effective use of this new technology. UIC-MWM materials fill some of that void. In creating our lessons, we have tried to develop good mathematics problems that make integral use of the calculator as an instructional tool.

Though calculators are used extensively in the lessons, use of the calculator is not an end in itself. The calculator has allowed us to develop challenging, multi-step problems that previously were accessible only to a relatively small group of mathematically-talented students. Our goal is to get all students involved in good mathematical problem solving. Through lessons like these, we will help put an end to any lingering doubts about the benefits (or dangers) of calculator use in math classes. Simply put, if schools want their students doing the problems found in *Maneuvers with Circles*, then calculators are a **requirement**.

UIC-MWM lessons generally stress topics that are ignored or inadequately covered in current textbooks. For example, many have a strong geometric flavor, partially because calculators liberate students from the complicated arithmetic that limited previous geometric study. Calculators also allow the use of several self-checking features that provide students with ongoing feedback telling them whether they are on the right track in solving a problem.

We have generated UIC-MWM materials so that they can be used in a variety of classroom environments. The lessons can be used in large group settings or in small cooperative groups. Each lesson has problems for novices and experts alike. There are many ways to stretch the lessons into larger investigations. You will find that the materials easily accommodate many different teaching and learning styles.

The mathematical content in UIC-MWM modules is richer than most current materials and is likely to be new to many teachers. As such, some teachers may feel more comfortable using the materials if they are accompanied by a staff development program. The Institute for Mathematics and Science Education at the University of Illinois at Chicago can assist schools in designing and/or presenting UIC-MWM staff development programs. Further information about UIC support services can be obtained by calling the Institute for Mathematics and Science Education at (312) 996-2448 or by writing to:

> UIC Institute for Mathematics and
>   Science Education (M/C 250)
> 840 West Taylor Street
> Chicago, IL 60607-7045

We would be remiss if we did not mention the strong institutional support that has contributed to the development of UIC-MWM materials. The development was generously supported by grants from the National Science Foundation. We also enjoyed the strong support and encouragement of the Department of Mathematics, Statistics, and Computer Science, the College of Liberal Arts and Science, the College of Education and the campus administration at UIC. The quality of the materials is also due, in large measure, to the assistance, suggestions, and feedback from many Chicago-area teachers who have worked with us throughout the materials development process. We are indebted to the staff of the MWM project, whose dedication and insight helped make this work a reality.

Finally, we wish to express our gratitude to Marty Gartzman, whose contributions to the conception of the project and the development of these materials have been, and continue to be, invaluable.

David A. Page
Kathryn Chval

Introduction

The Maneuvers with Mathematics (MWM) materials generate high interest among varied ability levels of students in the fifth through eighth grades. Students experiment, measure, and draw directly in the Student Lab Book. These hands-on activities help students gain a real understanding of mathematical concepts. Students apply these concepts as they solve multi-step problems. A coordinated sequence of multi-step problems is a hallmark of MWM. Many of the activities in the Student Lab Book encourage effective small-group interaction.

The goal of MWM is to replace or supplement units of current mathematics instruction with good calculator-based, problem-solving materials. MWM materials move teachers closer to the type of broad curriculum reform recommended in the *Curriculum and Evaluation Standards for School Mathematics* of the National Council of Teachers of Mathematics. The NCTM *Standards* encourages the use of calculators, mathematical reasoning, problem solving, communication about mathematics, and serious exploration of geometry and measurement. The *Standards* also encourages teachers to help students work together to make sense of mathematics and to help students rely on themselves to determine whether something is mathematically correct. According to the *Standards*, students must know and use appropriate methods of computation including estimation, mental computation, and the use of technology. These and other NCTM recommendations are incorporated throughout the Maneuvers with Mathematics materials.

Calculator Notes

Since the full-function (scientific) calculator will be new to many students, the use of specific functions is presented in the chapters as the need arises.

Important: Every student should have the same calculator. It should be a TI-30 SLR+™, TI-30 STAT™, TI-31™, or TI-30 Challenger™. **Note:** The TI-34™ calculator is not recommended for MWM materials because it has an "active equal sign," as shown in the following example.

Press	Window
5	5
×	5
2	2
=	10
=	20
=	40

Each time $\boxed{=}$ is pressed, the TI-34 performs the last operation on the number shown in the window.

Students must learn to press $\boxed{=}$ only once if they use calculators with an "active equal sign."

Order of Operations

Scientific calculators perform arithmetic operations in a mathematically correct order known as the *algebraic order of operations*. The standard order of operations follows.

- operations in parentheses (from inside out with nested parentheses)
- exponents, roots
- multiplication and division from left to right
- addition and subtraction from left to right

Most simple, four-function calculators do ***not*** follow order of operations. Instead, they do all operations from left to right. For example, subtract three 50° angles from 360°.

Press: $\boxed{360}$ $\boxed{-}$ $\boxed{50}$ $\boxed{×}$ $\boxed{3}$ $\boxed{=}$

A four-function calculator computes $360 - 50 \times 3 = 310 \times 3 = 930$, an incorrect answer. However, scientific calculators follow order of operations. First, multiplication and division are done in the order that they come from left to right. Then addition and subtraction are done from left to right. The same problem is shown below.

Press	Window
360	360
−	360
50	50
×	50
3	3
=	210

When | × | is pressed, the scientific calculator does not subtract 50 from 360. Instead, it waits, multiplies 50×3, and *then* subtracts this from 360.
The correct answer is 210.

You may want to give problems using order of operations.

$15 - \boxed{12 \div 3} \times 2 + 5$ Calculate multiplication and division, whichever comes first, from left to right.

$15 - 4 \times 2 + 5$

$15 - \boxed{4 \times 2} + 5$

$15 - 8 + 5$

$\boxed{15 - 8} + 5$ Next, calculate addition and subtraction, whichever comes first, from left to right. Notice you will obtain the wrong answer

$7 + 5$ if you add 8 and 5 first.

Student Lab Book

Special Features

1. Icons (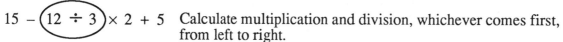) are placed in the left-hand margin to instruct students whether or not to use calculators, rulers, compasses, scissors, or mental computation. If the no-calculator icon appears, the students may use paper and pencil.

2. Starred problems (∗) combine several concepts into a challenging, multi-step problem. A starred problem does not mean "too challenging for some students." It merely implies that students must apply their skills to a new situation and do some "extra thinking."

3. Special instructions often appear below the answer line.

——————— Students are encouraged to label their answers.
Put in units.

——————— Students are given rounding instructions.
R to the nearest tenth.

——————— This indicates that the answer is a "messy" (many digit) number.
Copy window. Students copy the answer exactly as seen in the calculator window.

Self-Checking Techniques

1. A picture of the calculator window with one or more digits from the final answer is supplied. Students must find their mistakes if their answers do not "match."

2. In some problems, eight-digit data (i.e., "messy" numbers) are chosen so that the answer results in a "nice" number. A special note: *You'll know*, is written under the answer line. If a student's answer is "messy," he or she knows to go back and look for errors. Although students develop a sense that eight-digit data is not physically realistic, they appreciate these techniques as self-checking devices.

3. Many figures are drawn on a one-to-one scale. Students may check their calculations with their measurements. Moreover, they *know* what it is that they are calculating. A sketch represents the figure and cannot be measured.

4. Paired, parallel problems with "nice" and "messy" numbers are used to help estimate the "reasonableness" of answers. Students compare problems using "nice numbers" with similar problems constructed from "messy" numbers. Students are often told to use the following strategy, "If you can't solve it, make up an easier problem like it." They need many examples before they can actually practice this strategy effectively.

Problem-Solving Strategies

1. Multi-Step Problems
Students have grown accustomed to thinking of school mathematics as a series of unrelated, single-step exercises. As a result, students experience difficulty when they encounter multi-step problems. MWM gradually introduces these problems as a step-by-step process. In later problems, students must supply the intermediate steps.

2. Estimation
Students are encouraged to estimate before they calculate so that they can discriminate between reasonable and unreasonable answers.

3. Trial-and-Error Techniques
Trial and error is sometimes belittled as a poor problem-solving technique; often it is an excellent method. Calculators make solving problems through "trial and error" feasible. (Computers solve difficult problems through trial and error.)

4. Formulas
Students often think of geometric concepts (like area and perimeter) as a series of formulas (e.g., $2\pi r$ or πr^2) to be applied when the need arises. In MWM, formulas for the area and circumference of circles are never *explicitly* stated. Instead, problems are presented to build understanding of the ideas in several ways. Area and circumference are introduced through extensive use of figures drawn to scale. Estimated, measured, and calculated results are compared so that students know that the number in their calculator window has meaning. However, some students may happen to stumble upon formulas in a textbook or from some other resource. Encouraging proficient students to "show" how the formula works would be a way to discourage nonproficient students from trying to rely on a formula for magical results.

5. Data Tables
Data tables allow for a nice comparison of data and are excellent tools to facilitate estimation. Problems are generally sequenced in the tables so that they "tell a story." Since students may have difficulty visualizing the problems in the table, encourage them to draw sketches of the figures. Students should estimate the answers and discuss the relative size of the figure.

6. Keystrokes
Keystroke sequences are used in several ways. Students follow a designated sequence of keystrokes when new concepts or calculator techniques are introduced. Students are encouraged to list their keystrokes, find errors in a sequence of keystrokes, and to look for more efficient keystroke sequences. These analyses help students think about the steps required to solve a problem as well as prepare them for further work in mathematics.

Teacher Sourcebook

The Teacher's Sourcebook contains the following sections:

Teacher's Guide
The teacher's guide provides detailed hints and suggestions for each chapter of the Student Lab Book. These suggestions are based on classroom experience of pilot teachers.

1. Suggested Pacing: *Novice*, *apprentice*, and *expert* refer to pacing schedules geared for the inexperienced class to the experienced class.

2. Vocabulary: Vocabulary in the Student Lab Book is printed in bold and italic type. Understanding the idea is more important than memorizing a precise definition. The vocabulary list is for your reference.

3. Preliminary Activities: These activities outline skills necessary for the specific chapter.

4. Supplementary Activities: These optional activities are extensions of the concepts.

Transparencies (Blackline Masters)
Each transparency master explains its purpose and specifies the corresponding pages for the Student Lab Book. These blackline masters were designed to be photocopied on transparency film. Nearly all photocopy machines accept transparency film either in the paper bin or when hand fed. Different copy machines may require or recommend different types of transparency film.

You do not need to remove the pages you are copying from the book—just be certain that the page being copied lies flat against the glass of the copy machine. Before running the transparent film, it's a good idea to run sample copies on sheets of blank paper to assure the position, darkness, and quality of the copy.

Quizzes and Tests
Quizzes are intended to provide a quick assessment of student progress. The problems are presented in increasing difficulty. Quizzes are labeled as "Mid-Chapter Quiz" or "Quiz" (administered at the end of the chapter). The tests are cumulative and should be administered at the end of the specified chapters (Test A Chapter 3; Test B Chapter 6; Test C Chapter 10).

Some quizzes include a HINT or HINT SHEET that provides intermediate steps for the most challenging problems. When you copy the HINT SHEET, also copy the HINT DEFLECTOR on the back of the HINT SHEET. The HINT DEFLECTOR prevents the students from viewing the hint *through* the paper. Fold the bottom of the HINT SHEET to the dotted line and staple along the edges so that the hint cannot be viewed unless the staples are torn out. Every student has the option of whether to open the HINT SHEET. Although no definitive grading system is stated for the quizzes, it is recommended that if the HINT SHEET is opened and all the problems are solved correctly, the students still have the opportunity to earn the highest possible letter grade. Here are some other possible ways for grading a HINT SHEET:

1. deduct five points for opening the HINT SHEET and solving the problem correctly
2. add five points for *not* using the HINT SHEET and solving the problem correctly
3. give partial credit for correct answers to the intermediate steps on the HINT SHEET
4. give extra credit if students list more than one way to solve the problem

Teachers are encouraged to explore these and other approaches for grading the quizzes.

Quizzes and Tests Answer Key
This section provides reduced pages of the quizzes and the tests with answers.

Student Lab Book Answer Key
This section provides reduced Student Lab Book pages with answers.

Dear Parent/Guardian:

Your child will use *Maneuvers with Circles* in math class this year. This book is part of a series of materials developed by the University of Illinois at Chicago-Maneuvers with Mathematics (UIC-MWM) project. UIC-MWM lessons cover important content that reflects the national recommendations for curriculum improvement. For example, *Maneuvers with Circles* contains activities that help students build solid foundations for future work in mathematics.

UIC-MWM materials offer students a hands-on approach to mathematics. In *Maneuvers with Circles*, students measure circles and pieces of circles using rulers, compasses, and protractors. They then compare these measurements with their estimates and calculations. This approach successfully helps students apply mathematics and problem solving in their everyday lives.

I encourage you to follow along as your child progresses. Please note that, as you help your child with homework, UIC-MWM lessons are built on concepts developed in previous lessons. If you have any questions or concerns, feel free to contact me.

Sincerely,

Estimados Padres o Guardianes,

Su hija(o) estará utilizando *Maneuvers with Circles* (*Maniobras con Círculos*) en la clase de matemáticas este año. Este libro es parte de una serie de materiales desarollados por la Universidad de Illinois en Chicago-Maneuvers with Mathematics project (el proyecto -Maniobras con Matemáticas, UIC-MWM). Las lecciones de UIC-MWM cubren un contenido importante que refleja un mejoramiento al curriculum dado por recomendaciones nacionales, tales como actividades que ayudan a los estudiantes a construir fundaciones sólidas para el trabajo en las matemáticas.

Los materiales de UIC-MWM ofrecen a los estudiantes un método práctico a las matemáticas. En *Maniobras con Círculos*, por ejemplo, los estudiantes miden círculos y secciones de círculos usando reglas, compases y transportadores. Ellos comparan estas medidas con sus propios estimados y cálculos. Este método ayuda con éxito a los estudiantes a aplicar las matemáticas y resolver problemas en su vida diaria.

Les recomiendo que guien a su hija(o) en su progreso en la clase. Tome en cuenta que, mientras usted ayude a su hija(o) con la tarea, las lecciones de UIC-MWM estarán basadas en conceptos desarrollados en lecciones anteriores. Pongase en contacto conmigo si tiene alguna pregunta o preocupación.

Sinceramente,

Teacher's Guide

Chapter 1: Circumnavigate a Circle

Overview

Students use compasses to draw circles and explore several methods of estimating and calculating the circumference of a circle.

Student Materials

compass, ruler, scientific calculator, scissors, tape or glue, cylinders

Number of Periods Required/Suggested Schedule

Novice: 6 periods
- Day 1: Preliminary activities; pp. 1-5.
- Day 2: Pages 6-8.
- Day 3: Pages 9-11. Assign p. 15 (Problems 1-2).
- Day 4: Review homework; pp. 12-13; Mid-Chapter 1 Quiz.
- Day 5: Review Mid-Chapter 1 Quiz; pp. 14-16.
- Day 6: Chapter 1 Quiz.

Apprentice: 5 periods
- Day 1: Preliminary activities; pp. 1-6. Assign p. 7.
- Day 2: Review homework; pp. 8-10.
- Day 3: Pages 11-13. Assign p. 15 (Problems 1-2).
- Day 4: Review homework; Mid-Chapter 1 Quiz; p. 14. Assign p. 15 (Problems 3-5).
- Day 5: Review homework and Mid-Chapter 1 Quiz; p. 16; Chapter 1 Quiz.

Expert: 4 periods
- Day 1: Preliminary activities; pp. 1-6. Assign p. 7.
- Day 2: Review homework; pp. 8-11. Assign p. 15 (Problems 1-2).
- Day 3: Review homework; pp. 12-14. Assign pp. 15-16.
- Day 4: Review homework; Mid-Chapter 1 Quiz; Chapter 1 Quiz.

General Comments

When students communicate descriptions, such as the characteristics of circles or their parts, ask them to be as specific as possible. Allow students to point to or outline designated parts of a circle and then ask for words.

While using a compass, students should place several sheets of paper or a student lab book beneath the sheet on which they are drawing; this keeps the compass point from sliding or scratching the desk.

Encourage students to work together when using tools such as the compass and protractor. Students working cooperatively can help one another to learn techniques.

Teachers may find it helpful to appoint a student as "Compass Monitor" or "Tool Monitor" in a rotating position. This helps in several ways: pencils will be sharpened and ready at the start of the lesson, tools are less likely to be lost, and students have less opportunity to misuse the tools outside of the math lesson.

Encourage students to draw pictures for problems that do not have accompanying figures. Making sketches is an important problem-solving tool. Even crude, non-artistic sketches will help.

Use the calculator transparency on page 41 of this guide to help introduce the calculator. As a basic introduction to the TI-30 SLR+™ calculator, introduce the $\boxed{\text{AC/ON}}$ key and the keys for basic, arithmetic functions (+, −, ×, ÷, =). After turning on the calculator with $\boxed{\text{AC/ON}}$, students should get in the habit of clearing the calculator window with $\boxed{\text{CE/C}}$. This will help avoid future problems when they use the calculator's memory (introduced in Chapter 5). Later on, a source of error will be forgetting to push $\boxed{=}$ at the very end of a calculation. On the TI-30 SLR+™ calculator, a student can protect against this by pressing $\boxed{=}$ again "for good measure."

On the TI-30™, certain keys are activated by using the inverse key, $\boxed{\text{INV}}$. This is similar to the shift key on a typewriter. If a function appears above the key, it can be activated by pressing $\boxed{\text{INV}}$ first. Two keys that students will use frequently, $\boxed{\sqrt{x}}$ and $\boxed{\pi}$, use the $\boxed{\text{INV}}$ key. We have chosen *not* to include the $\boxed{\text{INV}}$ key in lists of keystrokes because of the variation between calculator keyboards.

Vocabulary

Understanding the idea involved is emphasized rather than memorizing a precise definition of a word. The following list is for *your* reference.

center point	The "middle" of a circle. Every point on the rim is the same distance from the center point.
circumference	The distance around the outside of a circle; the perimeter of a circle. Circumference is measured in linear (one dimensional) units (e.g. cm; in.; ft; etc.).
compass	A tool used to draw circles, pieces of circles, and sectors when given a center point and radius. It is also used to mark distances from given points.
diameter	The distance straight across a circle, passing through the center point. A diameter is formed by two radii on a straight line. A diameter cuts a circle in half.
perimeter	The distance all the way around a figure.
pi (π)	The ratio of a circle's circumference to its diameter. This is a constant for all circles. Pi begins 3.1415926536, and this is accurate enough even for scientific work.
polygon	A closed shape with three or more straight sides.
radius	The distance from the center of a circle to its rim. The plural form is *radii*.
regular polygon	A polygon in which all of the sides and all of the interior angles are equal. A perfectly symmetrical polygon.
side	One of the straight segments of a polygon.

Preliminary Activities

Students should use a ruler (yardstick, meter stick, etc.) to measure a variety of objects in the room. There are different types of rulers; some begin with the 0 mark at the left edge and some begin with the 0 mark indented. Students must be reminded to line up the 0 mark with the object they are measuring. Care must also be taken not to confuse inches with centimeters when they are on the same ruler. Occasionally a student may have an engineering scale with units close to centimeters that are not centimeters.

Conversion from cm to mm and back gives some children difficulty. For practice, name something that is 1 mm thick, then something that is 1 cm thick. It takes more mm than cm to reach a given length. Students should measure and record lengths in both mm and cm, and then see the difference in decimal point placement. On most rulers, the smallest marks are mm. A centimeter is made up of ten little millimeters.

For students who have no experience with decimal fractions, you may want to do a brief introduction to decimals. Students need to know that 0.6 is larger than 0.4372.

Many problems ask students to round their answers. Students should be familiar with rounding to the nearest whole number, tenth, hundredth, and thousandth.

Teaching Notes

page 1	Four of the shapes in Figure A are not circles; ask the students why not. Make sure students distinguish between a circle and a sphere. A ball is not a circle! Spheres are three-dimensional; circles are two-dimensional.
page 2	In Problem 5, students may ask if the word "could" implies an action on their part, and not a theoretical question (i.e. they may try to draw as many radii as possible).
page 3	Some students already familiar with the terminology related to circles might think there is one radius and two diameters in Figure H. Remind them that there are two radii in every diameter.

In Problem 8c, students are asked to "Put in units." They should include cm in their answer.

In Problem 8e, students could compare their new definition of a circle with their definition in Problem 2.

page 5	Use an eyeliner pencil in a compass for overhead transparencies. In Problems 13, 16a, and 17a, students are drawing *concentric circles*, circles with the same center point but different radii.
page 6	Students should be aware that the ruler in Problem 18a is not to scale.
page 7	Students who confuse radius and diameter in Problem 21 will discover their error when the circle runs into other items on the page.

Problem 22, Figure K is a sketch. In drawings referred to as "sketches," the dimensions are not drawn to a 1:1 scale. Therefore, calculated answers cannot be checked through measurement.

Problem 23 is the first use of a *You'll know* problem. *You'll know*s are "nice," whole number answers, such as 700 or 123, that come from "messy" numbers.

page 8	Transparency #1 reproduces Figures L, M, and N. Briefly review perimeter using a transparent ruler.

You may want to have class discussions to decide if the following statements are true or false: "All regular polygons are polygons." (True) "All polygons are regular polygons." (False)

page 9	In Problem 6, students should come up with their own solutions and compare their answers to the calculated answers they will find later.
	If students' rulers are not flexible, you can reproduce flexible rulers on transparencies using the blackline master on page 42 of this guide. If a string is used to measure the cylinder, make sure the string does not stretch.
pages 10-11	Use the Centimeter Grid Transparency on page 43 of this guide with Problems 7 and 9. Students may use the grid to set the compass for 3 cm instead of measuring with a ruler.
	Discuss the merits and/or failings of Ervin's method before proceeding to Lance's method.
	Show students examples of regular hexagons. Some floor or wall tiles are regular hexagons.
page 12	The interior hexagon in Figure U can be evenly divided into six congruent equilateral triangles. Knowing that the side length of the square is 5.5 cm, you can determine that the side length of each triangle is 2.75 cm. Because six of these sides build the perimeter of the hexagon, the perimeter is 16.5 cm.
	The easiest way to measure the diameter of a cylinder, as in Problem 17, is to find the longest distance across the circle; it may be off, but use this as the diameter. Another possibility is to wrap a strip of paper around the cylinder. Cut the strip so it is exactly the same length as the circumference. Fold the strip in half and cut. If you wrap this half strip around the cylinder, it will mark the two ends of the diameter.
page 13	Transparency #2 reproduces the table from Problem 20a. Doing science and math is not always an exact undertaking, as Problem 20 shows. Often times questions are answered through experimentation and finding an "average" answer.
page 14	Discuss the difference between *estimate* and *calculate*.
	Problem 23 is the first use of *rounding*. "*R*" refers to "Round."
	"Helping Digits" in Problem 24b is an MWM feature. If a student matches the given helping digits, it is highly likely that her answer is correct.
page 15	Ask students how they estimated their answers in Problem 3.
page 16	Transparency #3 reproduces Problems 6 and 7. If students can bypass the unknown diameter or radius and calculate the circumference directly, this is a first step towards the "one run" calculations coming later in the book.
	Students may notice that the data in the table is proportional. If the radius doubles, the diameter doubles and the circumference doubles. Looking at the table, if the radius is 440 cm, what is the diameter? (880 cm) What is the circumference? (2,764.6015 cm)

Supplemental Activities (Optional)

Debate the question: Which is better, a circle or a rectangle? (Circles are good for wheels, but not for bricks. Rectangles don't make good tires, etc.) Have students choose sides in a "Circle vs. Rectangle" debate.

Brainstorm possible substitutes for a compass: What if we don't have a compass? Could we use a string and a tack? Draftsmen use templates for small circles. What about for very large circles? What are the limits of our classroom tools?

Students can draw pictures using compasses and straight edges.

Research the number pi. Where does the odd symbol "π" come from? To how many digits has it been calculated? In August 1989, Japanese mathematician, Yasumasa Kaneda, calculated pi to 536,870,000 places; it took a supercomputer 67 hours and 13 minutes to print the number on 110,000 sheets of paper. Some reference sources may list enough digits to wrap around the room if written out on adding machine tape. Ask the students, "Is π a BIG number?" It isn't, so what is it? The decimal expression is long; the number is a little larger than 3.

Investigate the etymology of the word *circle*. List other words with the same *circ-* root: circumference, circumnavigate, circus, circumscribe, circuit, circulate, circumstance, circumvent, and circumspect.

Chapter 2: What's Inside?

Overview
Students estimate and calculate the area of circles.

Student Materials
compass, ruler, scientific calculator, scissors, tape or glue

Number of Periods Required/Suggested Schedule
Novice: 5 periods
>Day 1: Preliminary activities; pp. 17-19.
>Day 2: Pages 20-23. Assign p. 24.
>Day 3: Review homework; pp. 25-26; Mid-Chapter 2 Quiz. Assign p. 27.
>Day 4: Review homework and Mid-Chapter 2 Quiz; p. 28.
>Day 5: Chapter 2 Quiz.

Apprentice: 4 periods
>Day 1: Preliminary activities; pp. 17-22. Assign p. 23.
>Day 2: Review homework; pp. 24-26. Assign p. 27.
>Day 3: Review homework; p. 28; Mid-Chapter 2 Quiz.
>Day 4: Review Mid-Chapter 2 Quiz; Chapter 2 Quiz.

Expert: 3 periods
>Day 1: Preliminary activities; pp. 17-23. Assign pp. 24, 27.
>Day 2: Review homework; pp. 25-26; Mid-Chapter 2 Quiz. Assign p. 28.
>Day 3: Review homework and Mid-Chapter 2 Quiz; Chapter 2 Quiz.

General Comments
Students may have difficulty in the switch from linear quantities (circumference) to two-dimensional quantities (area). Students should pay special attention to units.

Several estimation strategies are suggested. Encourage students to evaluate strategies by asking, "Do you think this is a good method? Why or why not? Which method is most useful? Which method is most accurate? Which one will you use?"

Vocabulary

area   The amount of flat space a shape covers. Area is measured in square (two-dimensional) units (e.g. cm^2, in.^{2}, etc.).

x-squared (x^2)   A number multiplied by itself. Students will often say, "a number times itself," which is fine.

Preliminary Activities
Students can use unit grids and rulers to estimate, measure, and calculate the area of simple rectangular shapes: their desktops, books, etc. This gives them a physical sense of area.

To emphasize the "dimensional" difference between circumference and area, illustrate circumference with a flexible ruler (or flexible meter stick). Show the same sized circle drawn on cm grid paper, as shown at the top of the following page.

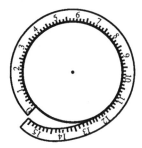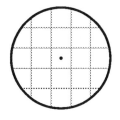

Length Around   Number of Squares

Teaching Notes

pages 17-18   Transparency #1 reproduces Figures A, B, and C. After students "eyeball" estimates for Problem 2, you may want them to "draw" cm grids on the figures. Demonstrate on the transparency how to draw a cm grid on the figures using a ruler. Grids are drawn in these shapes in Figure D. The centimeter grid transparency on page 43 of this guide can be used to estimate the area of the figures.

Use a transparent 25 cm² stamp, made from the blackline master on page 44, to show how to estimate area on Transparency #1. If possible, distribute 25 cm² transparent "stamps" to each student. Use the 25 cm² stamp to estimate the area of the circle in Problem 4b.

page 20   Watch to make sure that students are using the correct units. Students should think of area as the number of centimeter squares (or unit squares) that fit into a shape.

pages 21-22   Transparency #2 leads to Figure L to show that it takes more than the 3 corners to fit into the empty space. Therefore, the area of the circle is slightly more than the area of the three squares built along the radii.

Strongly emphasize the relationship between the radius and the side length of the square; they are the same!

In Problem 10d, discuss different students' reasoning. Have students consider whether some methods are more accurate than others.

page 23   Compare the answers for Problems 12 and 13. Why is there a difference? Do the students think the estimation technique is acceptable? Is such a technique acceptable when deciding how much paint to buy to paint a room-sized circle, or when designing a mechanical part for an airplane engine?

Problem 15 is the first time students are asked to write their keystrokes. Allow for a variety of strategies, and if students need more boxes let them draw them in.

page 24   Have students draw the square on the radius in Problem 16a.

page 25   For more experienced students, ask how they would calculate the area of the wood in Problem 21.

| 27 | x^2 | $-$ | 572.55526 | $=$ | 156.44474 cm² |

page 26　　　　Transparency #3 reproduces Problems 22-26.

After Problem 26, ask students to draw circles with radii of 5 cm and 7.0710678 cm (approximately 7.1 cm). Have the students calculate the area of each of these circles. The *area* of the second circle is twice the area of the first circle. To double the *area*, you do not double the *radius*. What happens to the area of a circle if the radius is *tripled*? (Area increases 9 times.)

page 28　　　　Ask for volunteers to list their keystrokes on the board for Problem 4.

Although students do not measure in Problem 6, they should be aware that the units are in square inches.

Supplemental Activities (Optional)

Students use classroom shapes as "stamps" to estimate the area of other shapes. For example, how many student desktops make up one chalkboard? How many math textbooks make up one student desktop? And, therefore, how many math textbooks make up one chalkboard?

Hand out sheets of paper with cm grid on one side and inch grid on the other side. Have students draw a shape on one side of the paper, then cut out the figure. Estimate the area of the shape in square centimeters, then flip the sheet to estimate the area in square inches. Why are the two numbers different? Are the *quantities* different? This exercise is to demonstrate that without proper units, it is impossible to obtain any "feel" for a quantity measured. This also shows the difference between square inches and square centimeters.

Draw a Jardine House as described on page 28 and compare this to the drawing below.

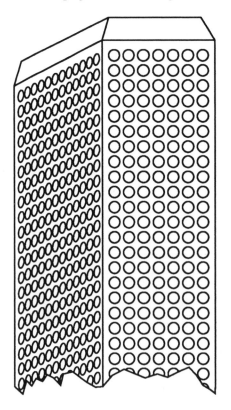

Chapter 3: In and About

Overview
Students work "backwards" as they calculate from area to circumference and circumference to area.

Student Materials
compass, ruler, scientific calculator

Number of Periods Required/Suggested Schedule
Novice: 7 periods
> Day 1: Preliminary activities; pp. 29-31.
> Day 2: Pages 32-35. Assign p. 36.
> Day 3: Review homework; pp. 37-38. Assign p. 39.
> Day 4: Review homework; Mid-Chapter 3 Quiz; p. 40. Assign p. 41.
> Day 5: Review homework and Mid-Chapter 3 Quiz, pp. 42-43. Assign p. 44.
> Day 6: Review homework; Chapter 3 Quiz.
> Day 7: Administer Test A.

Apprentice: 6 periods
> Day 1: Preliminary activities; pp. 29-32.
> Day 2: Pages 33-36. Assign p. 37.
> Day 3: Review homework; pp. 38-40. Assign p. 41.
> Day 4: Review homework; Mid-Chapter 3 Quiz; p. 42. Assign p. 43.
> Day 5: Review homework and Mid-Chapter 3 Quiz; p. 44; Chapter 3 Quiz.
> Day 6: Administer Test A.

Expert: 5 periods
> Day 1: Preliminary activities; pp. 29-32. Assign p. 33.
> Day 2: Review homework; pp. 34-37. Assign pp. 38-39.
> Day 3: Review homework; p. 40; Mid-Chapter 3 Quiz. Assign pp. 41-42.
> Day 4: Review homework and Mid-Chapter 3 Quiz; pp. 43-44; Chapter 3 Quiz.
> Day 5: Administer Test A.

General Comments
It is important that students have a concrete sense of circumference and area in order to comfortably work "backwards." Students are encouraged to estimate using 3 and then calculate using π. Going backwards is not algebra; it is just reversing the steps. (Forward: Open the door, walk into the room, and sit down in a chair. Reverse: Get up from the chair, walk out of the room, and shut the door behind you.)

The square root of x is introduced and used as students calculate the radius of a circle given the area of the circle.

When students list keystrokes on the board, periodically stop and ask, "What do you have here?" (area of the square built on the radius) After pressing the square root key, ask again, "What do you have here?" (radius) Do students know why they are pressing each key or are they just memorizing a procedure?

Vocabulary

square root of x   The inverse of x^2 (*x*-squared). What number multiplied by itself equals 9? 3 is the *square root* of 9.

Preliminary Activities

When a circle has a "nice" radius, will it have a nice area? A nice circumference? If a circle has a nice diameter, will it have a nice circumference? A nice area? Since pi is a "messy" number, the answer to all these questions is "Probably not." Students show this with drawings on grid paper and sketches.

Cut two strings that are each 60 cm long. One string represents the circumference of a circle. Use the other string to estimate the radius of a circle. About how many diameters build the circumference? (3) How many radii build 3 diameters? (6) Without measuring, how can you cut the string to make it a length close to the length of a radius? (Fold the string into thirds, then fold and cut one of these diameters in half. This is a good estimate for the radius of a circle.) Attach a piece of chalk to the end of this string. Draw a circle on the board. (The radius will be close to 10 cm.) Wrap the original 60 cm string around the circumference of the circle. How close is the string to the circumference of the circle?

Teaching Notes

page 29	Transparency #1 reproduces Problems 1, 2, and 3. In the table, students are directed for the first time to round to the nearest "hundredth." Sometimes people say, "Round to the second decimal place."
page 30	Students who have difficulty seeing the side length equals the diameter should draw and cut out a figure similar to Figure C. Students fold the square in half. Open up the square and the fold represents the diameter of the circle.
	If your students have not experienced square roots, provide more examples like Problems 5 and 6.
pages 31-32	Use Transparency #2 with Problems 7, 8, and 9. Transparency #2 can also be used to create additional trial and error problems. Encourage students already familiar with the square root key that trial-and-error is still a valuable tool in problem-solving. The $\boxed{\sqrt{x}}$ key is introduced. On some calculators, it may be necessary to press $\boxed{\text{INV}}$ (the "shift" key), to activate $\boxed{\sqrt{x}}$. You may want the students to write $\boxed{\text{INV}}$ as a keystroke.
page 34	In Problem 14a, $\boxed{\sqrt{x}}$ and $\boxed{x^2}$ "cancel."

Press:	6.76	$\sqrt{x}$	x^2
Window			

page 35	Students begin to work "backwards" problems. They need to know that about 3 (exactly π) of the squares built on the radius equals the area of the circle and about 3 (exactly π) diameters equals the circumference.
page 39	In Problem 25, discuss ways students estimated the area of the circle in Figure S. They have learned several in the previous chapter: counting squares, multiplying the squared radius by 3, etc.

page 40	Encourage students to draw sketches after they carefully read each problem.
	In Problem 28, this tree is considered to be the most massive living plant.
	The answer in Problem 28 is the first to show a rounded box. This indicates that a rounded answer is requested where helping digits are provided.
	In Problem 32a, students measure to the nearest whole centimeter, not to the nearest 0.1 cm. If a student finds this "strange," she is right.
page 41	"Averaging" is not formally taught in this book.
	In Problems 2f-2g, the average diameter of the two pools does not result in the average area of the two pools.
page 42	In Problem 4a, students draw the largest circle inside the rectangle. The center of the rectangle would be the center point of the circle. How do they find the center of a rectangle? Three possibilities might be to 1) Measure the rectangle and draw the middle lines for both length and height; the intersection is the center, 2) Draw the diagonals of the rectangle; the intersection is the center, or 3) Trial and error.
page 44	Before solving Problem 9, students compare the area of the square with the area of the circle. Is the area of the square larger or smaller than the area of the circle? (Larger)

Supplemental Activities (Optional)

In the table on page 29, the relationship between radius, diameter, and circumference are proportional. Area is not proportional. You may want students to graph the data. Proportional data results in straight line curves.

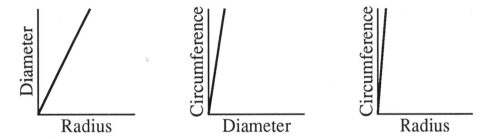

What does the area vs. circumference graph look like? Students could use data from the table on page 29 to make their graph.

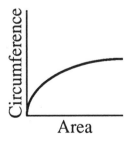

Which graphs above allow students to accurately make predictions (proportional data or straight-line curves)?

Chapter 4: Pieces of Circles

Overview
Students find the area of semicircles, quarter-circles, and figures built from quarter-circles.

Student Materials
compass, ruler, scientific calculator, scissors, tape or glue

Number of Periods Required/Suggested Schedule
Novice: 5 periods
    Day 1: Preliminary activities; pp. 45-47.
    Day 2: Pages 48-50. Assign p. 53.
    Day 3: Review homework; pp. 51-52 (Problems 1-5); Mid-Chapter 4 Quiz. Assign p. 52 (Problems 6-7).
    Day 4: Review homework and Mid-Chapter 4 Quiz; p. 54.
    Day 5: Chapter 4 Quiz.

Apprentice: 4 periods
    Day 1: Preliminary activities; pp. 45-48. Assign p. 53.
    Day 2: Review homework; pp. 49-51; Mid-Chapter 4 Quiz. Assign p. 52.
    Day 3: Review homework and Mid-Chapter 4 Quiz; p. 54.
    Day 4: Chapter 4 Quiz.

Expert: 3 periods
    Day 1: Preliminary activities; pp. 45-48. Assign p. 53.
    Day 2: Review homework; pp. 49-52; Mid-Chapter 4 Quiz. Assign p. 54.
    Day 3: Review homework and Mid-Chapter 4 Quiz; Chapter 4 Quiz.

General Comments
When finding the area of semicircles and quarter-circles, it is important for students to visualize the *whole* circle.

Encourage students to list keystrokes, even when keystrokes are not requested.

Vocabulary
quarter-circle   A one-fourth of a circle.

semicircle   Half of a circle cut along the diameter.

Preliminary Activities
Students draw and cut out circles. They try to divide the circle into pieces by folding and shading. Fold the circle into halves; shade one half. Fold the circle into fourths; shade one fourth.

Ask students, "How many quarters are there in a dollar? How many 50 cent pieces in a dollar?"

Teaching Notes
page 46   Problem 5d is an excellent opportunity to reinforce the order of operations.
    The answer key includes an equal sign ($\boxed{=}$) to find the area of the whole circle

prior to dividing by 2 to get a semicircle. There is no need for this because the calculator knows order of operations.

Transparency #1 reproduces Problem 5 on page 46 and Problem 6 on page 47.

page 47
In Problem 6a, students measure to the nearest whole cm, and not to the nearest 0.1 cm. It is unusual to see, "measure to the nearest whole cm" because it is a *coarse* measurement.

page 50
In Problem 15b, use the guide lines on the center to help draw the second diameter.

page 51
Transparency #2 reproduces page 51.

In Problem 2b, students may recognize the answer as pi. Why is it pi?

Another method that students might suggest is to find the area of a whole circle and multiply by $\frac{3}{4}$ (0.75), skipping the step of finding one quarter-circle's area.

It would be helpful to review Kendra's method after students learn to use memory in the next chapter.

page 52
In Problem 7, when students round the area, *two* digits change. 150.<u>79</u>645 rounds to 150.<u>80</u> .

page 54
In Figure U, the shaded regions form a whole circle. You may want students to cut out a copy of the figure and reconstruct it into a whole circle.

As an extension, find the area of the *unshaded* region in Figure U.

Supplemental Activities (Optional)

Ask students if they see a pattern emerging in the way they calculate the area of a semicircle and the way they calculate a quarter-circle. Do they have any ideas about "messy" sectors, ones that are not easily identifiable as simple fractions of a circle? How would they solve them? This topic will be covered in Chapter 6.

Have students write their own semicircle and quarter-circle problems.

Have students investigate the construction details of the Keck Telescope now operating in the Hawaiian Islands. It is made up of many hexagonal mirrors fitted together.

Chapter 5: Remember That Number

Overview
Students use the calculator's memory to help facilitate problem-solving and to prepare for using memory banks in advanced calculators and computers.

Student Materials
scientific calculator, ruler, protractor

Number of Periods Required/Suggested Schedule
Novice: 5 periods
> Day 1: Preliminary activities; pp. 55-57. Assign p. 58.
> Day 2: Review homework; pp. 59-61. Assign p. 62.
> Day 3: Review homework; pp. 63-64; Mid-Chapter 5 Quiz. Assign p. 65.
> Day 4: Review homework and Mid-Chapter 5 Quiz; pp. 66-67. Assign p. 68.
> Day 5: Review homework; Chapter 5 Quiz.

Apprentice: 5 periods
> Day 1: Preliminary activities; pp. 55-57. Assign p. 58.
> Day 2: Review homework; pp. 59-61. Assign p. 62.
> Day 3: Review homework; pp. 63-64; Mid-Chapter 5 Quiz. Assign pp. 65-66.
> Day 4: Review homework and Mid-Chapter 5 Quiz; pp. 67-68.
> Day 5: Chapter 5 Quiz.

Expert: 4 periods
> Day 1: Preliminary activities; pp. 55-60 (Problem 14). Assign pp. 60-61 (Problems 15-16).
> Day 2: Review homework; pp. 61-63; Mid-Chapter 5 Quiz. Assign pp. 64-65.
> Day 3: Review homework and Mid-Chapter 5 Quiz; pp. 66-68.
> Day 4: Review homework; Chapter 5 Quiz.

General Comments
Some students may have already investigated some of the calculator keys introduced in this chapter. They can be designated "mentors" for those who have difficulty. Students who practice saying or writing how they solved a problem using the calculator's memory enhance their mathematical communication. This chapter assists students in thinking ahead and planning how they will use the calculator's memory. They begin to plan calculator strategies before solving problems.

Transparency #1 is a blank table that can be used with the tables from the chapter or tables you create.

Vocabulary
memory — A feature on the calculator which allows you to save (store) a number that you will use later. More advanced calculators allow the user to store many different numbers in memory at the same time.

Preliminary Activities

Give the following problem on the board:
A figure is constructed of three semicircles
as shown at the right. Find the area of the
figure without writing down the area of
each semicircle. Ask students what they
"wish" the calculator would be able to do.

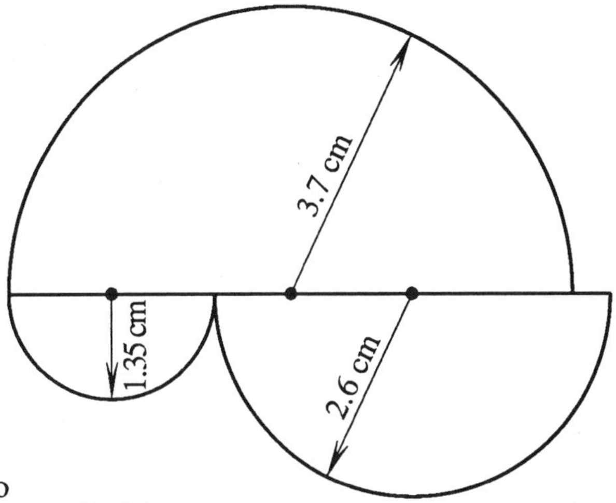

Teaching Notes

page 56

The transparency on page 41
reproduces a TI-30 SLR+™
calculator.

It is important to "train" students to
clear the calculator with $\boxed{\text{CE/C}}$ instead of $\boxed{\text{AC/ON}}$.
Pressing $\boxed{\text{AC/ON}}$ will erase the number in the window *and* the memory whereas the
$\boxed{\text{CE/C}}$ key clears the window but not the memory.

The calculator stores a number in memory as long as the calculator is on (as long
as the light level activates the photocell), until it is replaced by another number
using a memory key, or until $\boxed{\text{AC/ON}}$ is pressed.

Examples of using the $\boxed{\text{CE/C}}$ key:

Solve the following problem 3 + 5 = using your calculator.

Press: $\boxed{3}$ $\boxed{+}$ $\boxed{6}$ oops! $\boxed{\text{CE/C}}$ $\boxed{5}$ $\boxed{=}$

The calculator window shows 8. This is one way $\boxed{\text{CE/C}}$ helps correct a mistake.
But be careful. See what happens when $\boxed{\text{CE/C}}$ is pressed twice.

Press: $\boxed{3}$ $\boxed{+}$ $\boxed{6}$ $\boxed{\text{CE/C}}$ $\boxed{\text{CE/C}}$ $\boxed{5}$ $\boxed{=}$

The calculator window shows 5.

One important use of $\boxed{\text{EXC}}$ is to take a peek at the memory without losing the
number in the window. Students peek into the memory by pressing the $\boxed{\text{EXC}}$ key
once; then $\boxed{\text{EXC}}$ again to return the memory to its original position. "0" is in
memory until another number is stored.

Press: $\boxed{\text{AC/ON}}$ $\boxed{379}$ $\boxed{\times}$ $\boxed{\text{EXC}}$ $\boxed{=}$ (Answer: 0)

Operations with $\boxed{\text{EXC}}$ can be shown with the following example.

Press: $\boxed{4}$ $\boxed{\text{STO}}$ $\boxed{5}$ $\boxed{\times}$ $\boxed{\text{EXC}}$ $\boxed{=}$ (Answer: 20)

pages 57-58

In Problem 2c, 250 is the area of the circle. In Problems 3-6, have students tape a
piece of paper over the calculator window so that it creates a flap. (Make sure the
solar cells on the top of the calculator are not covered.) Students complete each
problem and then "peek" under the flap to check their answers. Group activities
allow students to devise their own problems.

pages 60-61

In some problems, students may need both the number in the window and the
number in memory. The $\boxed{\text{EXC}}$ key is recommended in those cases.

Teacher's Guide 17

Supplemental Activities (Optional)

Materials needed: paper or index cards. Select two students. One represents the memory and the other represents the calculator window. (Each wears a sign with "window" or "memory.")

If I press 6, what is in the window? The "window" student writes 6 on a card and holds it up. *What is in the memory?* The "memory" student holds a "0" card.

If I press [STO], *what is in the window? The memory?* The "window" student keeps the "6", but now the "memory" student writes and holds a "6" card and throws away the "0" because "0" is no longer in memory. The teacher writes the keystrokes on the board as students go along.

Give students keystrokes to a problem. Each keystroke is written on a separate index card. Then give them an answer and have them arrange the keystroke cards so that they arrive at the given answer. Group work is encouraged; students can create their own problems. If students have identical keystroke cards, "friendly" competition could develop.

The following example provides an extension to calculator keystrokes:

Press: [4] [+/-] (Window: − 4)

A student may ask, "Can I subtract a number from memory?"

The answer is yes. The [SUM] key can be converted into a "minus" key using negative numbers. Enter the number to be subtracted from memory. Then press [+/-] [SUM].

Example: [7] [STO] [5] [+/-] [SUM] [RCL] (Answer: 2)

Think of pressing [+/-] [SUM] as adding a negative number to what is in memory. Call [+/-] the "change sign" key to avoid confusion with [+] or [−].

Chapter 6: Circles, Sectors, and Angles

Overview

Students use a protractor to measure angles. Then students calculate the areas of whole circles, sectors, and figures built from sectors.

Student Materials

protractor, ruler, scientific calculator, scissors, tape or glue

Number of Periods Required/Suggested Schedule

Novice: 7 periods
Day 1: Pages 69-72.
Day 2: Pages 73-76. Assign p. 85.
Day 3: Review homework; pp. 77-79; Mid-Chapter 6 Quiz.
Day 4: Review Mid-Chapter 6 Quiz; pp. 80-82. Assign p. 83.
Day 5: Review homework; pp. 84, 86. Assign p. 87.
Day 6: Review homework; p. 88; Chapter 6 Quiz.
Day 7: Administer Test B.

Apprentice: 5 periods
Day 1: Pages 69-75. Assign pp. 76, 85.
Day 2: Review homework; pp. 77-79; Mid-Chapter 6 Quiz. Assign pp. 80-81.
Day 3: Review homework and Mid-Chapter 6 Quiz; pp. 82-84. Assign pp. 86-87.
Day 4: Review homework; p. 88; Chapter 6 Quiz.
Day 5: Administer Test B.

Expert: 4 periods
Day 1: Pages 69-75. Assign pp. 76, 85.
Day 2: Review homework; pp. 77-79; Mid-Chapter 6 Quiz. Assign pp. 80-81.
Day 3: Review homework and Mid-Chapter 6 Quiz; pp. 82-84; Chapter 6 Quiz.
    Assign pp. 86-88.
Day 4: Review homework; Administer Test B.

General Comments

Special attention should be taken to ensure that children are grasping that an angle is a measurement of the amount of "turning."

Estimating angles as less than or greater than 90° helps students determine which set of numbers on the protractor correspond to the angle they are measuring. Some students may have difficulty using a protractor with accuracy and will need more practice to develop their hand-eye coordination. In general, allow for a ±1° difference in answers when students measure with a protractor.

This chapter provides an excellent opportunity for students to use their verbal and written communication skills as they describe their problem-solving methods.

Vocabulary

central angle   An angle with its vertex located at the center point of a circle. It tells the student what part of a circle a sector is. When there is one central angle in a circle, there is automatically another central angle – the rest of the circle. It should always be clear which central angle is used (from arcs or shading). Most often it is the smaller angle.

congruent   An exact copy of any figure is *congruent* to the original figure. Congruent figures have the same size, shape, area, and perimeter — i.e., the same "everything," except for the location.

degree   A unit of angular measure. The symbol for degree is "°". There are 360 degrees (360°) in one full turn of a circle.

extending the sides   When measuring an angle whose sides are not long enough to be read by a protractor, it is necessary to draw the sides of the angle longer. This does not affect the size of the angle.

right angle   An angle that measures 90°. A corner of a piece of paper forms an accurate right angle.

sector   A piece of a circle formed by an angle whose two sides meet at the center point, the vertex, and the intersecting arc.

vertex   The point where two sides of an angle meet. We often make a vertex with a fairly big dot. The students should think of it as a tiny speck.

Teaching Notes

page 70   Central angles do not have to be measured clockwise; measuring counter-clockwise provides the same answer.

page 71   In Problem 3, students may erroneously think the length of the sides corresponds to the size of the angle. A student has "arrived" when she knows

that  is bigger than   .

Students should identify right angles in the room.

page 72   If students have difficulty seeing a circle as a rotation of 360° around a central point, use a compass. The point rests at a center point while the pencil makes a full turn around it.

page 73   Transparency #1 reproduces the sector in Figure N. Use this transparency to demonstrate the proper use of a protractor. As with rulers, students must line up the zero mark on a protractor with one side of the sector. On some protractors, the bottom edge is also the zero line; on other protractors, the bottom edge may *not* be the zero line. Caution must also be taken to read the correct value on the protractor.

Before measuring an angle, students should visually determine if the angle is less than or greater than 90°. This will help them check their measurement.

page 74   When naming a sector, such as in Problem 8, the middle letter represents the vertex of the internal angle.

page 75	Encourage students to estimate before measuring Figure R.
page 76	Use Transparency #1 to demonstrate extending sides and measuring angles. If students have difficulty "seeing" the internal angle, have them mark it by drawing an arc.
page 78	Transparency #2 reproduces Figures BB and CC. It may be helpful to shade the 60° sector a different color.
	Students must be careful with their drawings, or the final lines, after six sectors, might not match up.
page 81	Transparency #3 reproduces the table in Problem 11. The number of sectors in a circle in Problem 11f is a "messy" number. Students should not be led to believe that every sector evenly divides into a unit circle.
	Once the table is completed, students can "experiment" by solving for sectors that have central angles that are combinations of known sectors. For example, the area of a 22° sector can be found by adding together the areas of a 10° sector and a 12° sector, or by two 11° sectors.
page 82	The students find the area of a 1° sector and then multiply to find the area of larger sectors.
	Because of the thickness of the lines in Problem 14, measurements of the radius of the 1° sector will vary.
page 83	For more experienced students, a sector is a fraction of a circle. For example, Problem 17 can be thought of as $\frac{50}{360}$ of a circle; Problem 18 as $\frac{100}{360}$ of a circle.
	Simplifying or reducing fractions could also be introduced where $\frac{50}{360} = \frac{5}{36}$.
	Find the area of the whole circle and multiply by $\frac{5}{36}$.
page 85	Problem 1 is the first use of "could be" or "crazy." "Crazy" means impossible or not likely.
page 87	There are many ways to solve Problem 9. Encourage class discussion.
	For example, some students may choose to use $\frac{300}{360}$ or $\frac{5}{6}$ of a circle. Others may solve by subtracting the smaller sector from the whole circle.

Supplemental Activities (Optional)

The Angle Measuring Puzzle on page 23 provides extra practice. Its answer key follows on page 24.

Why are circles measured with 360°? Why not 400°? Why not 100°? The 360° system has its foundations in the length of the year: 365 days. The earth revolves approximately one degree around the sun each day. Early astronomers watched the sun move one degree against the background stars each day. With twelve months in the year, each month, or zodiacal constellation, marks off 30°. Also, for ease in geometry, a 90° right angle is easily divided in halves *and* thirds, whereas 100° is not. Imagine referring to a $33\frac{1}{3}$° angle! Still, engineers *do* use an angle measurement called a ***grad***. There are 100 grads in a right angle.

The following is an easy way to show sectors.

1. Cut out two circles of contrasting colors. Cut one slit along a radius of each circle.

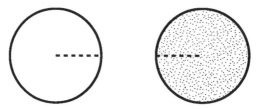

2. Attach the two circles along the slits. Rotate the circles to show the different-sized sectors.

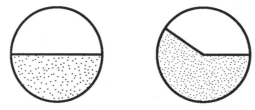

Another method of showing sectors is to use a fan that can be opened into a full circle. As a sector is described, open the fan to the approximate size.

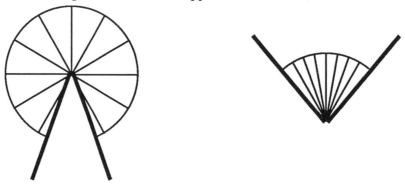

Paper clips and drinking straws can be used to illustrate angles. Bend open paper clips and place drinking straws of different lengths over each end. Demonstrate how side length has nothing to do with angle size. Relate this to the method of "extending the sides" and how this does not affect angle measurement.

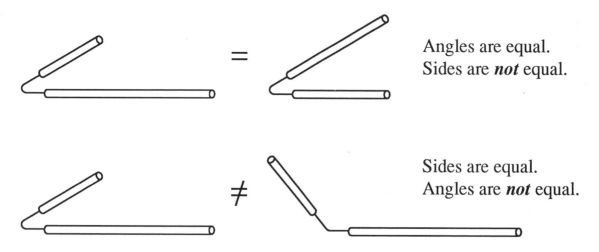

Angles are equal.
Sides are *not* equal.

Sides are equal.
Angles are *not* equal.

Angle Puzzle

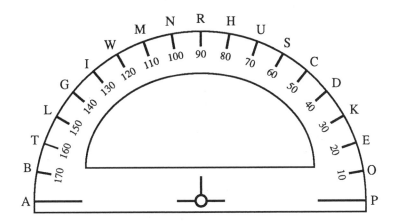

Measure the following angles and write the corresponding letter from the protractor above to find the secret message.

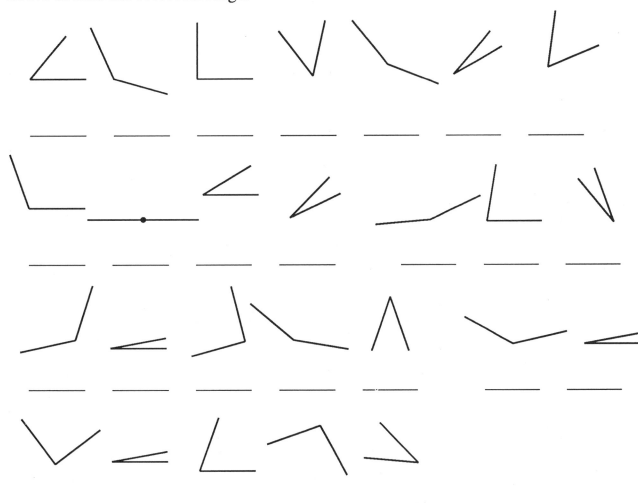

Angle Puzzle

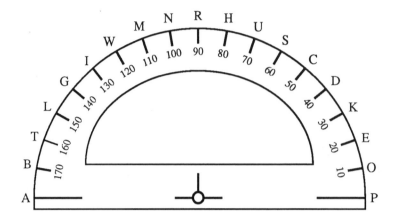

Measure the following angles and write the corresponding letter from the protractor above to find the secret message.

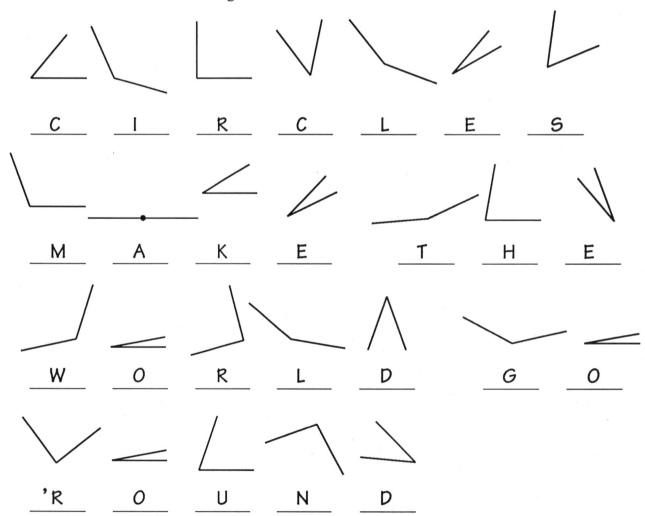

| C | I | R | C | L | E | S |

| M | A | K | E | | T | H | E |

| W | O | R | L | D | | G | O |

| 'R | O | U | N | D |

Chapter 7: Circles with Holes

Overview

Students calculate more complicated, multi-step area problems which deal with circles, rectangles, and triangles. A brief introduction to the area of right triangles is included. In this chapter, students see a close connection between physical "take away" and numerical subtraction.

Student Materials

compass, ruler, scientific calculator, scissors, tape or glue

Number of Periods Required/Suggested Schedule

Novice: 7 periods
    Day 1: Preliminary activities; pp. 89-91.
    Day 2: Pages 92-95.
    Day 3: Pages 96-99. Assign pp. 100, 104.
    Day 4: Review homework; p. 101; Mid-Chapter 7 Quiz.
    Day 5: Review Mid-Chapter 7 Quiz; pp. 102-103, 105. Assign p. 106.
    Day 6: Review homework; pp. 107-108.
    Day 7: Chapter 7 Quiz.

Apprentice: 6 periods
    Day 1: Preliminary activities; pp. 89-92. Assign pp. 93-94.
    Day 2: Review homework; pp. 95-99. Assign p. 100.
    Day 3: Review homework; pp. 101-102; Mid-Chapter 7 Quiz. Assign p. 104.
    Day 4: Review homework and Mid-Chapter 7 Quiz; pp. 103, 105. Assign p. 106.
    Day 5: Review homework; pp. 107-108.
    Day 6: Chapter 7 Quiz.

Expert: 5 periods
    Day 1: Preliminary activities; pp. 89-92. Assign pp. 93-94.
    Day 2: Review homework; pp. 95-100. Assign pp. 101, 104.
    Day 3: Review homework; pp. 102-103; Mid-Chapter 7 Quiz. Assign p. 105.
    Day 4: Review homework and Mid-Chapter 7 Quiz; pp. 106-107. Assign p. 108.
    Day 5: Review homework; Chapter 7 Quiz.

General Comments

It is important that students gain a physical sense of a hole by actually taking a figure and cutting out part of the inside. They must gain a sense that the inner shapes are being taken away, and that they are not merely shapes piled upon one another. Many students will need concrete activities.

Vocabulary

hypotenuse   The side opposite to the right angle and the longest side of a right triangle.

leg   The two shorter sides of a right triangle are legs. The legs form the right angle.

right triangle   A triangle with a right angle.

square root of x   The inverse of x-squared; what number times itself will give me x?
                      The square root of 9 is 3 or $\sqrt{9} = 3$ because $3 \times 3 = 9$. $\sqrt{144} = 12$.

Preliminary Activities

Make two copies of a small circle and a larger circle. Trace the small circle on each larger circle, but at different locations. Cut out the small circle from each large circle. Does each left-over part have the same area? (Yes)

Teaching Notes

page 89	Encourage students to come up with a wide variety of locations to cut the smaller circle out of Figure A. Most will try to place it directly at the center.
page 90	What if the small circle was removed as two separate semicircles? Would the area left over be the same? (Yes)
page 91	Transparency #1 reproduces Problems 10 and 11.
page 92	Encourage students to write the given dimensions on all figures. This will help them visualize the problems.
page 94	Students may need their memories refreshed on the use of the $\boxed{\sqrt{x}}$ key.
page 95	In Problem 20, students should realize there is no need to make any calculations or determine any properties of the figure, such as radius or side length of squares.
	Visualize Problem 21 as two independent three-quarter circles. If the student still can't "see" this, cover up one sector and solve each independently.
page 96	It is important that students know which side of the triangle is the hypotenuse; it will be used throughout the rest of the book.
page 97	This is a graphic demonstration of the "formula" for the area of a triangle, $\frac{1}{2} \times b \times h$, which is not formally introduced. "Pictures" are better than formulas. However, some students may happen to stumble upon the formula in a textbook or from some other resource. For students who have difficulty visualizing the area of a right triangle, have them complete the steps on this page. Pictures and procedures are better than formulas for the students' future in mathematics.
pages 98-99	Transparency #2 reproduces Figures U, V, and W.
	Beware! It is easy to forget to divide the area of the rectangle in half in order to find the area of a triangle. Remind the students from time to time.
page 100	Students should use the corner of a piece of paper or ruler to draw the right angle in Problem 14.
page 101	Problem 18 has extra information; there is no use for the 5 cm hypotenuse in finding area. If students ask, "Where does the 5 cm fit in?" respond with the same question. In "real life," a student must select relevant data from a large assortment of data.
page 102	Problem 20 may look different, but it is the same type of problem, only the hole will be subtracted from the sector.
page 103	Discuss the various strategies students used to solve Problem 23.

page 105	In Problems 3 and 4, students may have difficulty determining the dimensions of the rectangle. Encourage them to draw the diameters along the dimensions of the rectangles.
page 106	Figure MM is an optical illusion. The shaded part does not appear to have the same area as the white circle. Even after solving the problem, do students believe it?
	One way to think of Problem 7 is to imagine the pieces rearranged to make a square with two-centimeter sides and a circle with a 1 cm radius.
page 107	Students should follow the steps in Problem 9 without clearing their calculators.

Supplemental Activities (Optional)

Brainstorm a list of circular items with circular holes for Problem 1, page 104.

Students use a three-quarter circle to make up their own "circle with a hole" problem. They find the area of the circle and subtract the quarter-circle hole. This activity reinforces the "hole" idea, but do students find this method as a preferable way to solve the problem?

Chapter 8: Perimeter of Pieces

Overview

Students calculate perimeter of figures built from pieces of circles.

Student Materials

compass, ruler, scientific calculator, scissors, tape or glue

Number of Periods Required/Suggested Schedule

Novice: 6 periods

    Day 1: Pages 109-110. Assign p. 111 (Problem 7).

    Day 2: Review homework; pp. 111-112. Assign p. 113.

    Day 3: Review homework; pp. 114-116. Assign p. 120.

    Day 4: Review homework; p. 117; Mid-Chapter 8 Quiz.

    Day 5: Review Mid-Chapter 8 Quiz; pp. 118-119. Assign p. 122.

    Day 6: Review homework; p. 121; Chapter 8 Quiz.

Apprentice: 5 periods

    Day 1: Pages 109-111. Assign pp. 112-113.

    Day 2: Review homework; pp. 114-116. Assign pp. 117, 120.

    Day 3: Review homework; pp. 118-119; Mid-Chapter 8 Quiz. Assign p. 122.

    Day 4: Review homework and Mid-Chapter 8 Quiz; p. 121.

    Day 5: Chapter 8 Quiz.

Expert: 4 periods

    Day 1: Pages 109-112. Assign pp. 113, 120.

    Day 2: Review homework; pp. 114-117. Assign p. 118.

    Day 3: Review homework; pp. 119-121; Mid-Chapter 8 Quiz. Assign p. 122.

    Day 4: Review homework and Mid-Chapter 8 Quiz; Chapter 8 Quiz.

General Comments

"Pieces" give students more trouble than most figures. Often they do not "see" the problems as easily as circles with holes. Encourage them to visualize the complete circles before they attempt to find the perimeter of a piece.

For some students, it might be helpful to outline the perimeter of each figure in red, decreasing the possibility of counting non-existent sides.

When a figure has a hole, it is not customary to calculate its perimeter.

Teaching Notes

page 109   Transparency #1 reproduces Problems 2 and 3.

                      If flexible rulers are not available, make ruler transparencies from the blackline master on page 42 of this guide.

page 110   In Problem 6, the four semicircles in Figure D can also be seen as two complete circles, both with a diameter of 3 cm.

page 111	In Problem 7, the inner rectangle is used to construct the figure, but it is not included in the perimeter. Students should outline the perimeter of the figure to see that the inner rectangle is not included.

Some students may notice that the straight segment of a semicircle (diameter) is equal in length to the two straight portions of a quarter-circle (radii), or any other sector for that matter. Only the *arc length* depends on the central angle.

page 112	Figure H has the same perimeter as a circle that can be inscribed in the given square. What is the radius of this circle? (3 cm) Students can cut out the quarter-circles and rearrange them to create this circle.

page 113	Transparency #2 reproduces Problems 12 and 13. Teacher or students may want to color the figure to visualize the pieces.

page 114	Transparency #3 reproduces Problems 14, 15, and 16. These series of figures show the direct relationship between diameter and circumference. Consider the picture that follows. Both figures consist of semicircles built on a given length (1 ft). Although the figures are different, they have the same perimeter. Do they have the same area? (No)

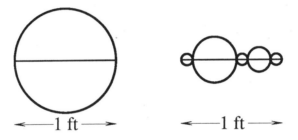

page 116	It is easy to lose track of which parts build the perimeter of a strip. As students calculate each part of the perimeter, they should outline and label the figure.

page 117	In Problem 9, you may want students to draw the circles that build the strip. It will be easier for students to "see" that the strip comes from two circles.

page 119	Transparency #4 reproduces page 119. It is impossible for students to "complete" the two circles that construct Figure T in their lab book. However, they can draw a freehand sketch in the margins.

page 120	Figure V can be rearranged into two whole circles to look like the following graphic.

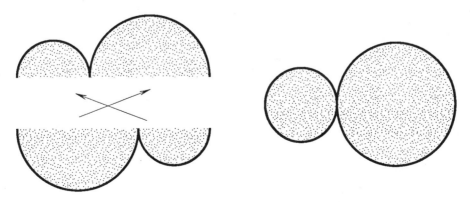

page 121   Basketball keys vary depending on the court; the key shown is for a professional league. Students could investigate the school court and draw their own basketball key.

page 122   Students should read the entire page before they begin Problem 6. Have them devise a strategy, using memory, that will tie all of the problems together.

Students might jump to the conclusion that the perimeter for Figure BB is the combined perimeter for Figure Z and Figure AA. This is true for *area*, but for perimeter, there are two overlapping edges that "disappear" when the pieces fit together.

Supplemental Activities (Optional)

To give the students a sense that a strip is indeed a part of a circle with a hole, cut out a semicircle from a sheet of contact paper. Draw a smaller semicircle on this sheet. Cut through the outer adhesive part, being careful not to cut through the back sheet. Peel away the inner semicircle while the students watch, emphasizing that the leftover piece, or strip, is a portion of a semicircle with a hole.

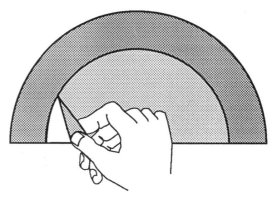

Find the perimeter and/or area of shapes around the classroom or school that are assembled from circles, semicircles, sectors, and strips. Give the students the area and perimeter of a shape and send them on a "Scavenger Hunt" with rulers, protractors, and calculators.

How do you cut a quarter-strip in half? If you cut on the dotted line, do you end up with exactly half of the quarter-strip? (No) Why or why not? Describe how you could cut this quarter-strip in half.

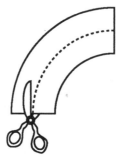

How would you find the *area* of a strip? The first step, just as with finding the perimeter, is to construct a "complete" figure of a circle with a hole. Find the area of an entire circle with a hole using methods learned in Chapter 7, and divide it into a sector using methods learned in Chapter 6. But, unlike perimeter, there is no need to worry about the flat edges of the strip; that is a linear dimension.

Chapter 9: Circles, Chords, and the Pythagorean Theorem

Overview
Students work with inscribed right triangles formed by chords and radii. Students use the Pythagorean Theorem in problem-solving activities.

Student Materials
ruler, scientific calculator, scissors, tape or glue

Number of Periods Required/Suggested Schedule
Novice: 5 periods
> Day 1: Pages 123-126.
> Day 2: Pages 127-130. Assign p. 132.
> Day 3: Review homework; p. 131; Mid-Chapter 9 Quiz.
> Day 4: Review Mid-Chapter 9 Quiz; pp. 133-134.
> Day 5: Chapter 9 Quiz.

Apprentice: 4 periods
> Day 1: Pages 123-126. Assign pp. 127-128.
> Day 2: Review homework; pp. 129-131. Assign p. 132.
> Day 3: Review homework; p. 133; Mid-Chapter 9 Quiz.
> Day 4: Review Mid-Chapter 9 Quiz; p. 134; Chapter 9 Quiz.

Expert: 3 periods
> Day 1: Pages 123-126, 129. Assign pp. 127-128.
> Day 2: Review homework; pp. 130-131; Mid-Chapter 9 Quiz. Assign pp. 132-133.
> Day 3: Review homework and Mid-Chapter 9 Quiz; p. 134; Chapter 9 Quiz.

General Comments
Students use the Pythagorean Theorem to find the length of the hypotenuse of a right triangle when both legs are given.

The Pythagorean Theorem is presented in a concrete manner. Squares are built along the legs and hypotenuse of a right triangle. Students see how the three squares are related to each other. Once students find the hypotenuse, they are able to solve multi-step problems involving right triangles and complex figures. Drawing, sketching, and writing out the keystrokes will reinforce the ideas in this chapter. Calculators make the Pythagorean Theorem an ideal topic for middle grade students. In earlier days, "taking the square root" was a nearly impossible task. With a calculator, it's easy.

Vocabulary

chord
A line segment whose end points lie on the rim of a circle. A diameter is a special chord that goes through the center of the circle.

Pythagorean Theorem
If any two sides of a right triangle are given, the third side can be determined. The Pythagorean Theorem states that the sum of the squares of the two legs of the triangle is equal to the square of the hypotenuse. The Pythagorean Theorem is written as an algebraic equation, $a^2 + b^2 = c^2$, where a and b are the lengths of the two legs, and c is the length of the hypotenuse.

Teaching Notes

page 124   In Problem 4c, line up one edge of a sheet of paper or ruler with Side *BC* and slide the paper until the corner of the sheet is at Point *C*. The other edge should then lie along Side *AC*.

In many problems, the ends of a chord are connected to the center of a circle to build a right triangle. It should be recognized that only special chords will form a right triangle when their ends are connected to the center point of a circle.

page 125   Squares can be constructed on any leg of a right triangle, but only unit squares like the one shown are immediately obvious. Other unit right triangles are 5, 12, 13 and 8, 15, 17. Emphasize that the hypotenuse usually won't be a "nice" number. Whenever possible, students should compare their calculations with their measurements. It will prevent some crazy answers. For example, if a student measures a hypotenuse as 14 cm but his calculator shows 196, he should think twice and see that he did not take the square root.

page 127   Transparency #1 reproduces Figure K.

page 129   In Figure L, the legs of Triangle *KLM* are equal. Why? (The legs are also radii of the circle and all radii of the same circle are equal.)

page 130   Triangle *RQP* is inscribed in the circle. Chord *RP* is a diameter. If Point *Q* were placed anywhere along the rim, the resulting triangle would be a right triangle.

page 131   Before solving Problem 18, ask students if the radius is less than, greater than, or equal to 5.6 cm. (less than) How do they know?

page 132   Students may be expecting a "You'll know" from the "messy" numbers in Problems 2 and 3, but, like the real world, the answer is another messy number.

page 133   In Problem 4, *JK* cuts Chord *GH* into two equal pieces. For the more experienced student, a line that is drawn from the center of a circle perpendicular to a chord will always bisect that chord.

If students need a hint on Problem 6, have them sketch in a few radii or diameters on the circle.

page 134   Transparency #2 reproduces Problems 7 and 8. The infield's dimensions are standard for all professional baseball fields, but the dimensions of the outfield differ. If students are interested, have them investigate the geometry of their favorite team's park.

Supplemental Activities (Optional)

Research the lives of Pythagoras and other Greek mathematicians. How did they become mathematicians; how were they trained? What role did mathematics play in Greek culture?

If two radii and a chord do not form a right triangle, can you use the Pythagorean Theorem? (No) Students may want to show this by designing their own problems, measuring, calculating, and "proving" that the Pythagorean Theorem works only with right triangles.

Draw a circle with a diameter. Show that a right triangle can be drawn anywhere along the rim of the circle if the diameter is the hypotenuse. Will the area of each right triangle be equal? (No) What about the perimeter? (No)

For a classroom party, a streamer will hang from one corner of the room to the opposite corner (assuming the room is rectangular). How long will the streamer be? Of course, we'll have to allow for twisting the streamer, so let's find the minimum length of the streamer. Students discuss in groups their plan of action. Students can measure the diagonal of the floor and the height of the room. Then they use the Pythagorean Theorem to calculate the length of the streamer.

Whole numbers that can be three sides of a right triangle (like 6, 8, 10 or 10, 24, 26) are called Pythagorean triples. Schools with a math club or other special project work may want to pursue Pythagorean triples in the library.

Up to this point, we have talked about the Pythagorean Theorem in terms of *squares* built along the sides of a right triangle, but what about circles, or semicircles built along the sides? As it turns out, the combined area of two semicircles built along the two legs equal the area of the semicircle built along the hypotenuse.

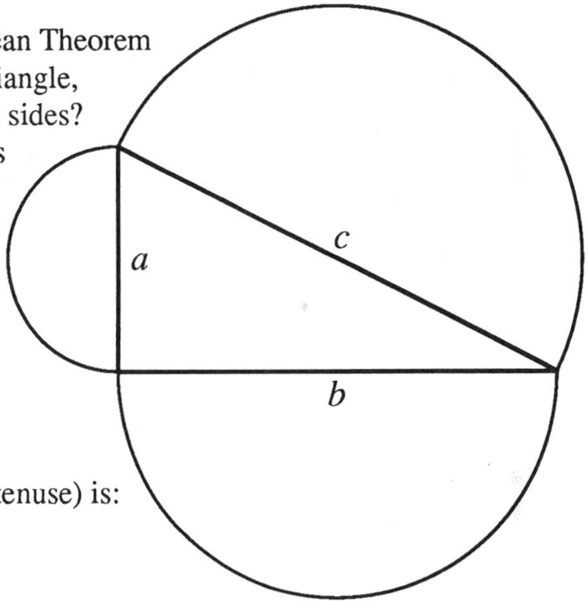

In the figure at the right, the area of the two smaller semicircles (built on the legs) is:

$$\pi \times \left(\frac{a}{2}\right)^2 \div 2 + \pi \times \left(\frac{b}{2}\right)^2 \div 2$$

The area of the largest semicircle (built on the hypotenuse) is:

$$\pi \times \left(\frac{c}{2}\right)^2 \div 2$$

Set the expressions equal and simplify:

$$\pi \times \left(\frac{a}{2}\right)^2 \div 2 + \pi \times \left(\frac{b}{2}\right)^2 \div 2 = \pi \times \left(\frac{c}{2}\right)^2 \div 2$$

$$\frac{\pi}{8} \times a^2 + \frac{\pi}{8} \times b^2 = \frac{\pi}{8} \times c^2$$

$$\frac{\pi}{8} \times \left(a^2 + b^2\right) = \frac{\pi}{8} \times \left(c^2\right)$$

Since both sides are multiplied by the same number, $\frac{\pi}{8}$, it can be divided out, leaving $a^2 + b^2 = c^2$, the Pythagorean Theorem!

Have students prove the same properties of *whole* circles built on the sides of a right triangle.

Notice the diameter of each circle is equal to the side on which the circle is built.

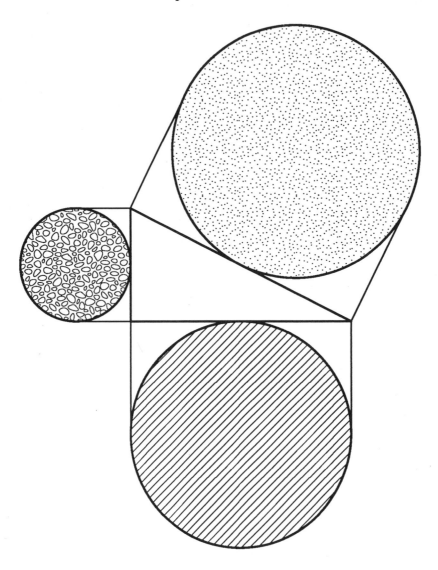

Chapter 10: Grazing Goats

Overview
Students solve for area of circles and parts of circles by doing classic problems.

Student Materials
compass, ruler, scientific calculator, shoe box lid (optional), string

Number of Periods Required/Suggested Schedule
Novice: 6 periods
    Day 1: Preliminary activities; pp. 135-138 (Problems 1-8). Assign p. 138 (Problem 9).
    Day 2: Review homework; pp. 139-141 (Problem 13). Assign p. 141 (Problem 14).
    Day 3: Review homework; pp. 142-143; Mid-Chapter 10 Quiz. Assign p. 145.
    Day 4: Review homework and Mid-Chapter 10 Quiz; pp. 144, 146. Assign p. 147.
    Day 5: Review homework; p. 148.
    Day 6: Administer Test C.

Apprentice: 5 periods
    Day 1: Preliminary activities; pp. 135-138. Assign p. 139.
    Day 2: Review homework; pp. 140-141. Assign p. 142.
    Day 3: Review homework; pp. 143-144; Mid-Chapter 10 Quiz. Assign p. 145.
    Day 4: Review homework and Mid-Chapter 10 Quiz; p. 146. Assign pp. 147-148.
    Day 5: Review homework; p. 148; Test C.

Expert: 4 periods
    Day 1: Preliminary activities; pp. 135-138. Assign pp. 139-140 (Problem 12).
    Day 2: Review homework; pp. 140-143. Assign pp. 144-145.
    Day 3: Review homework; pp. 146-147; Mid-Chapter 10 Quiz. Assign p. 148.
    Day 4: Review homework and Mid-Chapter 10 Quiz; Test C.

General Comments
The problems in this chapter center primarily around a tethered goat and the amount of area that the goat can reach. Students may have difficulty visualizing how the tethers change radii as they pass objects. It becomes much clearer if they have a physical model to use. A model is described in the Supplemental Activities. Use models with the early problems, moving on to compass methods.

It is important to emphasize the use of the calculator's memory.

If you choose to make up goat problems, be careful not to make the tether longer than half the perimeter of the rectangle, or other figure, involved... unless you want to venture into another category of much more difficult problems usually requiring trigonometry.

Of course, real goats on ropes are not even remotely involved in these problems. A goat on a rope merely makes a quick, elegant way to state an interesting problem.

Vocabulary
tether   A rope or chain that confines a goat. When astronauts go for a "space walk," they are tethered.

Preliminary Activities

During recess or gym, tie a rope to the belt loop of a student volunteer. Tie the other end to the corner of a building, a fence, or a jungle gym. Be sure to have objects for the tether to wrap around. Have the student walk until the rope is fully extended, then see where he/she can walk. This can be made into an educational "tag" game as described in the Supplemental Activities.

A goat on a tether works like a compass; the goat extends to the full length of its tether and sweeps out a part of a circle until it or its rope strikes an obstacle. A helpful demonstration tool using a shoe box lid is discussed in the Supplemental Activities.

Teaching Notes

page 135	If students have never used the pencil and string method to illustrate a compass, you might want them to use this method in Problems 1 and 2.
	In Figure A, the goat can reach anywhere within the encircled region. In Figure B, the goat cannot reach beyond the fence.
page 137	Transparency #1 reproduces Figure E.
	In Figure E, you may ask students what would happen if the side of the barn were less than 60 ft. (Billy would begin to wrap around the barn.)
page 138	In Problem 8, students can trace the grazing area with their compasses. However, when the pencil of the compass aligns with *BC*, the compass cannot "cross over" the barn. Only the length of *CD* can turn the corner of the barn. Adding the answers to Problems 8b and 8c should equal Problem 8a.
	Problem 9 is divided into two regions. It is important to stress that the regions change by *radius length* and the goat grazes on all regions combined.
page 139	Encourage students to write the radii measurements directly on Figure G.
	If students are having difficulty understanding why the radius changes as the tether bends a corner, try a physical model of a barn marked out with straight pins. Do not use a compass, but a string tied to a pencil. As the string wraps around the model barn, the tether gets caught and a new radius is created.
page 140	Students should extend the sides as far as possible so that the extended side intersects the tether line. If the extended side does not intersect with the tether line, a student is likely to "cross over" the edge of the barn.
page 141	Transparency #2 reproduces Figure J.
page 142	Transparency #3 reproduces Figure K. A scale line is provided in Problem 15. Students draw their own tether using this scale.
page 143	A general rule of thumb when estimating area, such as in Problem 16b, is that the more obstacles introduced (i.e. trees, fences, barns), the smaller the grazing area. Draw a line on Transparency #3 to represent the fence in Figure L.
page 144	Transparency #4 reproduces Figure M. This is not a guessing game; have students place their compasses on each corner of the barn, extended to the length of the tether. If the path of the compass overlaps the garden or trees, the goat should not be tethered there.

page 145	Figure N shows the first time a goat is tethered in the middle of a barn wall. Have students refer back to Problem 2 on page 135.
page 146	Compare the perimeter found in Problem 20 to the answer you would get if the goat were on a 60 ft tether without any fences; they are the same: 376.99112 ft. Does that seem unusual?
page 147	Ask students to estimate an answer to Problem 21 using what they learned in Problem 19 on the previous page. There are a variety of possible methods to Problem 21 using memory, but all require that a "messy" number be keyed in at least twice.
page 148	Transparency #5 reproduces Figure R.

Supplemental Activities (Optional)

To demonstrate a tether wrapping around a barn, tie a large knot at the end of a piece of string (tether). Place the knotted end into a corner slit of a shoe box lid (barn) and hold the lid against the chalkboard. Tie the other end of the string to a piece of chalk (goat). As the chalk is pulled around the barn, students will see how the tether "wraps."

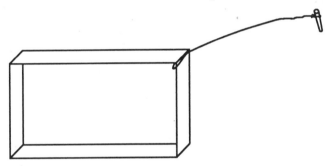

Play a game of "Tethered Goat Tag." Tie a tether to the belt loop of one student, the one chosen to be "The Goat." Tie the other end to a fence, building, or piece of playground equipment. Let all students know the length of the tether, and give them a few hints as to how to estimate distance through footsteps or paces. The object of the game is to be as close to "The Goat's" grazing area without standing in it. When the teacher signals, students have 30 seconds to find a place to stand. Once 30 seconds are up, the teacher shouts, "Freeze!" and the students cannot move. "The Goat" then walks around, tagging those frozen players that he/she can reach. To "win," a student has to be standing as close to "The Goat" without being tagged. The winner gets to be the next "Goat." For the next game, change the length of the tether, or tie it to a different location.

How much are these goats actually eating? A goat tied to a 125-foot tether in an open field grazes an area larger than a professional football field! That is quite a bit for one goat. A professional football field is 160 ft wide and 300 ft (100 yards) long, or 48,000 square feet. Every 10 yards on a football field marks off 4,800 square feet. What is the equivalent yardage on a football field of the grazed area from this chapter? The goat in Problem 18, page 145, grazes in an area larger than 2 football fields! Ask students if they think this is realistic. How long would it take the goat to graze that area? Students can estimate, or research, how much area a goat could graze in one day, then use the answer to determine the length of time a goat would need to finish off all the grass.

Flexible Ruler Transparency

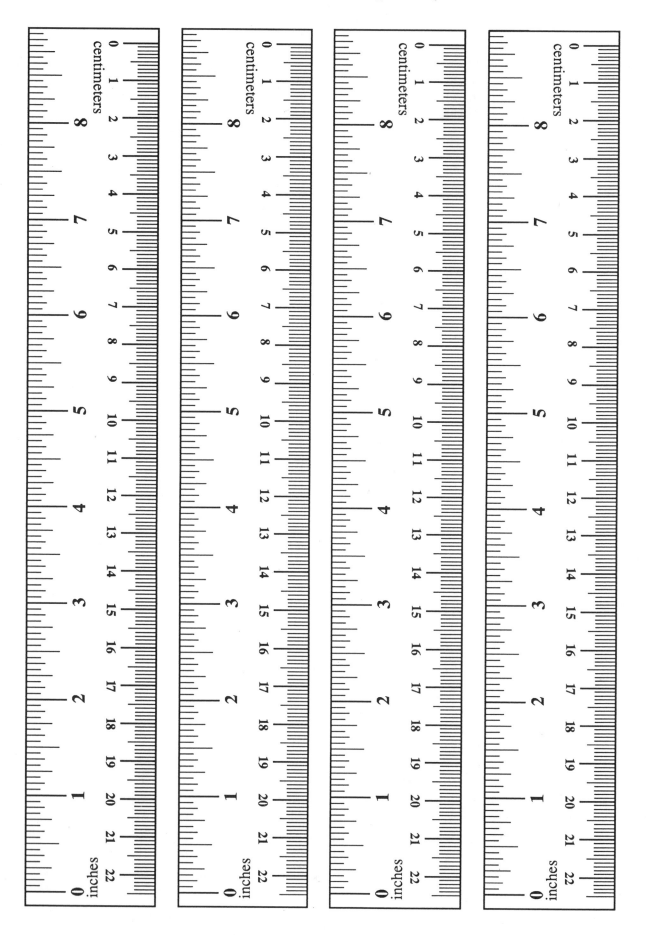

Transparencies (Blackline Masters)

Calculator Transparency

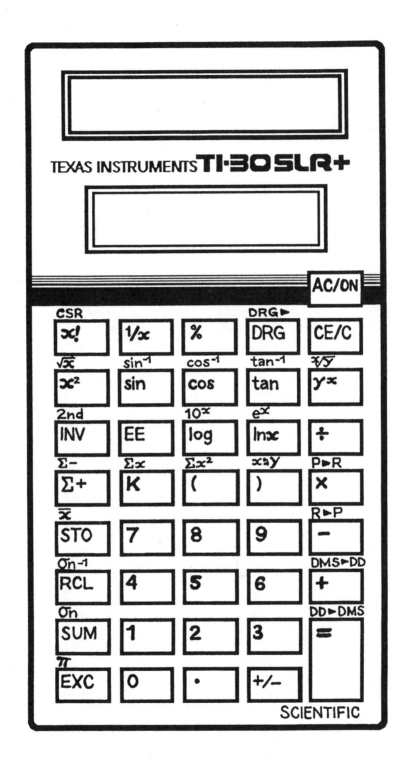

Flexible Ruler Transparency

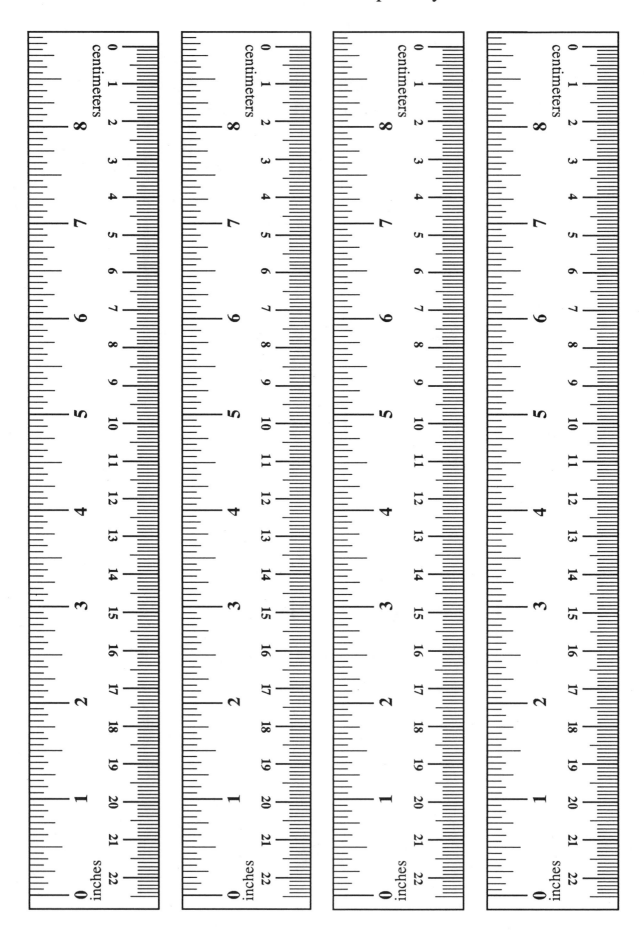

Centimeter Grid Transparency

25 cm² Transparency

Polygons

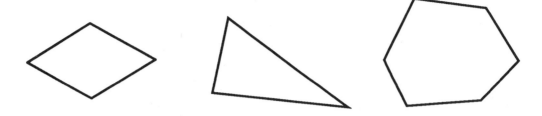

Regular Polygons

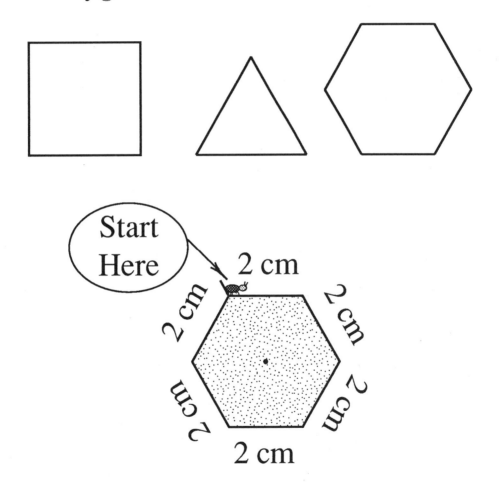

Perimeter _____ cm

Teacher's note: Label the lengths of the sides of each polygon. What is special about a regular polygon? Notice the first polygon has equal sides, but the angles are not equal. The equal sides and angles differentiate regular polygons from other polygons. Label each polygon with its perimeter.

Use with Student Lab Book page 8.

Cylinder	Measured Diameter *Put in units.*	Measured Circumference *Put in units.*
1		
2		
3		
4		
5		

20b. Compare the diameter and circumference columns. For each cylinder, about how many diameters equal the circumference?

Answer _____

Teacher's note: Use with Student Lab Book page 13.

Radius	Diameter	Circum-ference *Copy window.*	Keystrokes
2.75 cm			
	11 cm		
11 cm			
	44 cm		
44 cm			

7a. What happens to the length of the radius?

_____

7b. What happens to the length of the diameter?

_____

7c. What happens to the circumference?

_____

Teacher's note: Use with Student Lab Book page 16.

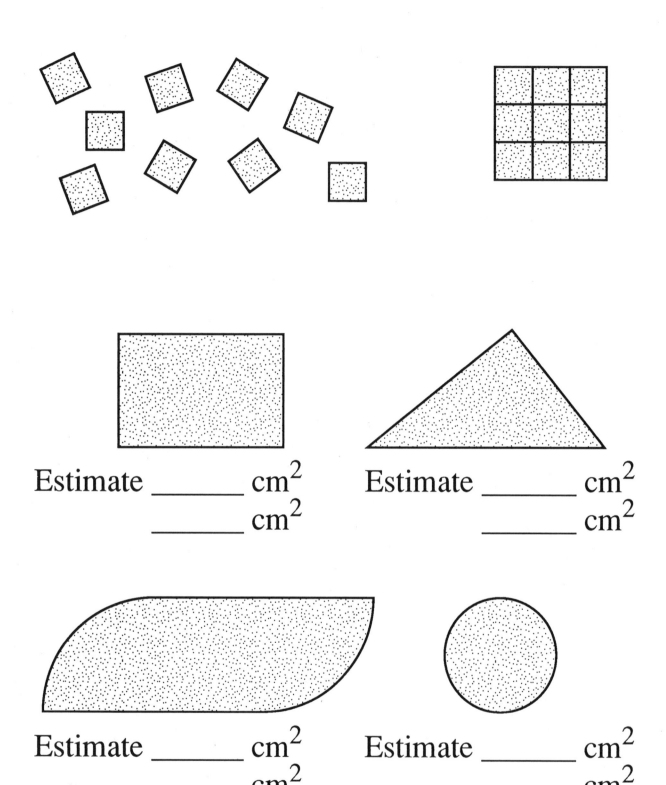

Estimate _____ cm^2
_____ cm^2

Estimate _____ cm^2
_____ cm^2

Estimate _____ cm^2
_____ cm^2

Estimate _____ cm^2
_____ cm^2

Teacher's note: Use the first answer line to estimate the area of each figure. Place a centimeter grid transparency over the figures to make an improved estimate. Write this estimate on the second line.

Use with Student Lab Book pages 17 and 18.

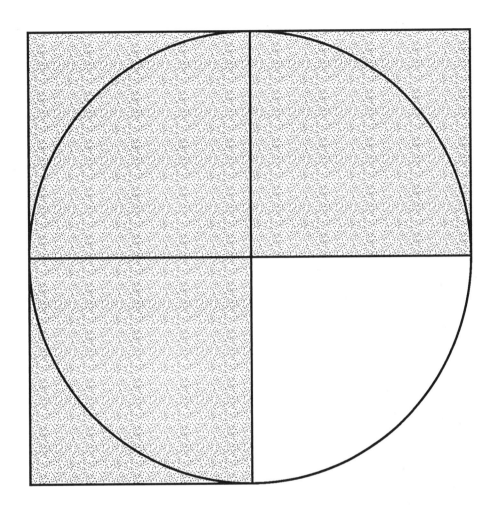

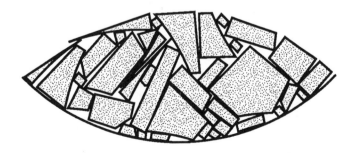

Teacher's note: To compare the area of the circle with the area of three squares, cut off the three outside corners. Place one corner along the radii, inside the empty quarter-circle. The other two corners were cut up to build the oval figure above. Place this figure inside the empty quarter-circle. The area of the circle is slightly more than the area of three squares.

Use with Student Lab Book pages 21 and 22.

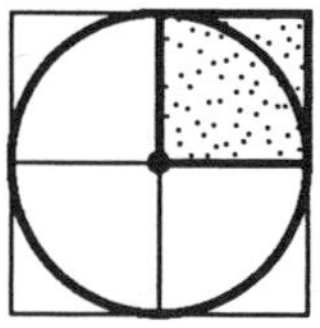

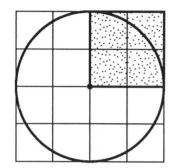 Area of square _____ cm²

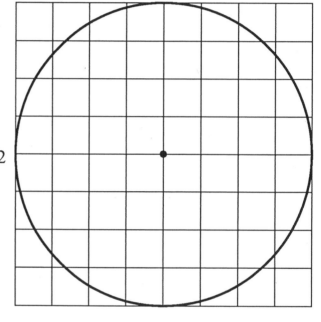 Area of square _____ cm²

Area of
square _____ cm²

Radius	Area of Square Built on Radius	Estimated Area of Circle
1 cm	1 cm²	3 × 1 cm² = 3 cm²
2 cm		
4 cm		
8 cm		

Teacher's note: Use with Student Lab Book page 26.

Radius	Diameter	Circumference _R to the nearest hundredth._	Area _R to the nearest hundredth._
0.25 cm			
	1 cm		
1 cm			
2 cm			
	8 cm		
8 cm			
16 cm			

2b. Predict the circumference of a circle with a 3 cm radius. _____ cm

2c. Predict the area. _____ cm^2

2d. Calculate the circumference. _____ cm

Nearest hundredth.

2e. Calculate the area. _____ cm^2

Nearest hundredth.

3. A circle has an area of 100 cm^2. Predict its circumference.

Prediction _____ cm

Teacher's note: Use with Student Lab Book page 29.

Chapter 3
Transparency #2

Side Length	Area *You want* ______________

Teacher's note: Use with Student Lab Book pages 31 and 32.

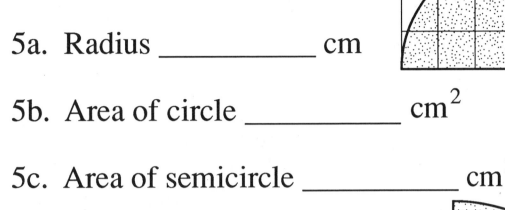

5a. Radius _____ cm

5b. Area of circle _____ cm^2

5c. Area of semicircle _____ cm^2

5d. List keystrokes.

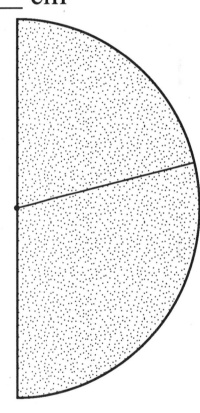

6a. Radius _____

Put in units.

6b. Area of circle 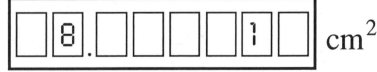 cm^2

6c. Area of semicircle  cm^2

Teacher's note: Use with Student Lab Book pages 46 and 47.

1. Estimate the area of the
    shaded figure.

    Estimate _____
    Put in units.

2a. Area of circle [ ][ ].[ ][6][6][ ][ ] cm^2

2b. Area of
    quarter-circle [ ].[1][ ][1][ ][ ][ ] cm^2

2c. Area of shaded figure _____ cm^2
    Copy window.

2d. [ ][ ][ ][ ][ ][ ][ ][ ][ ][ ]
    [ ][ ]

3. Kendra's keystrokes:

    [2][x^2][×][π][−]
    [2][x^2][×][π][÷][4][=]

3c. Explain Kendra's method. _____

_____

Teacher's note: In Problem 2, students multiply the area of one quarter-circle by three to
find the total area. In Problem 3, Kendra subtracts the area of one quarter-circle from the
whole circle.
Use with Student Lab Book page 51.

Chapter 5
Transparency #1

Press:	Window	Memory

Press:	Window	Memory

Teacher's note: Use with Student Lab Book pages 57-62, 66.

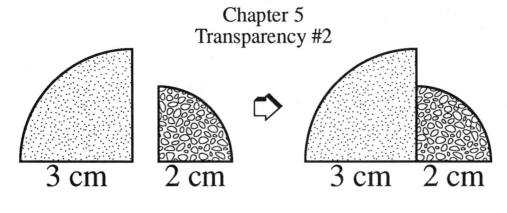

4a. Area of quarter-circle _____ cm^2 STO

4b. Area of quarter-circle _____ cm^2 SUM

4c. Press: RCL

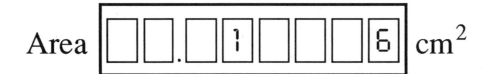

Area [   ][   ].[   ][1][   ][   ][6] cm^2

5a. Larger quarter-circle _____ cm^2 STO

5b. Radius _____ cm

5c. Smaller quarter-circle

[   ][8].[   ][   ][3][   ][   ] cm^2

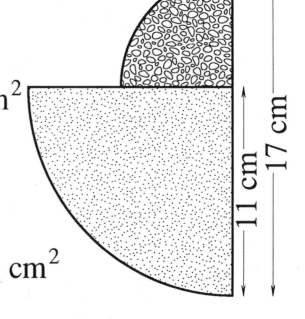

Press: SUM RCL

5d. Total area _____ cm^2

Nearest tenth.

Teacher's note: Use with Student Lab Book page 64.

6. Count square centimeters to estimate the area of the following figure.

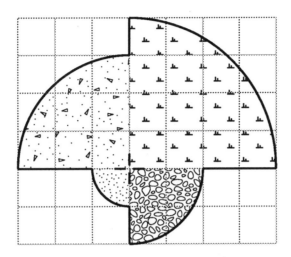

Estimate _____ cm^2

7. Calculate the area of the figure.

7a. Area of [image] _____ cm^2 Press: ☐

7b. Area of [image] _____ cm^2 Press: ☐

7c. Area of [image] _____ cm^2 Press: ☐

7d. Area of [image] _____ cm^2 Press: ☐

7e. Press ☐ or ☐ to find the total area.

Total area | | 3 | . | | 1 | | | cm^2

Teacher's note: Use with Student Lab Book page 65.

6.

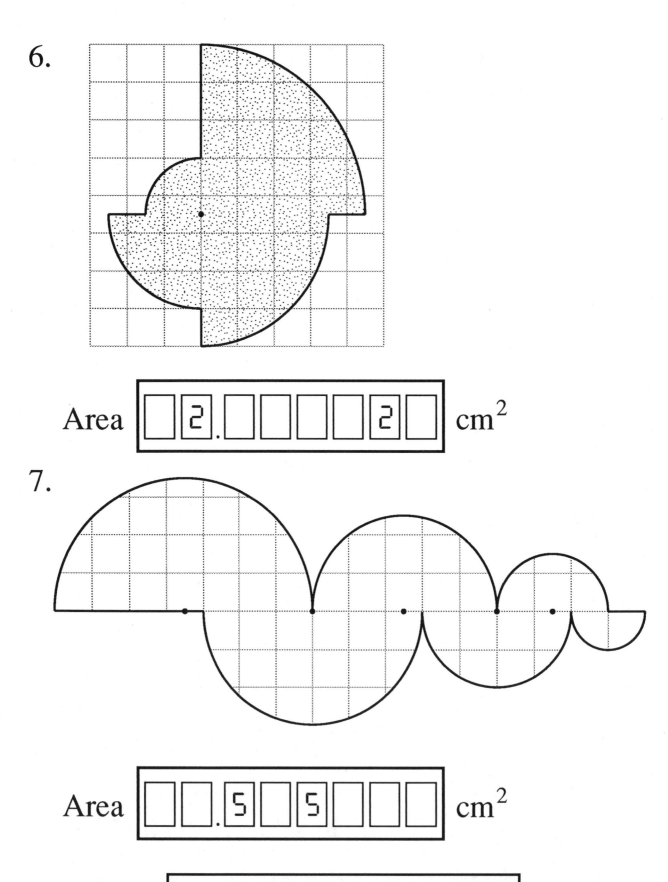

Area ☐ 2 . ☐ ☐ ☐ ☐ 2 ☐ cm^2

7.

Area ☐ ☐ . 5 ☐ 5 ☐ ☐ cm^2

Teacher's note: Use with Student Lab Book page 68.

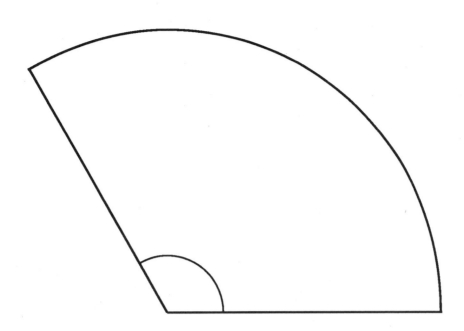

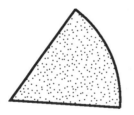

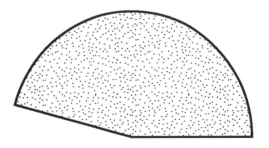

Teacher's note: Use top sector to demonstrate protractor use. Use bottom sectors to demonstrate extending and measuring.

Use with Student Lab Book pages 73, 75, and 76.

3. Find the number of 60° sectors in the circle.

    How many 60° sectors fit in the circle?

    Answer _____

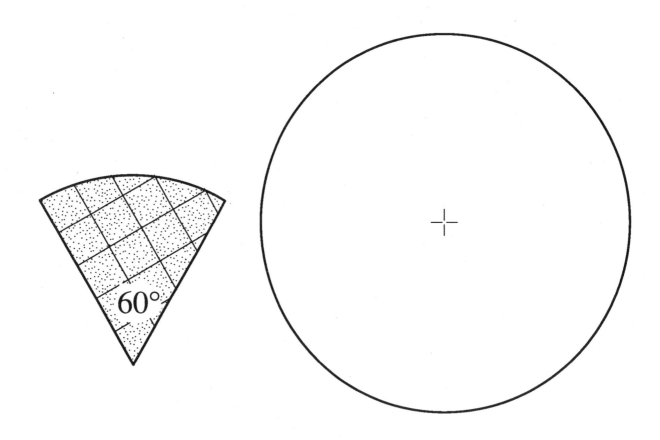

Degrees in Whole Circle	Angle	Number of Sectors	Area of Sector with Radius of 8 cm
360°	60°	6	201.06 cm^2 ÷ 6 = 33.51 cm^2
360°	45°		201.06 cm^2 ÷ =
	30°		
	15°		
	12°		
	11°		
	10°		

Teacher's note: Can the area of the sector be found when there is a "messy" number of sectors? Yes, as shown with the 11° angle.

Use with Student Lab Book page 81.

9. Estimate _____ cm²

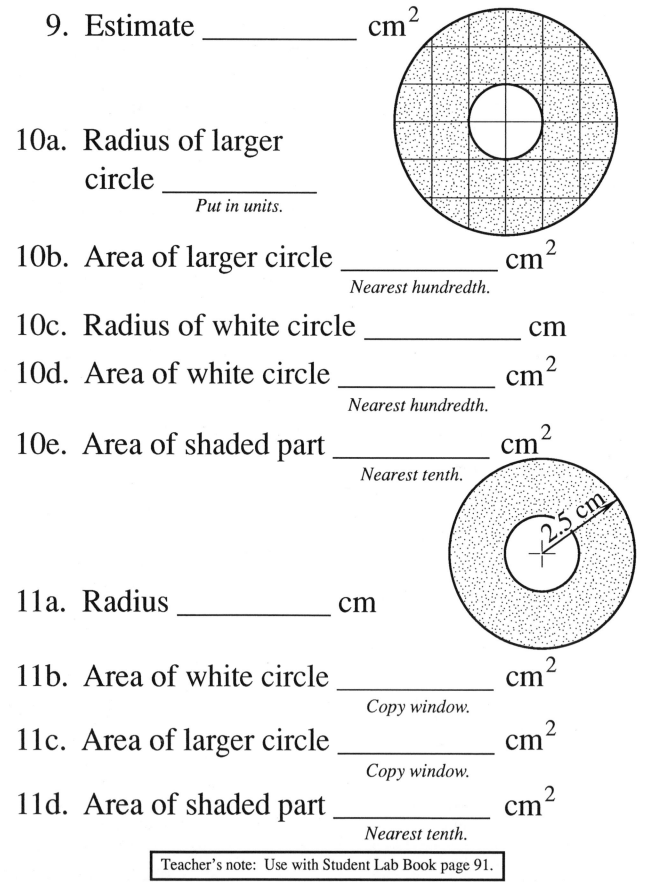

10a. Radius of larger
circle _____
Put in units.

10b. Area of larger circle _____ cm²
Nearest hundredth.

10c. Radius of white circle _____ cm

10d. Area of white circle _____ cm²
Nearest hundredth.

10e. Area of shaded part _____ cm²
Nearest tenth.

11a. Radius _____ cm

11b. Area of white circle _____ cm²
Copy window.

11c. Area of larger circle _____ cm²
Copy window.

11d. Area of shaded part _____ cm²
Nearest tenth.

Teacher's note: Use with Student Lab Book page 91.

4. Draw each rectangle. Find the area of each triangle.

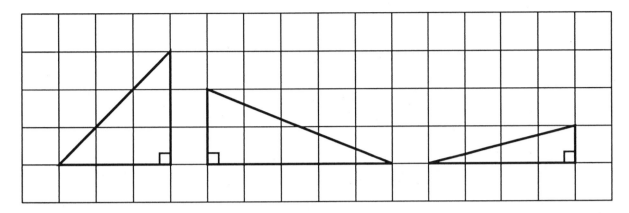

Area _____ cm²   Area _____ cm²   Area _____ cm²

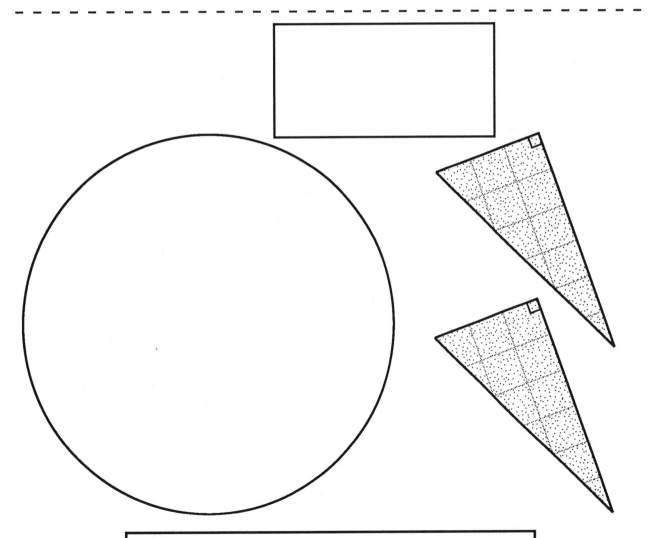

Teacher's note: Use with Student Lab Book pages 98 and 99.

2. The radius of the semicircle at the right is 3 cm. Measure the perimeter.

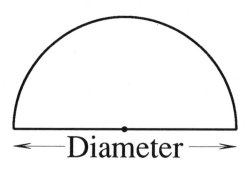

Measured perimeter _____ cm

3a. What is the length of curved part?

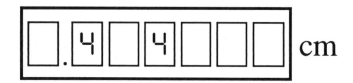
cm

3b. What is the length of the straight part?

Length of straight part _____ cm

3c. What is the perimeter? _____ cm

Nearest tenth.

Teacher's note: Use with Student Lab Book page 109.

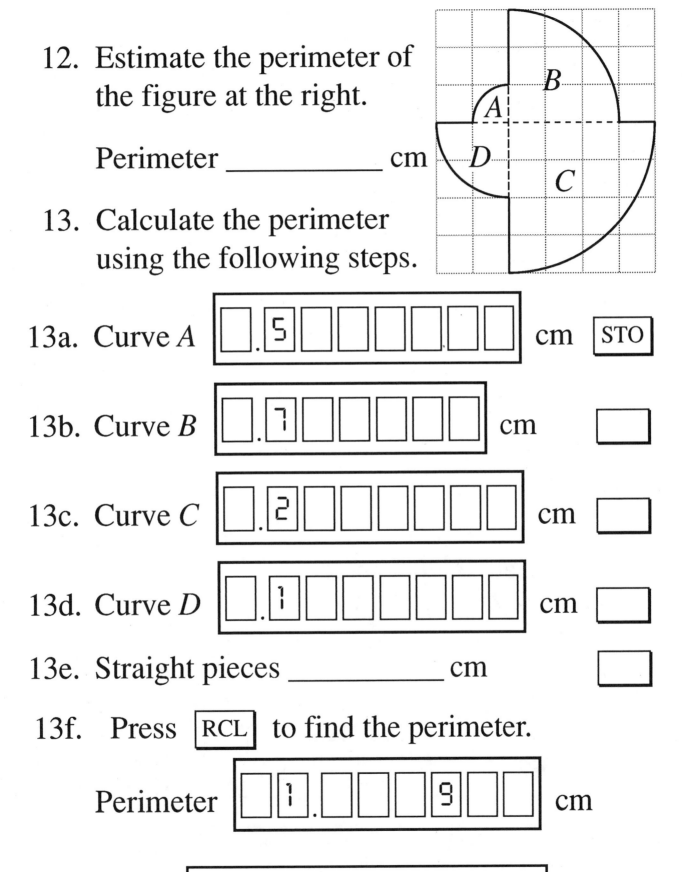

12. Estimate the perimeter of the figure at the right.

Perimeter _____ cm

13. Calculate the perimeter using the following steps.

13a. Curve A $\boxed{\square . 5 \square \square \square \square \square}$ cm $\boxed{\text{STO}}$

13b. Curve B $\boxed{\square . 7 \square \square \square \square}$ cm $\boxed{}$

13c. Curve C $\boxed{\square . 2 \square \square \square \square \square}$ cm $\boxed{}$

13d. Curve D $\boxed{\square . 1 \square \square \square \square \square}$ cm $\boxed{}$

13e. Straight pieces _____ cm $\boxed{}$

13f. Press $\boxed{\text{RCL}}$ to find the perimeter.

Perimeter $\boxed{\square 1 . \square \square 9 \square \square}$ cm

Teacher's note: Use with Student Lab Book page 113.

14. Calculate the circumference of the circle at the right.

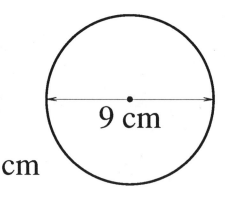

Circumference _____ cm

Copy window.

15. Calculate the perimeter of the shape at the right.

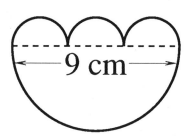

Perimeter of figure _____ cm

Copy window.

16. Calculate the perimeter of the figure at the right.

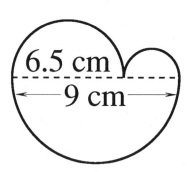

Perimeter | 8. 7 | cm

Teacher's note: In each figure, semicircles are built along both sides of the 9 cm diameter. The "perimeter" of each figure is the same.

Use with Student Lab Book page 114.

11. Estimate the perimeter of the following quarter-strip.

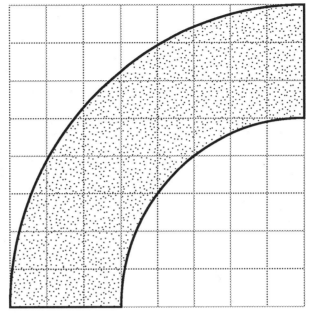

Estimated perimeter _____ cm

12. Calculate the perimeter of the quarter-strip.

12a. Large curve 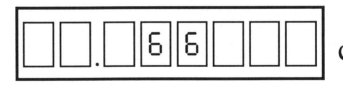 cm

12b. Small curve 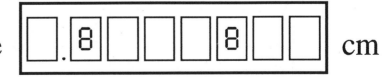 cm

12c. Straight parts _____ cm

12d. Perimeter _____ cm

Nearest tenth.

Teacher's note: Use with Student Lab Book page 119.

a. Build a square along each leg of the right triangle.
b. Shade or color one of the squares.
c. Cut out the triangle and the squares.
e. Cut and arrange the squares to build a larger square along the hypotenuse.

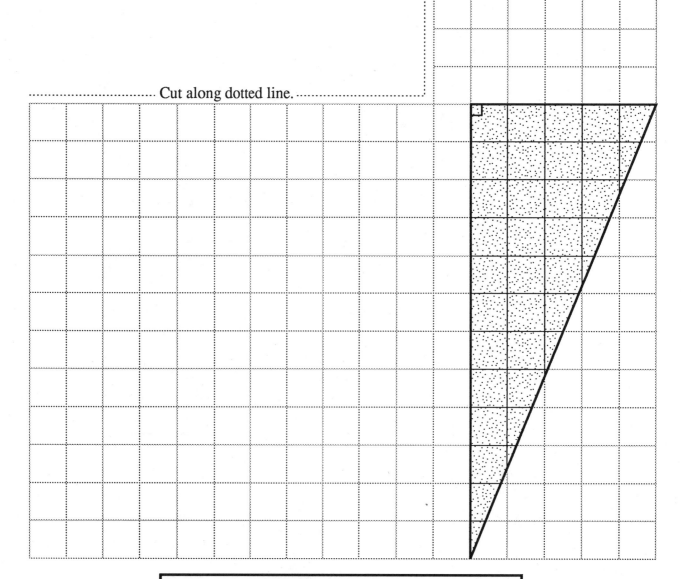

Cut along dotted line.

Teacher's note: Use with Student Lab Book page 127.

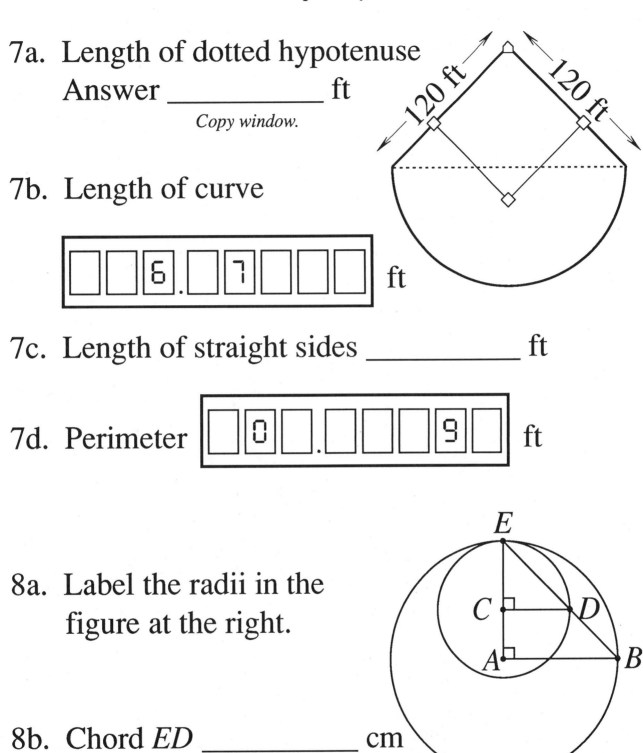

7a. Length of dotted hypotenuse
    Answer _____ ft

    Copy window.

7b. Length of curve

    ☐ ☐ 6 . ☐ 7 ☐ ☐ ☐ ft

7c. Length of straight sides _____ ft

7d. Perimeter ☐ 0 ☐ . ☐ ☐ 9 ☐ ft

8a. Label the radii in the
    figure at the right.

8b. Chord *ED* _____ cm

    Copy window.

8c. Chord *EB* _____ cm

    Copy window.

Teacher's note: Use with Student Lab Book page 134.

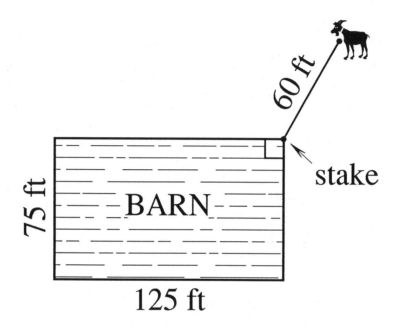

BARN

75 ft

125 ft

60 ft

stake

Area (□ 4 □ 2 . □) ft²

Nearest tenth.

Teacher's note: Use with Student Lab Book page 137.

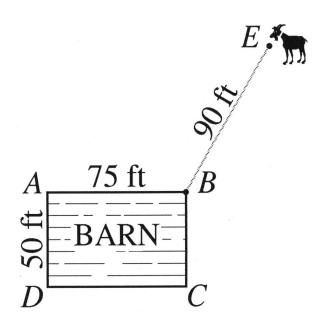

Total area 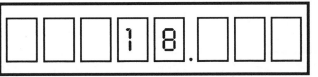 ft^2

Teacher's note: Use with Student Lab Book page 141.

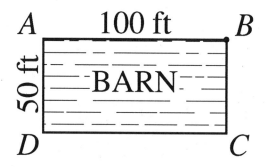

A 100 ft B

50 ft

BARN

D C

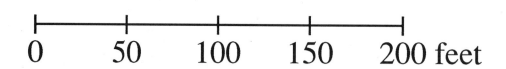

0   50   100   150   200 feet

Teacher's note: Make two copies of this transparency. Use one copy with Problem 15 on page 142. Use the second copy with Problem 16 on page 143. Draw in the 50 ft fence using the scale line. Put the two transparencies on top of each other to compare the different areas.

Use with Student Lab Book pages 142 and 143.

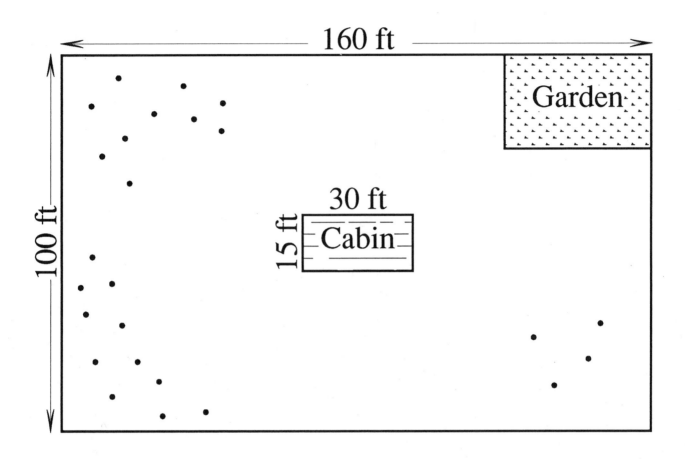

160 ft

100 ft

Garden

30 ft

15 ft

Cabin

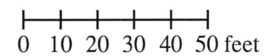

0   10   20   30   40   50 feet

Area _____ ft^2

Copy window.

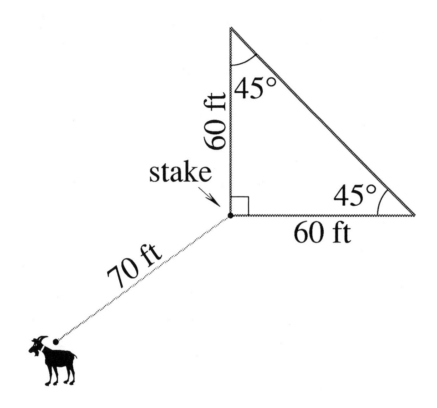

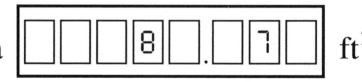

Grazing area [ ][ ][ ][8][ ].[7][ ] ft^2

Teacher's note: Use with Student Lab Book page 148.

Quizzes and Tests

HINT DEFLECTOR

(Use for Mid-Quizzes 3, 7, 9, and 10; Quizzes 2, 4, and 7)

HINT deflector SEE THROUGH STOPPER HINT deflector SEE THROUGH
SEE THROUGH STOPPER HINT deflector SEE THROUGH STOPPER HINT
HINT deflector SEE THROUGH STOPPER HINT deflector SEE THROUGH
SEE THROUGH STOPPER HINT deflector SEE THROUGH STOPPER HINT
HINT deflector SEE THROUGH STOPPER HINT deflector SEE THROUGH
SEE THROUGH STOPPER HINT deflector SEE THROUGH STOPPER HINT
HINT deflector SEE THROUGH STOPPER HINT deflector SEE THROUGH
SEE THROUGH STOPPER HINT deflector SEE THROUGH STOPPER HINT
HINT deflector SEE THROUGH STOPPER HINT deflector SEE THROUGH
SEE THROUGH STOPPER HINT deflector SEE THROUGH STOPPER HINT
HINT deflector SEE THROUGH STOPPER HINT deflector SEE THROUGH
SEE THROUGH STOPPER HINT deflector SEE THROUGH STOPPER HINT
HINT deflector SEE THROUGH STOPPER HINT deflector SEE THROUGH
SEE THROUGH STOPPER HINT deflector SEE THROUGH STOPPER HINT
HINT deflector SEE THROUGH STOPPER HINT deflector SEE THROUGH
SEE THROUGH STOPPER HINT deflector SEE THROUGH STOPPER HINT
HINT deflector SEE THROUGH STOPPER HINT deflector SEE THROUGH
SEE THROUGH STOPPER HINT deflector SEE THROUGH STOPPER HINT
HINT deflector SEE THROUGH STOPPER HINT deflector SEE THROUGH
SEE THROUGH STOPPER HINT deflector SEE THROUGH STOPPER HINT
HINT deflector SEE THROUGH STOPPER HINT deflector SEE THROUGH
SEE THROUGH STOPPER HINT deflector SEE THROUGH STOPPER HINT
HINT deflector SEE THROUGH STOPPER HINT deflector SEE THROUGH
SEE THROUGH STOPPER HINT deflector SEE THROUGH STOPPER HINT
HINT deflector SEE THROUGH STOPPER HINT deflector SEE THROUGH
SEE THROUGH STOPPER HINT deflector SEE THROUGH STOPPER HINT
HINT deflector SEE THROUGH STOPPER HINT deflector SEE THROUGH
SEE THROUGH STOPPER HINT deflector SEE THROUGH STOPPER HINT
HINT deflector SEE THROUGH STOPPER HINT deflector SEE THROUGH
SEE THROUGH STOPPER HINT deflector SEE THROUGH STOPPER HINT
HINT deflector SEE THROUGH STOPPER HINT deflector SEE THROUGH
SEE THROUGH STOPPER HINT deflector SEE THROUGH STOPPER HINT
HINT deflector SEE THROUGH STOPPER HINT deflector SEE THROUGH
SEE THROUGH STOPPER HINT deflector SEE THROUGH STOPPER HINT
HINT deflector SEE THROUGH STOPPER HINT deflector SEE THROUGH
SEE THROUGH STOPPER HINT deflector SEE THROUGH STOPPER HINT
HINT deflector SEE THROUGH STOPPER HINT deflector SEE THROUGH
SEE THROUGH STOPPER HINT deflector SEE THROUGH STOPPER HINT
HINT deflector SEE THROUGH STOPPER HINT deflector SEE THROUGH
SEE THROUGH STOPPER HINT deflector SEE THROUGH STOPPER HINT
HINT deflector SEE THROUGH STOPPER HINT deflector SEE THROUGH
SEE THROUGH STOPPER HINT deflector SEE THROUGH STOPPER HINT
HINT deflector SEE THROUGH STOPPER HINT deflector SEE THROUGH
SEE THROUGH STOPPER HINT deflector SEE THROUGH STOPPER HINT
HINT deflector SEE THROUGH STOPPER HINT deflector SEE THROUGH
SEE THROUGH STOPPER HINT deflector SEE THROUGH STOPPER HINT
HINT deflector SEE THROUGH STOPPER HINT deflector SEE THROUGH
SEE THROUGH STOPPER HINT deflector SEE THROUGH STOPPER HINT

HINT DEFLECTOR

(Use for Mid-Quizzes 3, 7, 9, and 10; Quizzes 2, 4, and 7)

HINT deflector SEE THROUGH STOPPER HINT deflector SEE THROUGH
SEE THROUGH STOPPER HINT deflector SEE THROUGH STOPPER HINT
HINT deflector SEE THROUGH STOPPER HINT deflector SEE THROUGH
SEE THROUGH STOPPER HINT deflector SEE THROUGH STOPPER HINT
HINT deflector SEE THROUGH STOPPER HINT deflector SEE THROUGH
SEE THROUGH STOPPER HINT deflector SEE THROUGH STOPPER HINT
HINT deflector SEE THROUGH STOPPER HINT deflector SEE THROUGH
SEE THROUGH STOPPER HINT deflector SEE THROUGH STOPPER HINT
HINT deflector SEE THROUGH STOPPER HINT deflector SEE THROUGH
SEE THROUGH STOPPER HINT deflector SEE THROUGH STOPPER HINT
HINT deflector SEE THROUGH STOPPER HINT deflector SEE THROUGH
SEE THROUGH STOPPER HINT deflector SEE THROUGH STOPPER HINT
HINT deflector SEE THROUGH STOPPER HINT deflector SEE THROUGH
SEE THROUGH STOPPER HINT deflector SEE THROUGH STOPPER HINT
HINT deflector SEE THROUGH STOPPER HINT deflector SEE THROUGH
SEE THROUGH STOPPER HINT deflector SEE THROUGH STOPPER HINT
HINT deflector SEE THROUGH STOPPER HINT deflector SEE THROUGH
SEE THROUGH STOPPER HINT deflector SEE THROUGH STOPPER HINT
HINT deflector SEE THROUGH STOPPER HINT deflector SEE THROUGH
SEE THROUGH STOPPER HINT deflector SEE THROUGH STOPPER HINT
HINT deflector SEE THROUGH STOPPER HINT deflector SEE THROUGH
SEE THROUGH STOPPER HINT deflector SEE THROUGH STOPPER HINT
HINT deflector SEE THROUGH STOPPER HINT deflector SEE THROUGH
SEE THROUGH STOPPER HINT deflector SEE THROUGH STOPPER HINT
HINT deflector SEE THROUGH STOPPER HINT deflector SEE THROUGH
SEE THROUGH STOPPER HINT deflector SEE THROUGH STOPPER HINT
HINT deflector SEE THROUGH STOPPER HINT deflector SEE THROUGH
SEE THROUGH STOPPER HINT deflector SEE THROUGH STOPPER HINT
HINT deflector SEE THROUGH STOPPER HINT deflector SEE THROUGH
SEE THROUGH STOPPER HINT deflector SEE THROUGH STOPPER HINT
HINT deflector SEE THROUGH STOPPER HINT deflector SEE THROUGH
SEE THROUGH STOPPER HINT deflector SEE THROUGH STOPPER HINT
HINT deflector SEE THROUGH STOPPER HINT deflector SEE THROUGH
SEE THROUGH STOPPER HINT deflector SEE THROUGH STOPPER HINT
HINT deflector SEE THROUGH STOPPER HINT deflector SEE THROUGH
SEE THROUGH STOPPER HINT deflector SEE THROUGH STOPPER HINT
HINT deflector SEE THROUGH STOPPER HINT deflector SEE THROUGH
SEE THROUGH STOPPER HINT deflector SEE THROUGH STOPPER HINT
HINT deflector SEE THROUGH STOPPER HINT deflector SEE THROUGH
SEE THROUGH STOPPER HINT deflector SEE THROUGH STOPPER HINT
HINT deflector SEE THROUGH STOPPER HINT deflector SEE THROUGH
SEE THROUGH STOPPER HINT deflector SEE THROUGH STOPPER HINT
HINT deflector SEE THROUGH STOPPER HINT deflector SEE THROUGH
SEE THROUGH STOPPER HINT deflector SEE THROUGH STOPPER HINT
HINT deflector SEE THROUGH STOPPER HINT deflector SEE THROUGH
SEE THROUGH STOPPER HINT deflector SEE THROUGH STOPPER HINT
HINT deflector SEE THROUGH STOPPER HINT deflector SEE THROUGH
SEE THROUGH STOPPER HINT deflector SEE THROUGH STOPPER HINT
HINT deflector SEE THROUGH STOPPER HINT deflector SEE THROUGH
SEE THROUGH STOPPER HINT deflector SEE THROUGH STOPPER HINT
HINT deflector SEE THROUGH STOPPER HINT deflector SEE THROUGH
SEE THROUGH STOPPER HINT deflector SEE THROUGH STOPPER HINT

Name _____ Date _____ Class _____

Mid-Chapter 1 Quiz

  1a. Use the center at the right to draw a circle that has a radius of 2.5 cm.

 1b. Without measuring, what is the length of the diameter?

Diameter _____ cm

 1c. Draw in a diameter and a radius. Label each with "diameter" or "radius."

 2a. A regular hexagon is built inside a circle at the right. One side is 2.2 cm. What is the perimeter of the hexagon?

Perimeter _____ cm

2b. Which is larger, the perimeter of the hexagon or the circumference of the circle?

Answer _____
Perimeter or Circumference

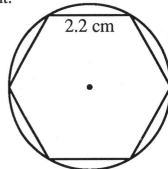

3. A line goes from the center of the large circle to its rim in the following sketch. The line also goes through the center of the small circle.

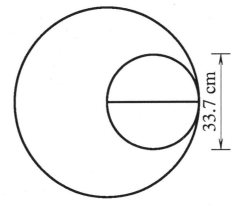

3a. What is the radius of the small circle?

Radius of small circle _____ cm

3b. What is the diameter of the large circle?

Diameter of large circle _____ cm

Chapter 1 Quiz

1a. Christos put a piece of wire along half the circumference of a circle. Which is longer, the length of the wire or the diameter of the circle?

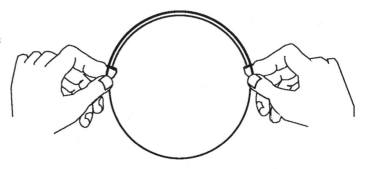

Answer _____
Wire or Diameter

1b. Explain your answer. _____

_____

1c. Barry bent a different wire as shown at the right. Rank the diameter, Christos' wire, and Barry's wire from longest to shortest.

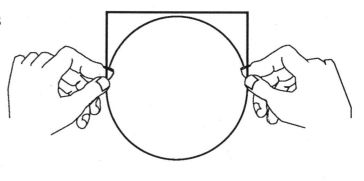

_____ _____ _____
Longest *Shortest*

2a. Estimate the circumference of the following circle.

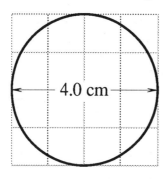

4.0 cm

Estimate _____ cm

2b. Explain what method you used to estimate the circumference.

_____

_____

3a. The diameter of the sketch at the right is 6.0 cm. Estimate the circumference of the circle.

Estimate _____ cm

3b. Calculate the circumference of the circle.

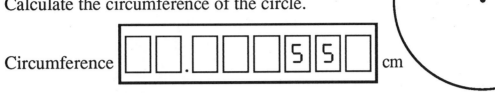

Circumference [ ][ ].[ ][ ][ ][5][5][ ] cm

3c. List your keystrokes for Problem 3b.

[ ][ ][ ][ ][ ]

4. The circles in the following sketches have circumferences of 6 cm, 12 cm, 24 cm, and 48 cm.

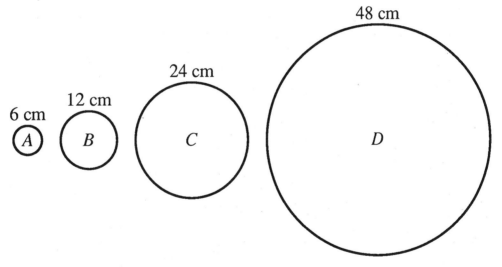

6 cm (A) 12 cm (B) 24 cm (C) 48 cm (D)

4a. Which circle has a diameter of 3.8197186 cm? _____

A, B, C, or D

4b. List your keystrokes for Problem 4a.

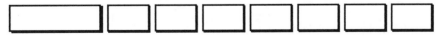

4c. Which circle has a radius of 3.8197186 cm? _____
A, B, C, or D

4d. List your keystrokes for Problem 4c.

Mid-Chapter 2 Quiz

Show your work whenever you use a calculator.

 1a. Estimate the area of the circle in the following figure.

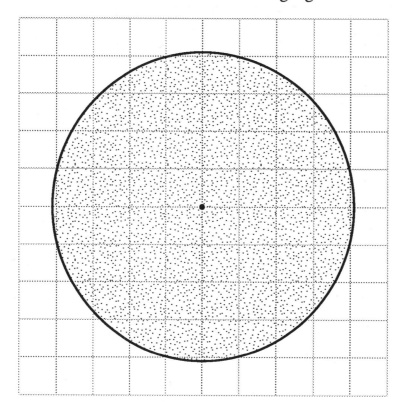

Estimated area _____ cm^2

1b. Briefly tell how you estimated the area in Problem 1a.

_____

 2a. The radius of the circle is 4.1 cm. Calculate the area of the circle.

Area ☐☐.☐☐☐☐☐ cm^2

2b. List your keystrokes for Problem 2a.

4.1						

You do not need to use all the keystroke boxes.

3. The following sketch shows a circle in a square. The circle has a radius of 4.9 cm. Calculate the area of the circle.

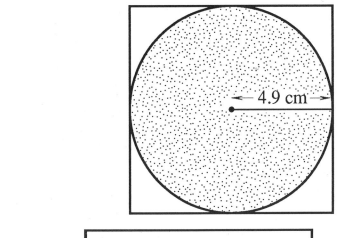

Area of circle | □ □ . 4 □ 9 □ □ | cm²

4a. What is the side length of the square above? _____ cm

Label the sketch.

4b. What is the area of the square? _____ cm²

5. The following sketch shows four identical circles in a square. The *diameter* of each circle is 4.9 cm. Calculate the total area of the four circles.

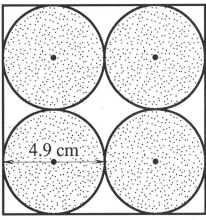

4.9 cm

Area of four circles | □ 5 . □ 2 □ □ □ | cm²

6. What is the area of the square? _____ cm²

Chapter 2 Quiz

 1a. Estimate the area of the sketch at the right.

Estimate _____ cm²

 1b. Calculate the area of the sketch.

Area _____ cm²
Copy window.

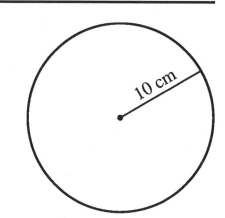

 2a. Estimate the area of the circle at the right.

Estimate _____ cm²

 2b. The diameter of the circle is 5.88 cm. What is the radius of the circle?

Radius _____ cm

2c. Calculate the area of the circle.

Area _____ cm²
Copy window.

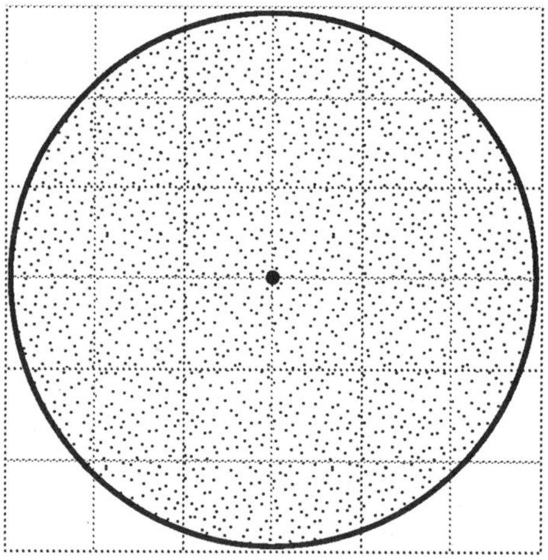

2d. List the keystrokes you used to calculate the area of the circle.

5.88							

3. In the sketch at the right, two small circles are built on the diameter of a large circle. The diameter of the large circle is 8.2 cm. Calculate the area of the smaller circles.

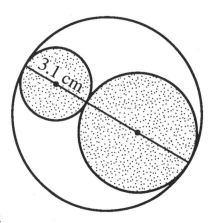

3a. Area of smallest circle  cm²
R to the nearest hundredth.

3b. Area of middle circle 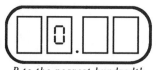 cm²
R to the nearest hundredth.

4. A square is built along the diameter in the sketch at the right. The perimeter of the square is 200 cm. Calculate the area of the circle. Show your work.

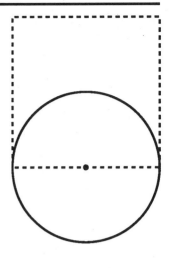

Area of circle ⬚⬚6⬚.⬚ cm²

R to the nearest tenth.

[If you cannot solve Problem 4 within a few minutes, open the HINT below. If you open the HINT and solve Problem 4, you will receive partial credit.]

H-I-N-T

4a. The distance around the square (or perimeter) is 200 cm. What is the side length of the square?

Side length _____ cm

The answer is more than 40 cm.

4b. What is the diameter of the circle?

Diameter _____ cm

4c. What is the radius of the circle?

Radius _____ cm

4d. Calculate the area of the circle.

Area of circle ⬚⬚6⬚.⬚ cm²

R to the nearest tenth.

Side Length

Mid-Chapter 3 Quiz

1. A square is built around a circle in the figure at the right. The area of the square is 25 cm^2.

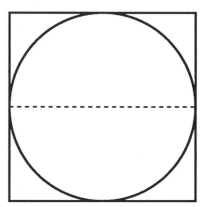

1a. What is the side length of the square?

   Side length _____ cm

1b. What is the diameter of the circle?

   Diameter _____ cm

1c. What is the radius of the circle?

   Radius _____ cm

2. The square in the sketch at the right has an area of 102 cm^2.

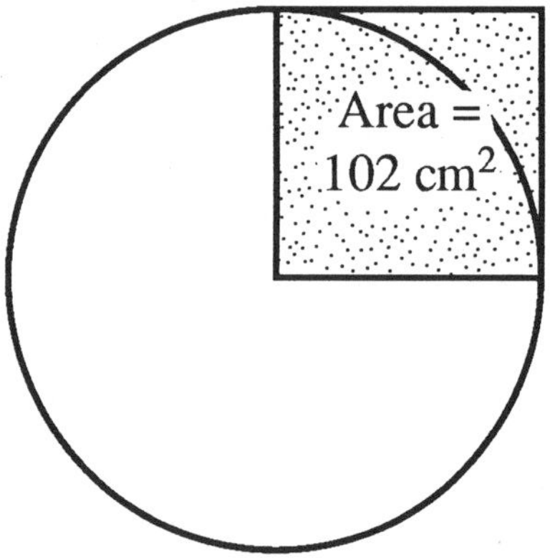

2a. Circle the best estimate for the area of the circle.

   200 cm^2 300 cm^2 400 cm^2

2b. Calculate the radius of the circle.

Radius 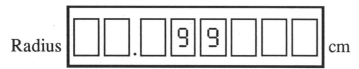 cm

2c. Find the area of the circle.

Area  cm^2

Compare with Problem 2a.

2d. List the keystrokes you used to find the area of the circle. Draw in your own keystroke boxes.

3. Two squares are built along the radii in the circle at the right. The area of the circle is 11.103645 cm^2. Calculate the area of the shaded part.

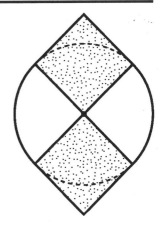

Area of shaded part ☐.☐6☐☐ cm^2

[If you cannot solve Problem 3 within a few minutes, open the HINT below. If you open the HINT and solve Problem 3, you will receive partial credit.]

H-I-N-T

- -

3a. The area of the circle is 11.103645 cm^2. What is the area of *one* square built on the radius?

Area of *one* square _____ cm^2
Copy window.

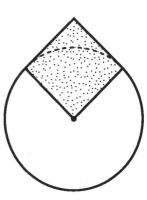

3b. The area of the shaded part at the right is built from two of these squares. What is the area of the shaded part?

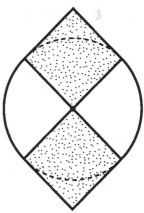

Area of shaded part ☐.☐6☐☐ cm^2

Chapter 3 Quiz

 1a. The area of the circle at the right is 11.34 cm^2.
Calculate the area of the square built on the radius.

Area _____ cm^2
R to the nearest tenth.

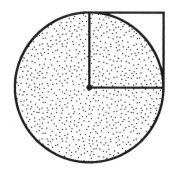

 1b. What is the radius of the circle?

Radius _____ cm
R to the nearest tenth.
Measure to check.

 2. The circumference of the circle in the sketch at
the right is 120 cm. Use the following steps to
calculate the radius of the circle.

2a. Diameter 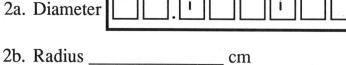 cm

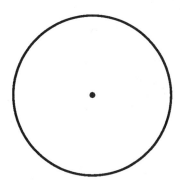

2b. Radius _____ cm
R to the nearest tenth.

3. The area of the square in the sketch at
the right is 240.25 cm^2. The square is
built along the diameter of each circle.
What is the circumference of *one* of the
circles?

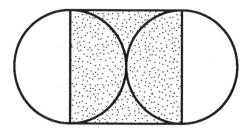

Circumference 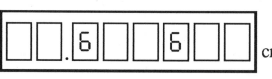 cm

4. The area of the square equals the area of the circle
in the figure at the right. The side length of the
square is 2.774 cm. Calculate the radius of the circle.

←2.774 cm→

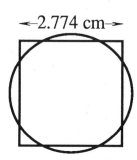

Radius  cm

---

Test A

1. The two circles in the sketch at the right are drawn on a playground. The dashed line shows a path that travels through the center of the small circle and the center of the large circle. The diameter of the small circle is 275 cm and the radius of the large circle is 188 cm.

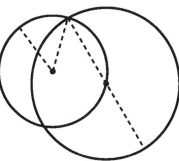

 1a. What is the radius of the small circle? _____ cm

1b. What is the diameter of the large circle? _____ cm

1c. What is the total distance of the dashed line? _____ cm

 2a. Estimate the *circumference* of the circle at the right.

Estimate _____ cm

 2b. The radius of the circle is 3.5 cm. Calculate the circumference.

Circumference ⌈ ⌈ ⌈ . 9 ⌈ ⌉ cm

R to the nearest hundredth.

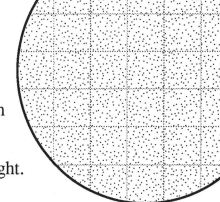

 2c. Estimate the *area* of the circle at the right.

Estimate _____ cm^2

2d. What method did you use to estimate the area of the circle?

_____

 2e. Calculate the area of the circle. ⌈ 8 . 8 ⌈ ⌈ ⌈ ⌉ cm^2

3. Explain why the figure at the right is not a circle.

_____

_____

4a. Three squares are built along the diameter of the following circle. The area of each square is written on the figure. Measure the diameter of the circle.

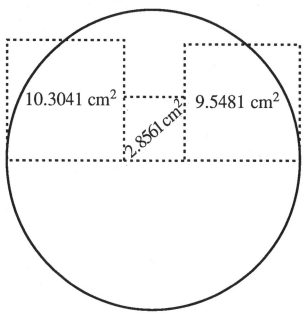

10.3041 cm²   2.8561 cm²   9.5481 cm²

Measured diameter _____ cm

 4b. Calculate the length of this circle's diameter.

Calculated diameter _____ cm

5. The area of the circle at the right is 26.786476 cm².

 5a. Measure the radius of the circle.

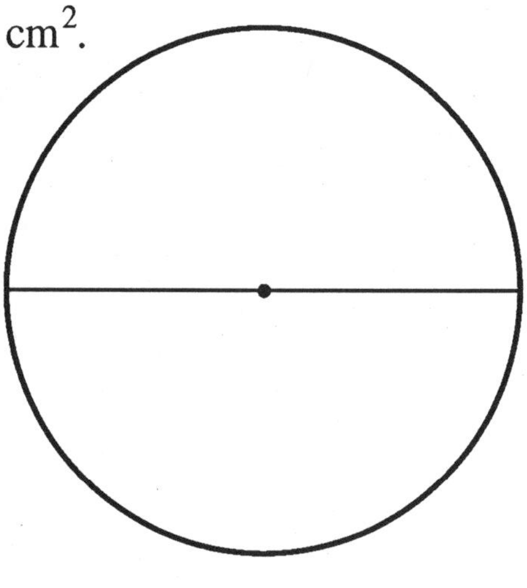

Measured radius _____ cm

 5b. List the keystrokes to calculate the radius of this circle.

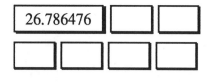

26.786476		

Radius _____ cm

Compare with Problem 5a.

5c. Calculate the circumference of the circle.

Circumference [ ][8].[ ][ ][9][ ][ ] cm

6. A circle and a square each has an area of 25 cm².

 6a. Calculate the diameter of a circle with an area of 25 cm².
List the keystrokes you used.

Diameter _____ cm
R to the nearest tenth.

6b. What is the side length of a square with an area of 25 cm²?

Side length _____ cm

6c. Which is larger, the diameter of the circle or the side length of the square?

Answer _____
Diameter or Side length

  6d. Draw a square and a circle, each with an area of 25 cm².

 7. One of the largest clocks in the world is in Japan. Its circumference is 185.52 ft. Calculate the area of this huge clock face.

Area [7 3 .] ft²
R to the nearest tenth.

Mid-Chapter 4 Quiz

 1a. Use the center on the following grid to draw a circle with a diameter of 4.6 cm.

 1b. Measure the diameter to check your drawing.

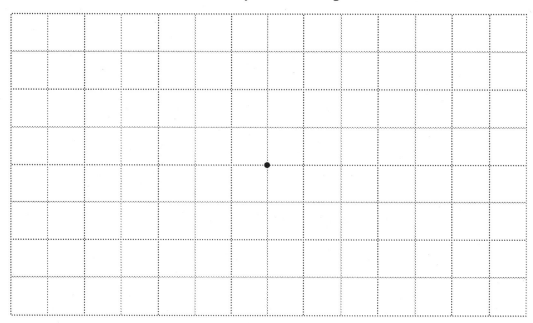

2. How long is a radius of your circle?

   Radius _____ cm

 3. Calculate the area of the whole circle.

   Area | | |.| |1| | |0| | | cm²

 4. Shade a semicircle in your drawing. Circle the best estimate for the area of the semicircle.

   3 cm²   10 cm²   15 cm²   20 cm²

 5. Calculate the area of the semicircle.

   Area of semicircle | |.| | | cm²

   R to the nearest hundredth.
   Compare with Problem 4.

6. A square is built along the radius of the semicircle at the right. The area of the square is 10.24 cm^2. Calculate the area of the semicircle.

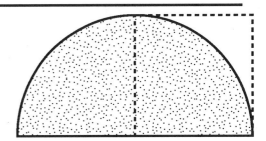

Area  cm^2

7a. Shade a quarter-circle in the sketch at the right.

7b. The radius of the circle is 3.53 cm. Find the area of the quarter-circle.

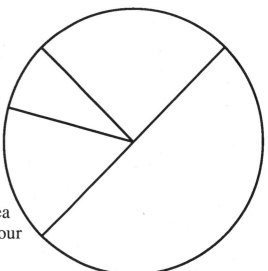

Area 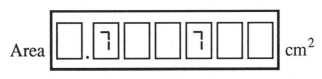 cm^2

7c. List the keystrokes you used to find the area of the quarter-circle in one run. Draw in your own keystroke boxes.

8. A square is built around a quarter-circle in the sketch at the right.

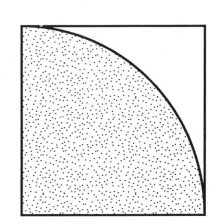

8a. The area of the square is 102.01 cm^2. Find the side length of the square.

Side length _____ cm

8b. Calculate the area of the quarter-circle.

Area of quarter-circle  cm^2

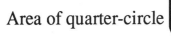
R to the nearest hundredth.

Chapter 4 Quiz

1. The figure at the right is built from three quarter-circles.

1a. Estimate the area of the figure.

Estimate _____ cm^2

1b. The radius of each quarter-circle is 2.8 cm. Calculate the area of the figure.

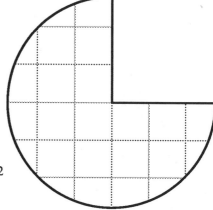

Area  cm^2

1c. List the keystrokes you used to find the area of this figure.

2. The following figure is built from quarter-circles. The radius of each quarter-circle is 2.5 cm. Calculate the area of the figure. Show your work.

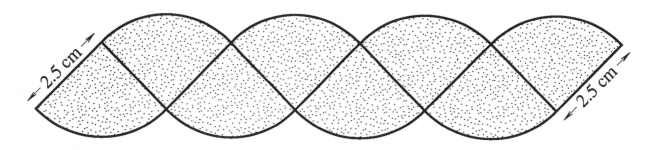

Area ☐☐.2☐ cm^2

R to the nearest hundredth.

3. Circle the best estimate for the
　　 shaded area at the right.

　　　100 cm^2

　　　80 cm^2

　　　60 cm^2

　　　40 cm^2

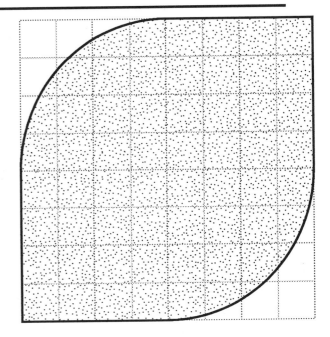

 4. In the figure above, the "curves" are pieces of circles. Calculate the area
　　 of the entire figure. Label the area of each part on the figure above.
　　 Show your work.

Area 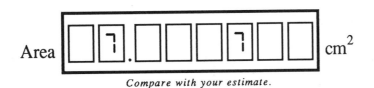 cm^2

Compare with your estimate.

[If you cannot solve Problem 4 within a few minutes, open
the HINT SHEET. If you open the HINT SHEET and solve
Problem 4, you will receive partial credit.]

H-I-N-T S-H-E-E-T

[If you open the HINT SHEET and solve Problem 4, you will receive partial credit.]

. . . .

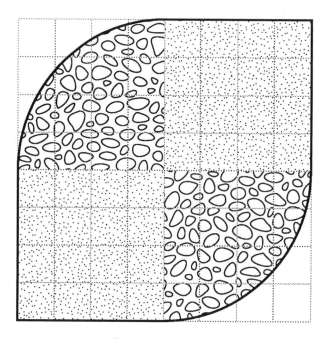

 4a. Find the total area of the ⠿⠿⠿ regions. _____ cm²

4b. The ⠿⠿⠿ regions are quarter-circles. What is the area of both quarter-circles?

Area of both quarter-circles [☐ ☐ . 1 ☐ 2 ☐ ☐ ☐] cm²

4c. Calculate the total area of the figure.

Area [☐ 7 . ☐ ☐ ☐ 7 ☐ ☐] cm²

Compare with Problem 3.

Mid-Chapter 5 Quiz

 Do not use a calculator on this quiz.

1. Sima looked at the figure at the right and pressed the following keystrokes.

| 3.7256 | STO | × | 2 | = |

1a. What is in memory, the diameter of the small circle or the diameter of the large circle?

Answer _____
Small or Large

1b. What part of the large circle is in memory, the radius or the diameter?

Answer _____
Radius or Diameter

1c. What is in the window, the diameter of the small circle or the diameter of the large circle?

Answer _____
Small or Large

2. Complete the following tables.

Press:	AC/ON	100	STO	÷	2	=	EXC	RCL
Window								
Memory								

Press:	AC/ON	97	STO	14	EXC	SUM	EXC	RCL
Window								
Memory								

3. The sketch at the right is built from three circles.
   Terrence pressed the following keystrokes.

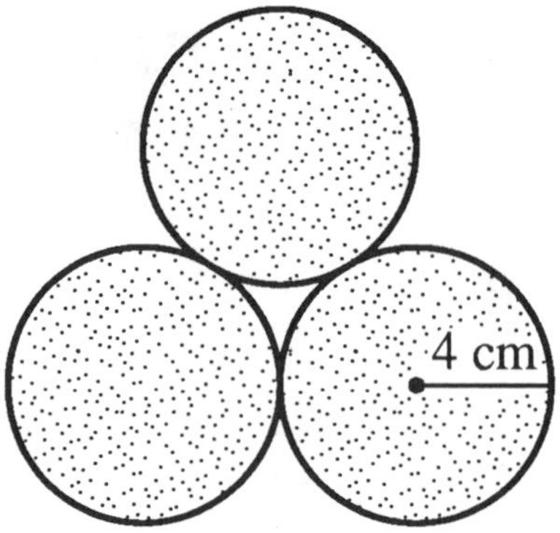

   | AC/ON | 4 | x^2 | × | π | = |

   | STO | SUM | SUM | EXC |

3a. What is in the window, the area of one circle
    or the area of the entire figure?

    Answer _____

Circle or Figure

3b. What is in memory, the area of one circle or the area of the entire figure?

    Answer _____

Circle or Figure

4. Look at the following keystrokes for the figure above.

   | AC/ON | 4 | x^2 | × | π | = | STO | SUM | SUM | RCL |

4a. Which area is in the window? _____

Circle or Figure

4b. Which area is in memory? _____

Circle or Figure

5. Jake pressed the following keystrokes for the same figure above.
   Notice that Jake did not press STO.

   | AC/ON | 4 | x^2 | × | π | = | SUM | SUM | SUM | RCL |

5a. Jayni said, "You end up with too many circles."

    Is Jayni right? _____

Yes or No

5b. Explain your answer. _____

    _____

Name _____ Date _____ Class _____

Chapter 5 Quiz

1. Juliet used the following keystrokes to do the problem at the right.

$2.843865 \times 2.843865 + 2.843865$

| 2.843865 | × | 2.843865 | + | 2.843865 | = |

1a. What did Juliet see in her window? _____
Copy window.

1b. Write a different set of keystrokes for Juliet's problem. Do not key in the messy number again.

| 2.843865 | | | | | | | |
You do not need to use all the keystroke boxes.

1c. Use your keystrokes above. What do you see in the window?

Answer _____
Copy window.

2. In the sketch at the right, a square is built on the radius of the semicircle. List your keystrokes to find the area of the figure. Key in the messy number only once.

| 2.81437 | | | | | |

| | | | | | | |

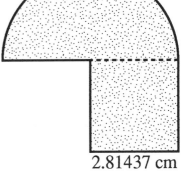

2.81437 cm

Area | | | . | 3 | | 2 | | | | cm²

3. The sketch at the right is built from a semicircle and two quarter-circles. Calculate the area of the figure.

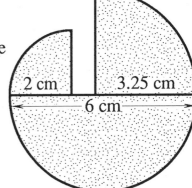

2 cm   3.25 cm

6 cm

Area | | | . | 5 | | | 5 | | | cm²

Mid-Chapter 6 Quiz

 1. The following sectors have central angles of 30°, 60°, 90°, and 175°. Without using a protractor, label each sector with the correct angle measure.

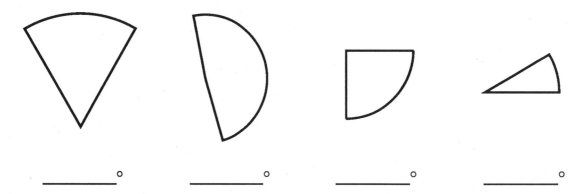

_____ °   _____ °   _____ °   _____ °

2. Measure the central angles of the following sectors. Remember to extend the lines.

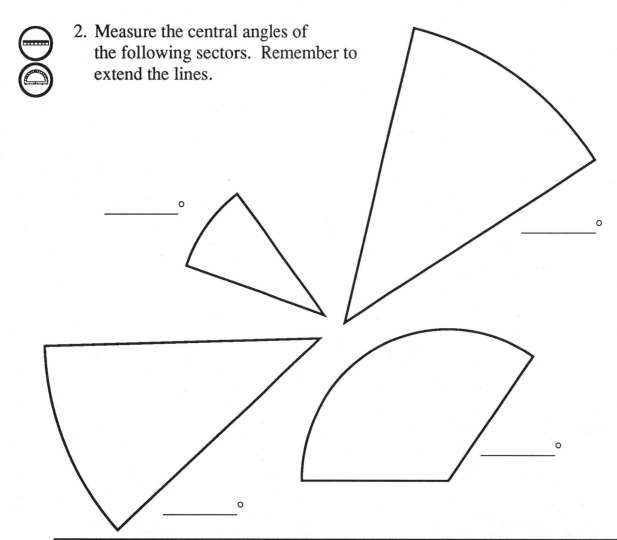

3. The circle at the right is cut into 2 sectors.
Find the degree measure of the
central angle for the *shaded* sector.
Show your work.

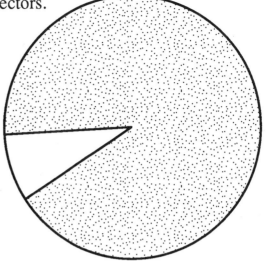

Answer _____°

 4a. The central angle of the sector at the right is 45°.
How many 45° sectors fit in a full circle?

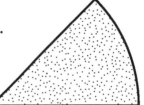

Answer _____ sectors

4b. Trevor copied 1,121 of these 45° sectors on his computer. How many *full circles* could he build from these 45° sectors? Show your work.

Answer _____ full circles

Chapter 6 Quiz

1. A circle has a radius of 4 cm. How many 20° sectors build this circle? Show your work.

    Answer _____ sectors

2. Calculate the area of the 25° sector at the right. Show your work.

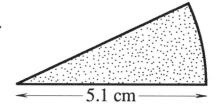

5.1 cm

Area of sector  cm²

3. The circle at the right is cut into six sectors. Each sector labeled "B" has a central angle equal to 68°. All the sectors labeled "A" have equal central angles. What is the angle measure of each sector labeled "A"?

    Answer _____ °

4. The sketch at the right is built from two sectors. Calculate the area of the figure. Show your work.

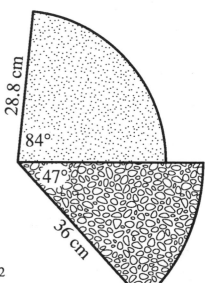

28.8 cm

84°

47°

36 cm

Area  cm²

Test B

1. The radius of the circle at the right is 1.4081 cm.
   Look at the following keystrokes.

   | 1.4081 | | STO | | SUM |

   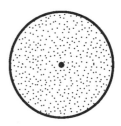

   What does the number in memory represent? _____
   Radius or Diameter

2. Jodi pressed the keystrokes below while looking at the circle in the
   following sketch. Press her keystrokes to find out what is in the window
   and memory after the last keystroke is pressed.

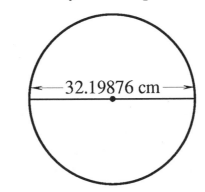

←——— 32.19876 cm ———→

| 32.19876 | | ÷ | | 2 | | = | | STO | | x^2 | | × | | π | | = | | EXC |

2a. What does the number in the window represent? _____
    Radius, Diameter, or Area

2b. What does the number in the memory represent? _____
    Radius, Diameter, or Area

2c. At the end above, Randy pressed |RCL| instead of |EXC|. What did the
    number in Randy's calculator window represent?

    Answer _____
    Radius, Diameter, or Area

2d. What did the number in Randy's calculator memory represent?

    Answer _____
    Radius, Diameter, or Area

3. Use the following sectors to complete Problems 3a through 3d.
   Remember to extend the sides of the sectors when necessary.

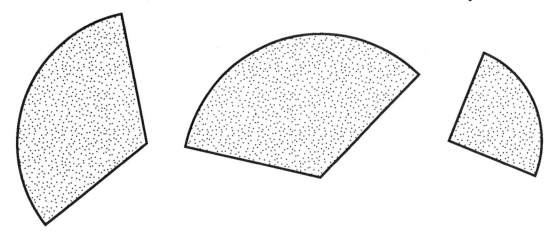

3a. Measure the radius of the 122° sector to the nearest 0.1 cm.

   Radius of 122° sector _____ cm

3b. Measure the radius of the 90° sector to the nearest 0.1 cm.

   Radius of 90° sector _____ cm

3c. Measure the radius of the 117° sector to the nearest 0.1 cm.

   Radius of 117° sector _____ cm

3d. One of the sectors is a quarter-circle. Find the area of the quarter-circle.

   Area of quarter-circle _____ cm^2
                          R to the nearest tenth.

4. The sketch at the right is built from a square
   and four quarter-circles. Find the area of the
   figure using your calculator's memory.
   List your keystrokes.

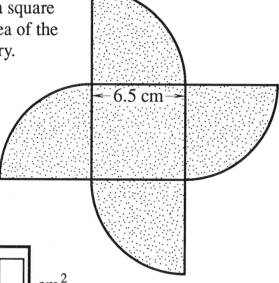

6.5 cm

Area  cm^2

5. The following figure is built from two sectors.

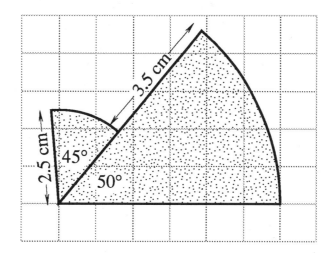

 5a. Estimate the area of the figure.

Estimate _____ cm²

 5b. Calculate the area of the figure.

Area  cm²

Compare with your estimate.

6. The sketch at the right is built from a square, a semicircle, and a quarter-circle. The edge of the square sits along the radius of the quarter-circle and the diameter of the semicircle. Calculate the area of the figure. Show your work. Use the calculator's memory.

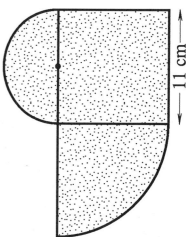

Area 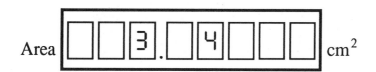 cm²

Mid-Chapter 7 Quiz

 1a. Calculate the area of the following circle.

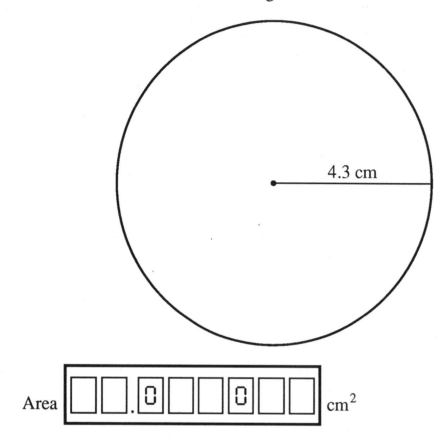

4.3 cm

Area $\boxed{.00}$ cm^2

1b. Round your answer to the nearest tenth.

Area _____ cm^2

2a. Draw a circle with a radius of 2.5 cm anywhere inside of the circle above.

2b. Shade the circle you drew.

2c. Calculate the area of the part that is **not** shaded. Show your work.

Area $\boxed{8.}$ cm^2

R to the nearest tenth.

3a. Estimate the area of the shaded part
　　at the right.

　　Estimate _____ cm^2

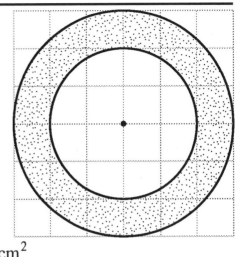

3b. The shaded part is built from two circles.
　　Calculate the area of the shaded part.
　　Show your work.

Area  cm^2

4. A square is built around a circle at the right.
　 Find the area of the shaded region.
　 Show your work.

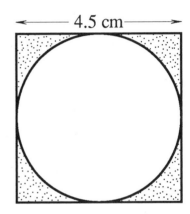

← 4.5 cm →

Area (☐.3☐) cm^2
R to the nearest hundredth.

[If you cannot solve Problem 4 within a few minutes, open the
HINT below. If you open the HINT and solve Problem 4, you
will receive partial credit.]

H-I-N-T

- -

4a. What is the area of the square? _____ cm^2

4b. How long is the diameter of the circle? _____ cm

4c. How long is the radius of the circle? _____ cm

4d. What is the area of the circle? ☐☐.☐☐43☐☐ cm^2

4e. What is the area of the shaded region? ☐.3☐ cm^2
R to the nearest hundredth.

Chapter 7 Quiz

1. Josh shaded and cut two congruent, right triangles from a circle in the sketch at the right. Find the area of the paper left over using the following steps.

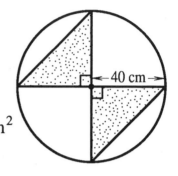

40 cm

1a. Area of circle $\boxed{5}\boxed{}\boxed{}\boxed{}.\boxed{5}\boxed{}\boxed{}\boxed{}$ cm^2

1b. Total area of both triangles _____ cm^2

1c. Area of paper left over $\boxed{}\boxed{4}\boxed{}\boxed{}.\boxed{}\boxed{4}\boxed{}\boxed{}$ cm^2

2. The diameter of the large circle at the right is 6.4 cm. Each quarter-circle has a radius of 2 cm. Find the area of the unshaded part. Show your work.

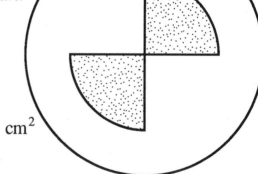

Area $\boxed{}\boxed{}.\boxed{8}\boxed{8}\boxed{}\boxed{}\boxed{}\boxed{}$ cm^2

3a. The right triangle has a sector hole in the sketch at the right. The radius of the sector is 30 cm. Calculate the area of the shaded part.

Area _____ cm^2

You'll know.

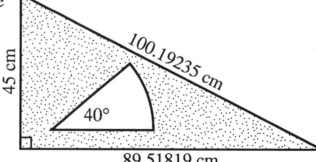

45 cm

100.19235 cm

40°

89.51819 cm

3b. List your keystrokes. Draw in your own keystroke boxes.

4. The circle at the right has a radius of 4 cm.
The hole is built from 3 different sectors with
radii of 2.5 cm, 1.5 cm, and 3.5 cm.
Calculate the area of the shaded part.
Show your work.

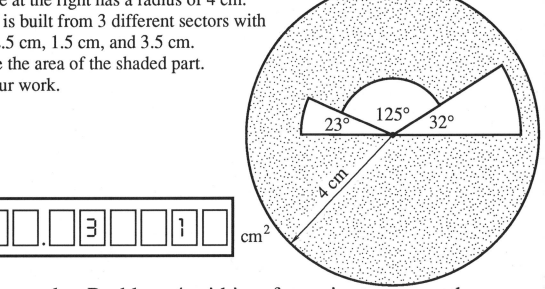

Area [☐☐ . ☐ 3 ☐☐☐] cm^2

[If you cannot solve Problem 4 within a few minutes, open the
HINT below. If you open the HINT and solve Problem 4, you
will receive partial credit.]

H-I-N-T

. . . .

4a. Measure and label the radius of each sector in the figure above.

4b. Calculate the area of each sector. Use the calculator's memory.

Area of 23° sector _____ cm^2 [STO]
              Copy window.

Area of 125° sector _____ cm^2 [SUM]
               Copy window.

Area of 32° sector _____ cm^2 [SUM]
              Copy window.

4c. Calculate the area of the circle.

Area of circle [☐☐ . 2 ☐☐ 4 ☐☐] cm^2

4d. Calculate the area of the shaded part.

Area of shaded part [☐☐ . ☐ 3 ☐☐ 1 ☐] cm^2

Mid-Chapter 8 Quiz

1. Calculate the perimeter of the quarter-circle at the right. Show your work.

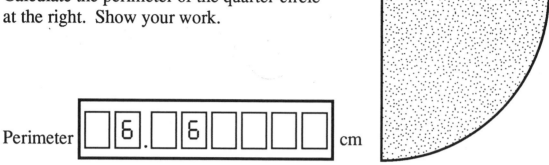

4.5 cm

Perimeter ⬜ 6 . ⬜ 6 ⬜ ⬜ ⬜ cm

2a. The following figure is built from two quarter-circles and a square. Draw in lines to show the quarter-circles and the square.

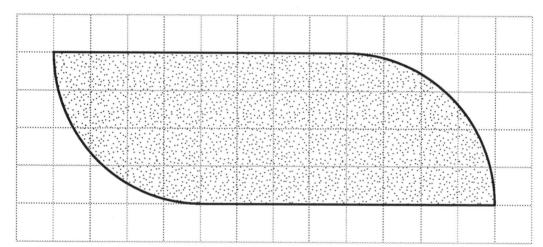

2b. Estimate the perimeter of the figure.

Estimated perimeter _____ cm

3. Use the following steps to calculate the perimeter of the figure above.

3a. Length of both curved parts ⬜ ⬜ . ⬜ 6 6 ⬜ ⬜ cm

3b. Length of straight parts _____ cm

3c. Perimeter ⬜ ⬜ . ⬜ cm

R to the nearest tenth.

4a. The following figure is built from two quarter-circles. Calculate the perimeter of the figure.

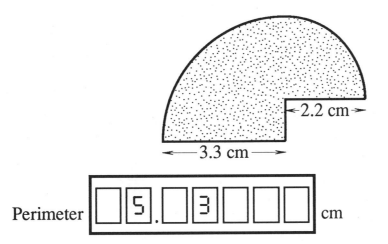

←2.2 cm→

←——— 3.3 cm ———→

Perimeter [ ][5].[ ][3][ ][ ] cm

4b. List the keystrokes you used to find the perimeter of the figure. Draw in your own keystroke boxes.

5a. The following figure is built from a square and two semicircles. The area of the square is 23.642 cm^2. Calculate the side length of the square.

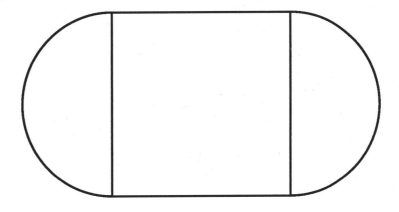

Side length _____ cm

Copy window.
Label the figure.

5b. Calculate the perimeter of the figure.

Perimeter _____ cm

R to the nearest whole number.

Chapter 8 Quiz

1. Use the following steps to calculate the perimeter of the shaded half-strip at the right.

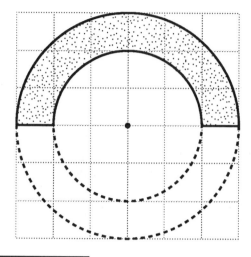

1a. Length of large curve  cm

1b. Length of small curve $\boxed{}.\boxed{}\boxed{8}\boxed{}\boxed{8}\boxed{}\boxed{}$ cm

1c. Length of straight parts _____ cm

1d. Perimeter $\boxed{}\boxed{}.\boxed{0}\boxed{}\boxed{9}\boxed{}\boxed{}$ cm

2. The sketch at the right is built from four semicircles and a square. The semicircles are built along the sides of the square.

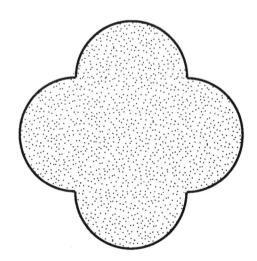

2a. Draw in lines on the figure to show the semicircles and square.

2b. The area of the square is 100 cm². Calculate the perimeter of the figure.

Perimeter 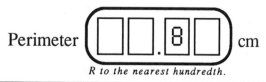 cm

R to the nearest hundredth.

3. Calculate the perimeter of the quarter-strip
   at the right. Show your work.

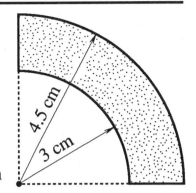

Perimeter  cm

4a. Ali used two of the quarter-strips above
    to build the half-strip at the right.
    Ali said, "Since I know the perimeter
    of one quarter-strip, I'll multiply
    by 2 to find the perimeter of
    the half-strip."

What was Ali's mistake? _____

_____

4b. What is the perimeter of the half-strip?

Perimeter _____ cm
          Copy window.

5. The figure at the right is built from two
   congruent semicircles. Calculate the perimeter
   of the figure. The dotted lines are not part of
   the perimeter. Show your work.

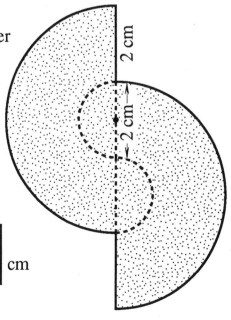

Perimeter  cm

Mid-Chapter 9 Quiz

Show your work when you use a calculator.

1a. The circle at the right has a radius of 2.1 cm. Chord *AB* is the hypotenuse of the right triangle. Measure the length of Chord *AB* to the nearest 0.1 cm.

Measured length _____ cm

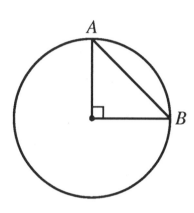

1b. Calculate the length of Chord *AB*.

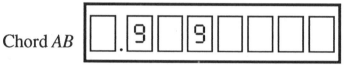

Chord *AB*

Compare with your measurement in Problem 1a.

2. In the following figure, a circle is built around a square. The diameter of the circle cuts the square into two right triangles.

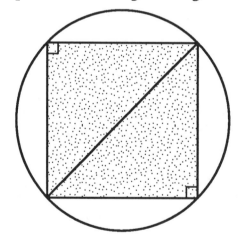

2a. The perimeter of the square is 16.44 cm. Find the side length of the square and label the side length on the figure.

Side length _____ cm

2b. Calculate the diameter of the circle.

Diameter [ ].[8][ ][2][ ][ ][ ] cm

3. The sketch at the right is built from a right triangle
   and a semicircle. Calculate the area of the figure.

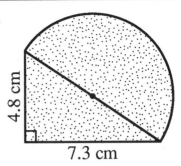

4.8 cm

7.3 cm

Area of figure  cm²

[If you cannot solve Problem 3 within a few minutes, open the
HINT below. If you open the HINT and solve Problem 3, you
will receive partial credit.]

H-I-N-T

. . . .

3a. Area of triangle   ☐ ☐ . 5 ☐   cm²

3b. Diameter of semicircle   ☐ . 7 ☐ ☐ 7 ☐ ☐   cm

3c. Area of semicircle   ☐ ☐ . ☐ 7 4 ☐ ☐   cm²

3d. Area of figure   ☐ 7 . ☐ 9 ☐ ☐ ☐   cm²

Chapter 9 Quiz

Show your work when you use a calculator.

1. A right triangle is built on the diameter of
   a semicircle at the right. Use the
   following steps to calculate the
   perimeter of the semicircle.

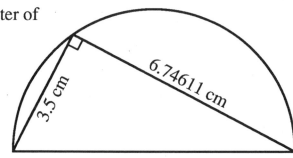

1a. Length of straight part _____ cm

1b. Length of curve  cm

1c. Perimeter _____ cm
    R to the nearest tenth.

2a. The shaded figure at the right is built from
    a quarter-circle and a right triangle.
    Calculate the perimeter of the shaded figure.
    Label each part as you go.

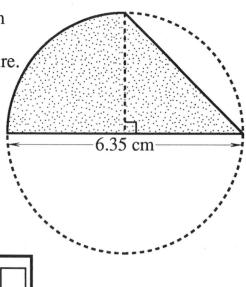

Perimeter  cm

2b. List your keystrokes. Draw your own keystroke boxes.

3. The following shaded semicircle fits along the hypotenuse of a right triangle as shown below. Calculate the perimeter of the shaded semicircle.

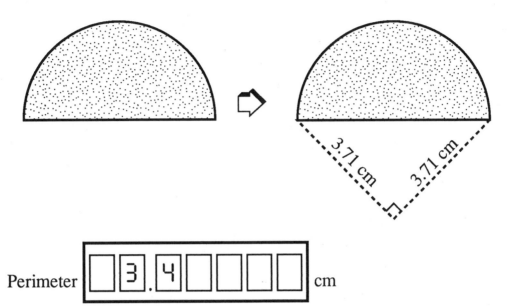

Perimeter ⬚ 3 . 4 ⬚ ⬚ ⬚ ⬚ cm

4. Semicircles are built along the sides of a right triangle in the figure at the right. Find the perimeter of the figure.

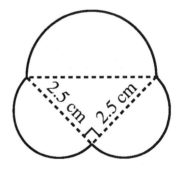

Perimeter ⬚ 3 . 4 ⬚ ⬚ ⬚ ⬚ cm

5. Two congruent right triangles are built along the diameter of a semicircle in the sketch at the right. Calculate the perimeter of the figure.

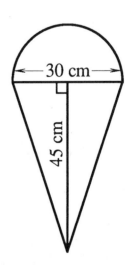

Perimeter ⬚ ⬚ 1 . ⬚ ⬚ 2 ⬚ ⬚ cm

Mid-Chapter 10 Quiz

 1. A goat is tied to the corner of a barn in the sketch at the right. The shaded region shows the area the goat can graze. Calculate the grazing area.

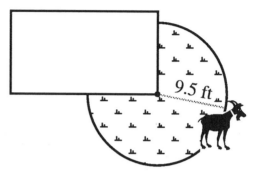

Area  ft²

R to the nearest hundredth.

 2. A goat is tied to a doghouse with a 5-foot tether in the following sketch. Draw and shade the goat's grazing region.

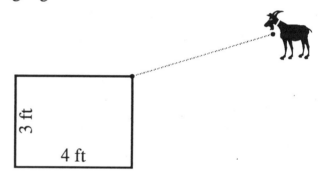

3 ft

4 ft

 3. Calculate the grazing area using the following steps.

3a. Area of three-quarter circle  ft²

3b. Area of smaller quarter-circle 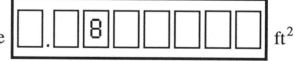 ft²

3c. Area of larger quarter-circle 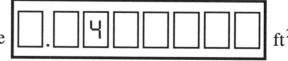 ft²

3d. Total grazing area _____ ft²

R to the nearest hundredth.

4. A goat is tethered to a diamond-shaped barn. Each wall is 10 feet long. The goat's tether is also 10 feet long. The following sketch shows the region the goat can graze. Calculate the area of the shaded region. Show your work.

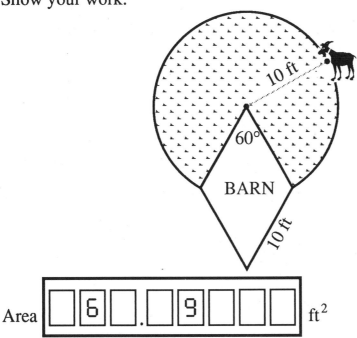

Area ⬚ 6 ⬚ . ⬚ 9 ⬚ ⬚ ft^2

[If you cannot solve Problem 4 within a few minutes, open the HINT below. If you open the HINT and solve Problem 4, you will receive partial credit.]

H-I-N-T

. . . .

4a. Find the area of the whole circle with a radius of 10 feet.

Area _____ ft^2
          Copy window.

4b. Look at the shaded sector. What is the central angle of this shaded sector? Remember, a complete circle is 360°.

Central angle _____ °

4c. Calculate the area of the shaded region.

Area ⬚ 6 ⬚ . ⬚ 9 ⬚ ⬚ ft^2

Test C

Show your work when you use a calculator.

1. In the following circle, two right triangles build a rectangle. The two triangles share a hypotenuse, which is also the diameter of the circle.

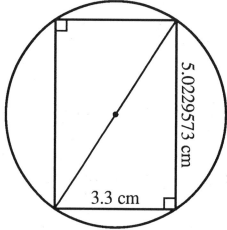

 1a. Calculate the diameter of the circle.

Diameter _____ cm

1b. Calculate the circumference of the circle.

Circumference | □ | □ | . | □ | □ | 0 | 9 | □ | □ | cm

2. The shaded ring below is built from two circles. Calculate the area of the shaded ring.

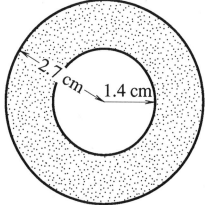

Area | □ | □ | . | □ | 4 | 4 | □ | □ | □ | cm²

3. A circular hole is cut out of a 78° sector in the following figure. Calculate the area of the shaded region.

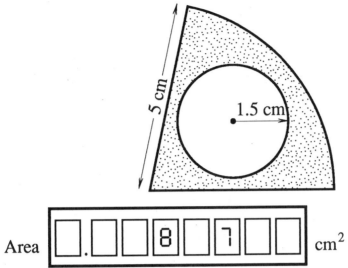

Area [ ][.][ ][ ][8][7][ ][ ] cm²

4. A right triangle is built inside a quarter-circle in the figure at the right. The radius of the quarter-circle is 3.5 cm. Calculate the area of the shaded part. Show your work.

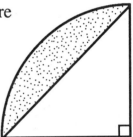

Area 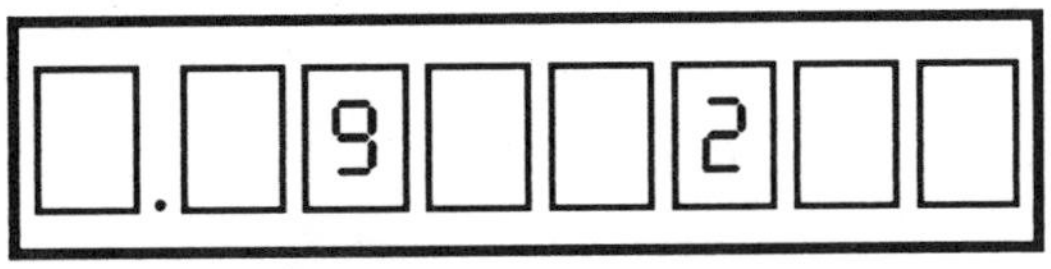 [ ][.][9][ ][ ][2][ ][ ] cm²

5. The sketch at the right is built from two congruent quarter-circles and two right triangles. Calculate the perimeter of the figure.

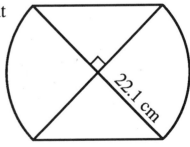

Perimeter [ ][3][ ][.][ ][3][ ][ ][ ] cm

6a. A goat is tethered to a rectangular barn in the following sketch.
    Draw and shade in the region that the goat is able to graze.
    Remember to extend the sides when necessary.

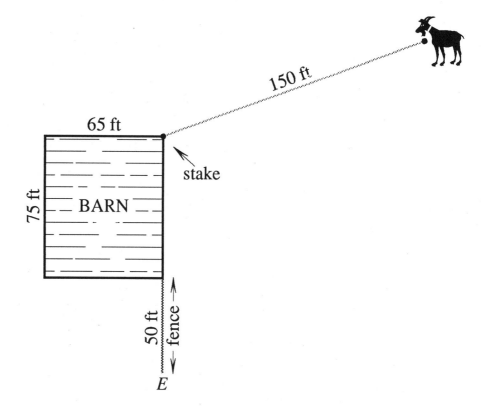

6b. Calculate the grazing area.

Grazing area [ ][9][ ][9].[ ][ ] ft²

Quizzes and Tests Answer Key

Mid-Chapter 1 Quiz

1a. Use the center at the right to draw a circle that has a radius of 2.5 cm.

1b. Without measuring, what is the length of the diameter?

Diameter _____5_____ cm

1c. Draw in a diameter and a radius. Label each with "diameter" or "radius."

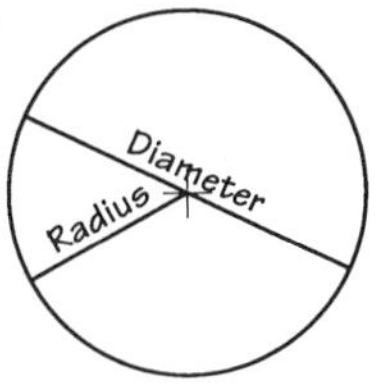

2a. A regular hexagon is built inside a circle at the right. One side is 2.2 cm. What is the perimeter of the hexagon?

Perimeter _____13.2_____ cm

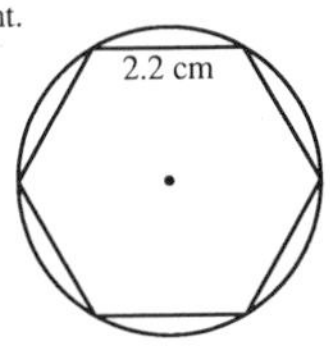

2b. Which is larger, the perimeter of the hexagon or the circumference of the circle?

Answer __Circumference__
Perimeter or Circumference

3. A line goes from the center of the large circle to its rim in the following sketch. The line also goes through the center of the small circle.

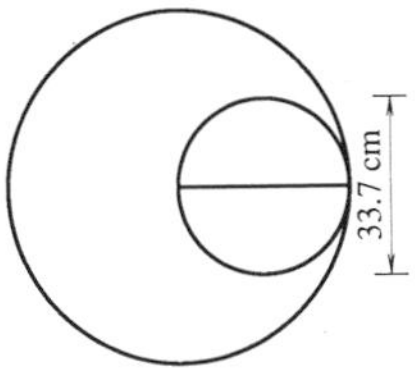

33.7 cm

3a. What is the radius of the small circle?

Radius of small circle _____16.85_____ cm

3b. What is the diameter of the large circle?

Diameter of large circle _____67.4_____ cm

Chapter 1 Quiz

1a. Christos put a piece of wire along half the circumference of a circle. Which is longer, the length of the wire or the diameter of the circle?

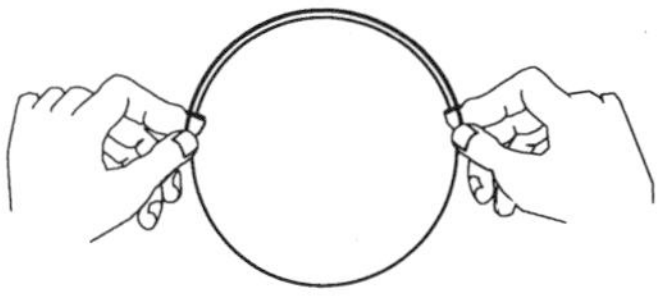

Answer _____Wire_____
Wire or Diameter

1b. Explain your answer. __Answers will vary. Looks longer, straight across is shorter than going around.__

1c. Barry bent a different wire as shown at the right. Rank the diameter, Christos' wire, and Barry's wire from longest to shortest.

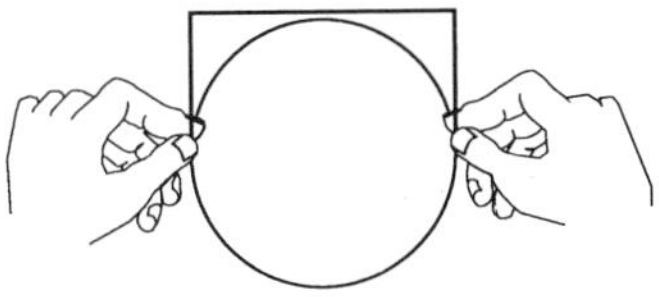

__Barry's wire__   __Christos' wire__   __diameter__
Longest   Shortest

2a. Estimate the circumference of the following circle.

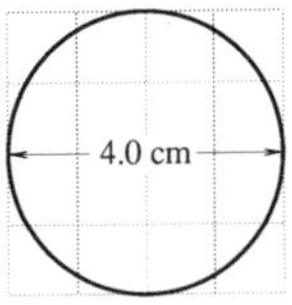

4.0 cm

Estimate _____12 - 14_____ cm

2b. Explain what method you used to estimate the circumference. __Answers will vary.__ __The perimeter of the square is 16 cm. The circle's circumference is smaller. About 3 diameters (4 cm × 3) make up the circumference.__

3a. The diameter of the sketch at the right is 6.0 cm. Estimate the circumference of the circle.

Estimate _____18 - 22_____ cm

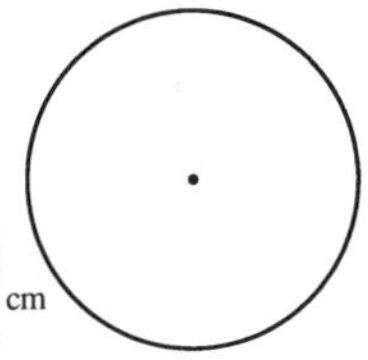

3b. Calculate the circumference of the circle.

Circumference | 1 | 8 | . | 8 | 4 | 9 | 5 | 5 | 6 | cm

3c. List your keystrokes for Problem 3b.

| 6 | × | π | = | |

4. The circles in the following sketches have circumferences of 6 cm, 12 cm, 24 cm, and 48 cm.

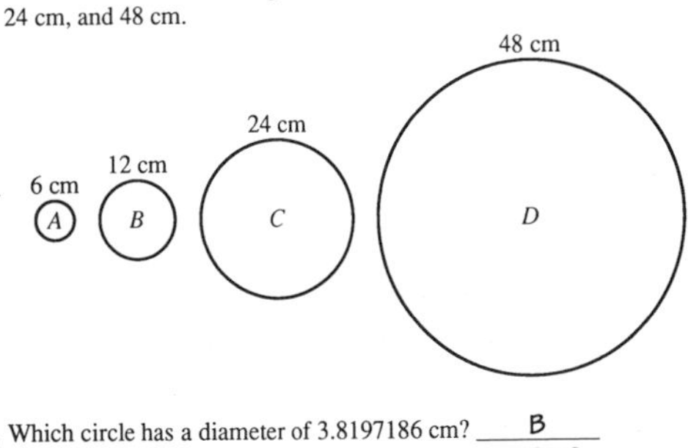

48 cm

24 cm

6 cm 12 cm

A   B   C   D

4a. Which circle has a diameter of 3.8197186 cm? ___B___
A, B, C, or D

4b. List your keystrokes for Problem 4a.

| 3.8197186 | × | π | = | | | |

4c. Which circle has a radius of 3.8197186 cm? ___C___
A, B, C, or D

4d. List your keystrokes for Problem 4c.

| 3.8197186 | × | 2 | × | π | = | | |

Mid-Chapter 2 Quiz

Show your work whenever you use a calculator.

1a. Estimate the area of the circle in the following figure.

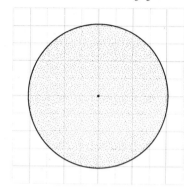

Estimated area ___48 - 55___ cm²

1b. Briefly tell how you estimated the area in Problem 1a. **Answers will vary.**

Counted square centimeters. or Built square on the radius
(4 × 4) and multiplied the area of the square by 3.

2a. The radius of the circle is 4.1 cm. Calculate the area of the circle.

Area ⬚5 2 . 8 1 0 1 7 3⬚ cm²

2b. List your keystrokes for Problem 2a.

⬚4.1⬚ ⬚x²⬚ ⬚×⬚ ⬚π⬚ ⬚=⬚ ⬚ ⬚ ⬚ ⬚
You do not need to use all the keystroke boxes.

---

3. The following sketch shows a circle in a square. The circle has a radius of 4.9 cm. Calculate the area of the circle.

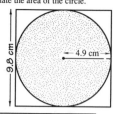

Area of circle ⬚7 5 . 4 2 9 6 4⬚ cm² **4.9** x² × π =

4a. What is the side length of the square above? ___9.8___ cm **4.9 × 2 =**
Label the sketch.

4b. What is the area of the square? ___96.04___ cm² **9.8** x²

5. The following sketch shows four identical circles in a square. The **diameter** of each circle is 4.9 cm. Calculate the total area of the four circles.

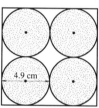

Area of four circles ⬚7 5 . 4 2 9 6 4⬚ cm² **4.9 ÷ 2 = x²**
                                                × π × 4 =

6. What is the area of the square? ___96.04___ cm² **4.9 × 2 = x²**

Chapter 2 Quiz

Estimates will vary.

1a. Estimate the area of the sketch at the right.

Estimate ___300___ cm²

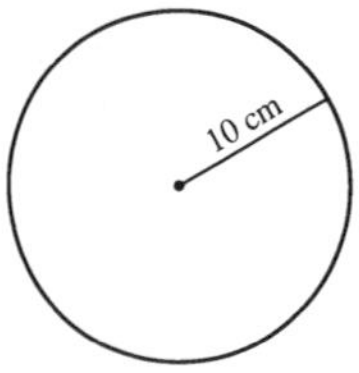

1b. Calculate the area of the sketch.

Area ___314.15927___ cm²
Copy window.

2a. Estimate the area of the circle at the right.

Estimate ___27 - 30___ cm²

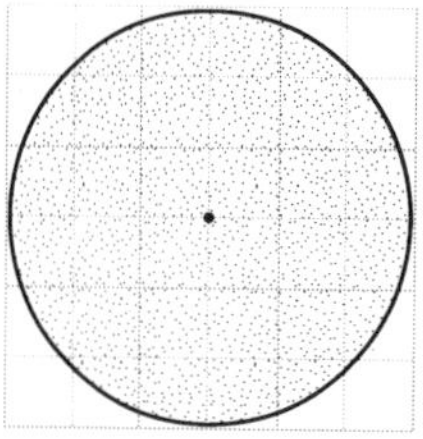

2b. The diameter of the circle is 5.88 cm. What is the radius of the circle?

Radius ___2.94___ cm

2c. Calculate the area of the circle.

Area ___27.15467___ cm²
Copy window.

2d. List the keystrokes you used to calculate the area of the circle.

⬚5.88⬚ ⬚÷⬚ ⬚2⬚ ⬚=⬚ ⬚x²⬚ ⬚×⬚ ⬚π⬚ ⬚=⬚ ⬚ ⬚

3. In the sketch at the right, two small circles are built on the diameter of a large circle. The diameter of the large circle is 8.2 cm. Calculate the area of the smaller circles.

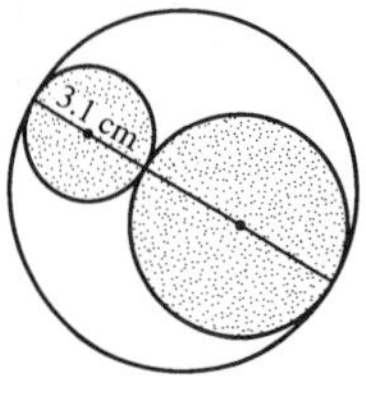

3a. Area of smallest circle ⬚7 . 5 5⬚ cm²
R to the nearest hundredth.

3b. Area of middle circle ⬚2 0 . 4 3⬚ cm²
R to the nearest hundredth.

---

4. A square is built along the diameter in the sketch at the right. The perimeter of the square is 200 cm. Calculate the area of the circle. Show your work.

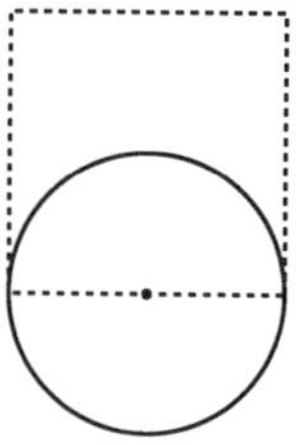

200 ÷ 4 ÷ 2 = x² × π =

Area of circle ⬚1 9 6 3 . 5⬚ cm²
R to the nearest tenth.

[If you cannot solve Problem 4 within a few minutes, open the HINT below. If you open the HINT and solve Problem 4, you will receive partial credit.]

H-I-N-T

- -

4a. The distance around the square (or perimeter) is 200 cm. What is the side length of the square?

Side length ___50___ cm **200 ÷ 4 =**
The answer is more than 40 cm.

4b. What is the diameter of the circle?

Diameter ___50___ cm

4c. What is the radius of the circle?

Radius ___25___ cm **50 ÷ 2 =**

Side Length

4d. Calculate the area of the circle.

Area of circle ⬚1 9 6 3 . 5⬚ cm² **25** x² × π =
R to the nearest tenth.

Mid-Chapter 3 Quiz

1. A square is built around a circle in the figure at the right. The area of the square is 25 cm².

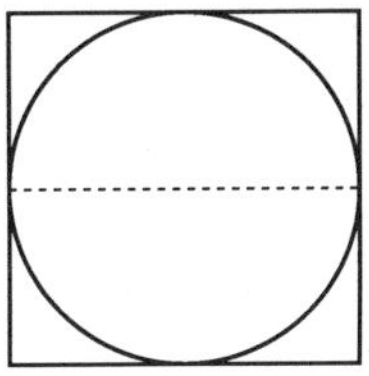

1a. What is the side length of the square?

Side length _____ **5** _____ cm

1b. What is the diameter of the circle?

Diameter _____ **5** _____ cm

1c. What is the radius of the circle?

Radius _____ **2.5** _____ cm

2. The square in the sketch at the right has an area of 102 cm².

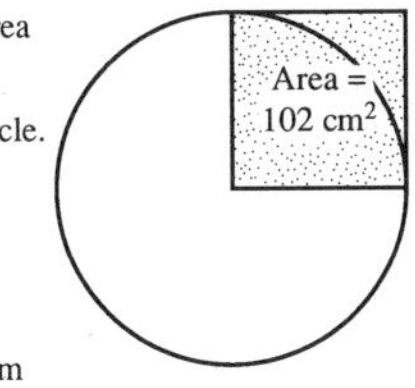

Area = 102 cm²

2a. Circle the best estimate for the area of the circle.

200 cm²   (**300 cm²**)   400 cm²

2b. Calculate the radius of the circle.

Radius | 1 | 0 | . | 0 | 9 | 9 | 5 | 0 | 5 | cm

2c. Find the area of the circle.

Area | 3 | 2 | 0 | . | 4 | 4 | 2 | 4 | 5 | cm²

Compare with Problem 2a.

2d. List the keystrokes you used to find the area of the circle. Draw in your own keystroke boxes.

| 102 | × | π | = | or

| 102 | √x | x² | × | π | = |

---

3. Two squares are built along the radii in the circle at the right. The area of the circle is 11.103645 cm². Calculate the area of the shaded part.

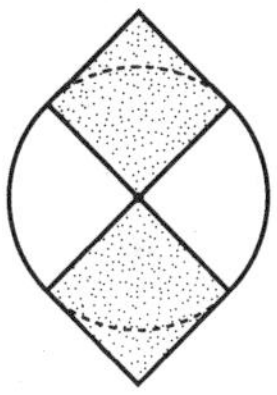

Area of shaded part | 7 | . | 0 | 6 | 8 | 8 | cm²

[If you cannot solve Problem 3 within a few minutes, open the HINT below. If you open the HINT and solve Problem 3, you will receive partial credit.]

H-I-N-T

- -

3a. The area of the circle is 11.103645 cm². What is the area of *one* square built on the radius?

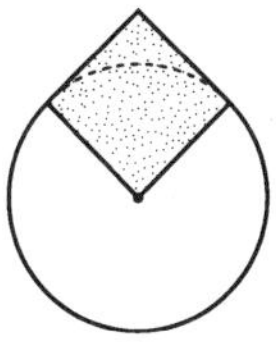

Area of *one* square _____ **3.5344** _____ cm²

Copy window.

11.103645 ÷ π =

3b. The area of the shaded part at the right is built from two of these squares. What is the area of the shaded part?

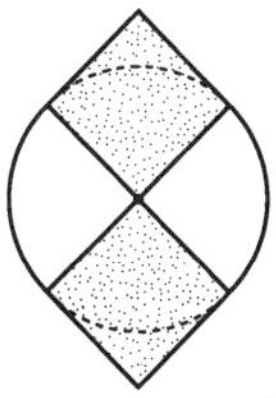

Area of shaded part | 7 | . | 0 | 6 | 8 | 8 | cm²

3.5344 × 2 =

Chapter 3 Quiz

1a. The area of the circle at the right is 11.34 cm². Calculate the area of the square built on the radius.

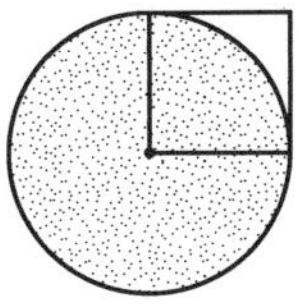

Area _____ **3.6** _____ cm²

R to the nearest tenth.

1b. What is the radius of the circle?

Radius _____ **1.9** _____ cm

R to the nearest tenth. Measure to check.

2. The circumference of the circle in the sketch at the right is 120 cm. Use the following steps to calculate the radius of the circle.

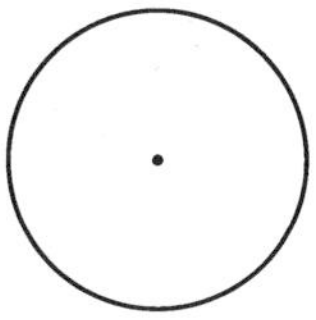

2a. Diameter | 3 | 8 | . | 1 | 9 | 7 | 1 | 8 | 6 | cm

2b. Radius _____ **19.1** _____ cm

R to the nearest tenth.

3. The area of the square in the sketch at the right is 240.25 cm². The square is built along the diameter of each circle. What is the circumference of *one* of the circles?

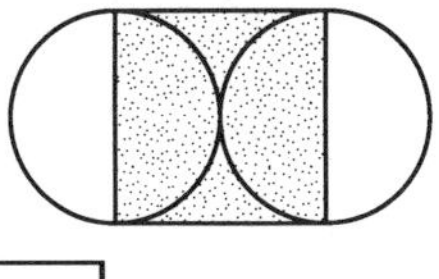

Circumference | 4 | 8 | . | 6 | 9 | 4 | 6 | 8 | 6 | cm

4. The area of the square equals the area of the circle in the figure at the right. The side length of the square is 2.774 cm. Calculate the radius of the circle.

←2.774 cm→

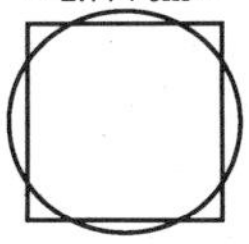

Radius | 1 | . | 5 | 6 | 5 | 0 | 6 | 1 | 9 | cm

Test A

1. The two circles in the sketch at the right are drawn on a playground. The dashed line shows a path that travels through the center of the small circle and the center of the large circle. The diameter of the small circle is 275 cm and the radius of the large circle is 188 cm.

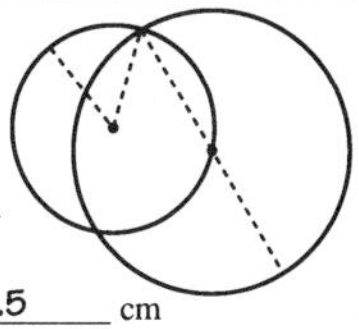

1a. What is the radius of the small circle? _____ **137.5** _____ cm

1b. What is the diameter of the large circle? _____ **376** _____ cm

1c. What is the total distance of the dashed line? _____ **651** _____ cm

2a. Estimate the *circumference* of the circle at the right.

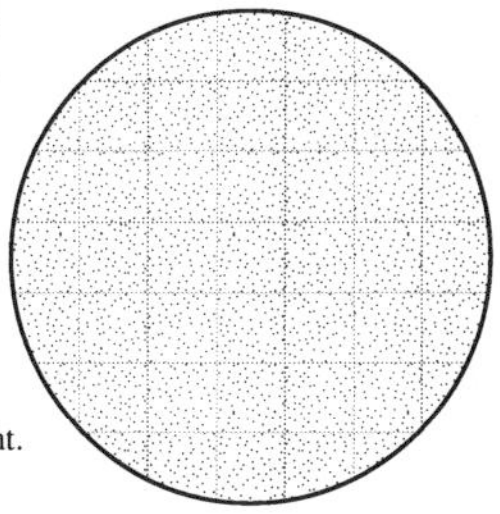

Estimate _____ **20 - 25** _____ cm

2b. The radius of the circle is 3.5 cm. Calculate the circumference.

Circumference | 2 | 1 | . | 9 | 9 | cm

R to the nearest hundredth.

2c. Estimate the *area* of the circle at the right.

Estimate _____ **27 - 48** _____ cm²

2d. What method did you use to estimate the area of the circle? **Answers will vary.**

Counted square cm. or Estimated area of square on radius then multiplied by 3.

2e. Calculate the area of the circle. | 3 | 8 | . | 4 | 8 | 4 | 5 | 1 | cm²

3. Explain why the figure at the right is not a circle.

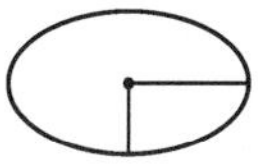

Distance from center point to any where on the rim is not the same.

4a. Three squares are built along the diameter of the following circle. The area of each square is written on the figure. Measure the diameter of the circle.

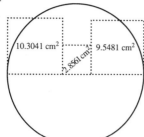

10.3041 cm²   2.8561 cm²   9.5481 cm²

Measured diameter ___7.9, 8.0, 8.1___ cm

4b. Calculate the length of this circle's diameter.

Calculated diameter _____7.99_____ cm

5. The area of the circle at the right is 26.786476 cm².

5a. Measure the radius of the circle.

Measured radius ___2.8, 2.9, 3.0___ cm

5b. List the keystrokes to calculate the radius of this circle.

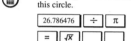

Radius _____2.92_____ cm
Compare with Problem 5a.

5c. Calculate the circumference of the circle.

Circumference | 1 | 8 |.| 3 | 4 | 6 | 9 | 0 | 1 | cm

---

6. A circle and a square each has an area of 25 cm².

6a. Calculate the diameter of a circle with an area of 25 cm². List the keystrokes you used.

| 25 | ÷ | π | = | √x | × | 2 | = |

Diameter _____5.6_____ cm
R to the nearest tenth.

6b. What is the side length of a square with an area of 25 cm²?

Side length _____5_____ cm

6c. Which is larger, the diameter of the circle or the side length of the square?

Answer _____Diameter_____
Diameter or Side length

6d. Draw a square and a circle, each with an area of 25 cm².

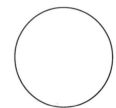

7. One of the largest clocks in the world is in Japan. Its circumference is 185.52 ft. Calculate the area of this huge clock face.

Area (2 | 7 | 3 | 8 |.| 9) ft²
R to the nearest tenth.

Name _____ Date _____ Class _____   1

Mid-Chapter 4 Quiz

1a. Use the center on the following grid to draw a circle with a diameter of 4.6 cm.

1b. Measure the diameter to check your drawing.

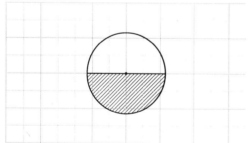

2. How long is a radius of your circle?

Radius _____2.3_____ cm

3. Calculate the area of the whole circle.

Area | 1 | 6 |.| 6 | 1 | 9 | 0 | 2 | 5 | cm²

4. Shade a semicircle in your drawing. Circle the best estimate for the area of the semicircle.

3 cm²   (10 cm²)   15 cm²   20 cm²

5. Calculate the area of the semicircle.

Area of semicircle (8 |.| 3 | 1) cm²
R to the nearest hundredth.
Compare with Problem 4.

---

6. A square is built along the radius of the semicircle at the right. The area of the square is 10.24 cm². Calculate the area of the semicircle.

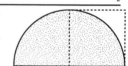

Area | 1 | 6 |.| 0 | 8 | 4 | 9 | 5 | 4 | cm²

7a. Shade a quarter-circle in the sketch at the right.

Students may shade any quarter-circle.

7b. The radius of the circle is 3.53 cm. Find the area of the quarter-circle.

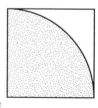

Area | 9 |.| 7 | 8 | 6 | 7 | 6 | 8 | cm²

7c. List the keystrokes you used to find the area of the quarter-circle in one run. Draw in your own keystroke boxes.

| 3.53 | x² | × | π | ÷ | 4 | = |

8. A square is built around a quarter-circle in the sketch at the right.

8a. The area of the square is 102.01 cm². Find the side length of the square.

Side length _____10.1_____ cm

8b. Calculate the area of the quarter-circle.

Area of quarter-circle (8 | 0 |.| 1 | 2) cm²
R to the nearest hundredth.

Chapter 4 Quiz

1. The figure at the right is built from three quarter-circles.

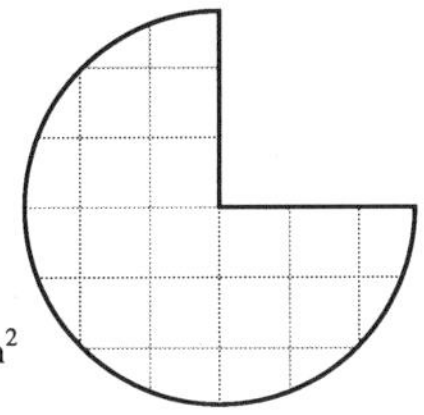

1a. Estimate the area of the figure.

Estimate ___16 - 19___ cm²

1b. The radius of each quarter-circle is 2.8 cm. Calculate the area of the figure.

Area | 1 | 8 | . | 4 | 7 | 2 | 5 | 6 | 5 | cm²

1c. List the keystrokes you used to find the area of this figure.

2. The following figure is built from quarter-circles. The radius of each quarter-circle is 2.5 cm. Calculate the area of the figure. Show your work.

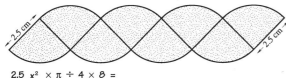

2.5 x^2 × π ÷ 4 × 8 =

or

2.5 x^2 × π × 2 =

Area | 3 | 9 | . | 2 | 7 | cm²

R to the nearest hundredth.

---

3. Circle the best estimate for the shaded area at the right.

100 cm²

80 cm²

(60 cm²)

40 cm²

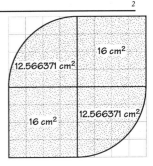

12.566371 cm²   16 cm²

16 cm²   12.566371 cm²

4. In the figure above, the "curves" are pieces of circles. Calculate the area of the entire figure. Label the area of each part on the figure above. Show your work.

4 x^2 × π ÷ 2 + 32 =

or

4 x^2 × π ÷ 4 = 12.566371 cm² × 2 + 16 + 16 =

Area | 5 | 7 | . | 1 | 3 | 2 | 7 | 4 | 1 | cm²

Compare with your estimate.

[If you cannot solve Problem 4 within a few minutes, open the HINT SHEET. If you open the HINT SHEET and solve Problem 4, you will receive partial credit.]

H-I-N-T S-H-E-E-T

[If you open the HINT SHEET and solve Problem 4, you will receive partial credit.]

· ·

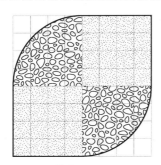

4a. Find the total area of the ▨ regions. ___32___ cm²

4b. The ▨ regions are quarter-circles. What is the area of both quarter-circles?

Area of both quarter-circles | 2 | 5 | . | 1 | 3 | 2 | 7 | 4 | 1 | cm²

4c. Calculate the total area of the figure.

Area | 5 | 7 | . | 1 | 3 | 2 | 7 | 4 | 1 | cm²

Compare with Problem 3.

Mid-Chapter 5 Quiz

Do not use a calculator on this quiz.

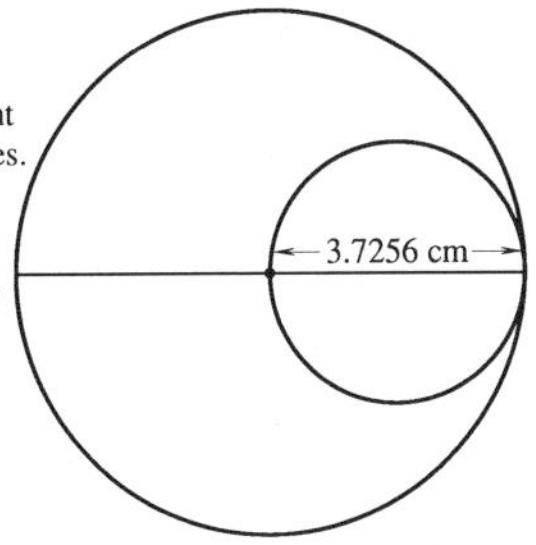

1. Sima looked at the figure at the right and pressed the following keystrokes.

| 3.7256 | STO | × | 2 | = |

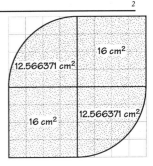

← 3.7256 cm →

1a. What is in memory, the diameter of the small circle or the diameter of the large circle?

Answer ___Small___
Small or Large

1b. What part of the large circle is in memory, the radius or the diameter?

Answer ___Radius___
Radius or Diameter

1c. What is in the window, the diameter of the small circle or the diameter of the large circle?

Answer ___Large___
Small or Large

2. Complete the following tables.

Press:	AC/ON	100	STO	÷	2	=	EXC	RCL
Window	0	100	100	100	2	50	100	50
Memory	0	0	100	100	100	100	50	50

Press:	AC/ON	97	STO	14	EXC	SUM	EXC	RCL
Window	0	97	97	14	97	97	111	97
Memory	0	0	97	97	14	111	97	97

3. The sketch at the right is built from three circles. Terrence pressed the following keystrokes.

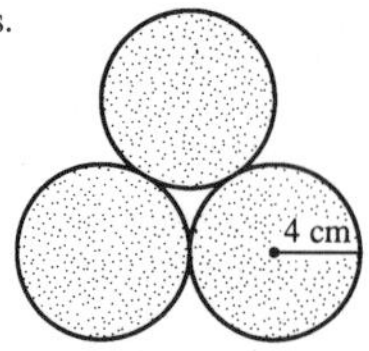

| AC/ON | 4 | x^2 | × | π | = |

| STO | SUM | SUM | EXC |

3a. What is in the window, the area of one circle or the area of the entire figure?

Answer ___**Figure**___
Circle or Figure

3b. What is in memory, the area of one circle or the area of the entire figure?

Answer ___**Circle**___
Circle or Figure

4. Look at the following keystrokes for the figure above.

| AC/ON | 4 | x^2 | × | π | = | STO | SUM | SUM | RCL |

4a. Which area is in the window? ___**Figure**___
Circle or Figure

4b. Which area is in memory? ___**Figure**___
Circle or Figure

5. Jake pressed the following keystrokes for the same figure above. Notice that Jake did not press STO.

| AC/ON | 4 | x^2 | × | π | = | SUM | SUM | SUM | RCL |

5a. Jayni said, "You end up with too many circles."

Is Jayni right? ___**No**___
Yes or No

5b. Explain your answer. **The first sum that Jake pressed was just to put what is in the window into memory.**

The answer to "4 x^2 × π" was added to "0" in memory.

Name _____ Date _____ Class _____

Chapter 5 Quiz

1. Juliet used the following keystrokes to do the problem at the right.   2.843865 × 2.843865 + 2.843865

| 2.843865 | × | 2.843865 | + | 2.843865 | = |

1a. What did Juliet see in her window? ___10.931433___
Copy window.

1b. Write a different set of keystrokes for Juliet's problem. Do not key in the messy number again.   **Keystrokes will vary.**

| 2.843865 | STO | x^2 | + | EXC | = | | |
You do not need to use all the keystroke boxes.

1c. Use your keystrokes above. What do you see in the window?

Answer ___10.931433___
Copy window.

2. In the sketch at the right, a square is built on the radius of the semicircle. List your keystrokes to find the area of the figure. Key in the messy number only once.   **Keystrokes will vary.**

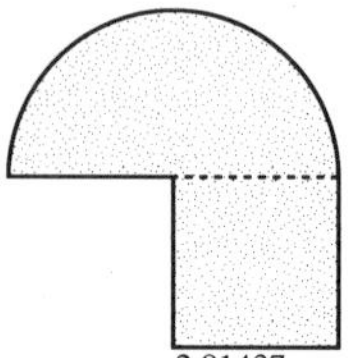

| 2.81437 | x^2 | STO | × | π | ÷ |

| 2 | = | SUM | EXC | | | |

Area | 2 | 0 | . | 3 | 6 | 2 | 4 | 5 | 1 | cm²

2.81437 cm

3. The sketch at the right is built from a semicircle and two quarter-circles. Calculate the area of the figure.

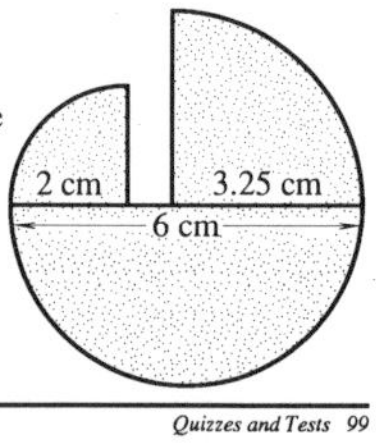

2 cm   3.25 cm
6 cm

Area | 2 | 5 | . | 5 | 7 | 4 | 5 | 2 | 8 | cm²

Name _____ Date _____ Class _____ *1*

Mid-Chapter 6 Quiz

1. The following sectors have central angles of 30°, 60°, 90°, and 175°. Without using a protractor, label each sector with the correct angle measure.

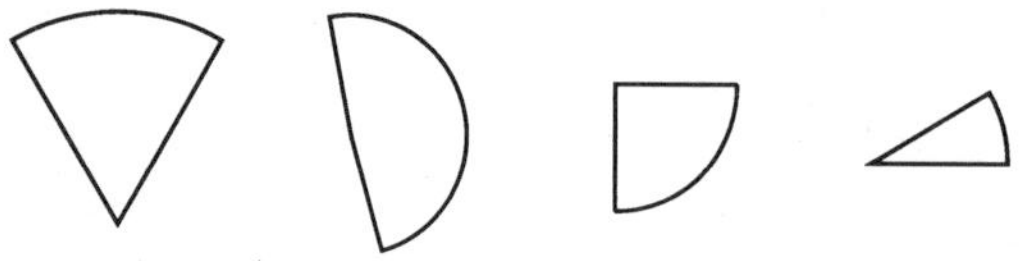

___60___ °   ___175___ °   ___90___ °   ___30___ °

2. Measure the central angles of the following sectors. Remember to extend the lines.

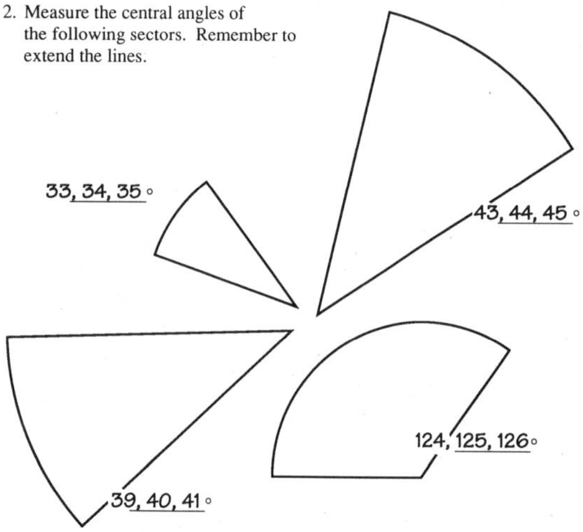

33, 34, 35 °

43, 44, 45 °

124, 125, 126 °

39, 40, 41 °

---

3. The circle at the right is cut into 2 sectors. Find the degree measure of the central angle for the **shaded** sector. Show your work.

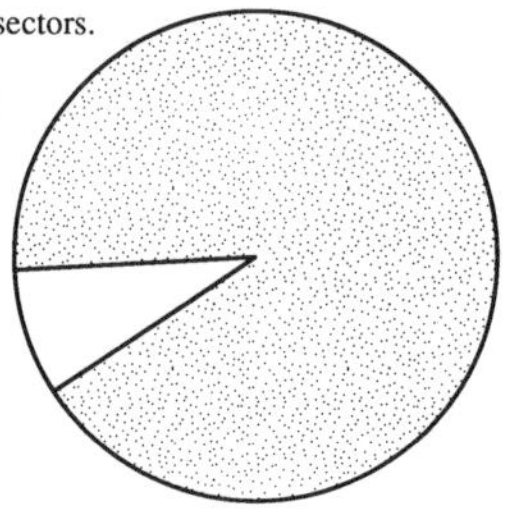

360° − 29° = 331°
or
360° − 30° = 330°
or
360° − 31° = 329°

Answer ___329, 330, 331___ °

4a. The central angle of the sector at the right is 45°. How many 45° sectors fit in a full circle?

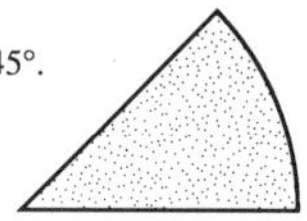

Answer ___8___ sectors

4b. Trevor copied 1,121 of these 45° sectors on his computer. How many **full circles** could he build from these 45° sectors? Show your work.

1,121 × 45° = 50,445°
50,445° ÷ 360° = 140.125
or
1,121 ÷ 8 = 140.125

Answer ___140___ full circles

Chapter 6 Quiz

1. A circle has a radius of 4 cm. How many 20° sectors build this circle? Show your work.

   $360° \div 20° = 18$

   Answer _____ 18 _____ sectors

2. Calculate the area of the 25° sector at the right. Show your work.

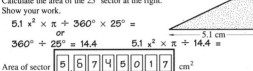

   $5.1 \; x^2 \times \pi \div 360° \times 25° =$
   or
   $360° \div 25° = 14.4$ $5.1 \; x^2 \times \pi \div 14.4 =$

   Area of sector [5].[6][7][4][5][0][1][7] cm²

3. The circle at the right is cut into six sectors. Each sector labeled "B" has a central angle equal to 68°. All the sectors labeled "A" have equal central angles. What is the angle measure of each sector labeled "A"?

   Answer _____ 52 _____ °

4. The sketch at the right is built from two sectors. Calculate the area of the figure. Show your work.

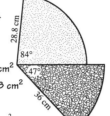

   $36 \; x^2 \times \pi \div 360° \times 47° = 531.55748 \; cm^2$
   $28.8 \; x^2 \times \pi \div 360° \times 84° = 608.01128 \; cm^2$

   Area [1][1][3][9].[5][6][8][8] cm²

Test B

1. The radius of the circle at the right is 1.4081 cm. Look at the following keystrokes.

   [1.4081] [STO] [SUM]

   What does the number in memory represent? __ Diameter __
   Radius or Diameter

2. Jodi pressed the keystrokes below while looking at the circle in the following sketch. Press her keystrokes to find out what is in the window and memory after the last keystroke is pressed.

   [32.19876] [÷] [2] [=] [STO] [x^2] [×] [π] [=] [EXC]

   2a. What does the number in the window represent? __ Radius __
   Radius, Diameter, or Area

   2b. What does the number in the memory represent? __ Area __
   Radius, Diameter, or Area

   2c. At the end above, Randy pressed [RCL] instead of [EXC]. What did the number in Randy's calculator window represent?

   Answer __ Radius __
   Radius, Diameter, or Area

   2d. What did the number in Randy's calculator memory represent?

   Answer __ Radius __
   Radius, Diameter, or Area

---

3. Use the following sectors to complete Problems 3a through 3d. Remember to extend the sides of the sectors when necessary.

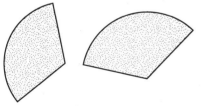

   3a. Measure the radius of the 122° sector to the nearest 0.1 cm.
   Radius of 122° sector __ 3.7, 3.8, 3.9 __ cm

   3b. Measure the radius of the 90° sector to the nearest 0.1 cm.
   Radius of 90° sector __ 2.4, 2.5, 2.6 __ cm

   3c. Measure the radius of the 117° sector to the nearest 0.1 cm.
   Radius of 117° sector __ 3.4, 3.5, 3.6 __ cm

   3d. One of the sectors is a quarter-circle. Find the area of the quarter-circle.
   Area of quarter-circle __ 4.5, 4.9, 5.3 __ cm²
   R to the nearest tenth.

4. The sketch at the right is built from a square and four quarter-circles. Find the area of the figure using your calculator's memory. List your keystrokes.

   [6.5] [x^2] [STO] [+] [RCL] [×] [π] [=]

   or

   $6.5 \; x^2 + 6.5 \; x^2 \times \pi =$

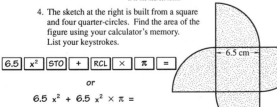

   Area [1][7][4].[9][8][2][2][9] cm²

---

5. The following figure is built from two sectors.

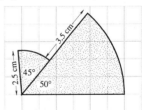

   5a. Estimate the area of the figure.
   Estimate __ 16 - 20 __ cm²

   5b. Calculate the area of the figure.
   $2.5 \; x^2 \times \pi \div 360° \times 45° = 2.4543693$
   $2.5 + 3.5 = 6$
   $6 \; x^2 \times \pi \div 360° \times 50° = 15.707963$

   Area [1][8].[1][6][2][3][3] cm²
   Compare with your estimate.

6. The sketch at the right is built from a square, a semicircle, and a quarter-circle. The edge of the square sits along the radius of the quarter-circle and the diameter of the semicircle. Calculate the area of the figure. Show your work. Use the calculator's memory.

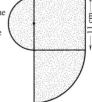

   $11 \times 11 = 121$ [STO]
   $5.5 \; x^2 \times \pi \div 2 = 47.516589$ [SUM]
   $11 \; x^2 \times \pi \div 4 = 95.033178$ [SUM] [RCL]

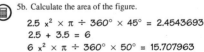

   Area [2][6][3].[5][4][9][7][7] cm²

Name _____ Date _____ Class _____ *1*

Mid-Chapter 7 Quiz

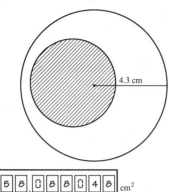

1a. Calculate the area of the following circle.

4.3 cm

Area ⎣5⎦⎣8⎦.⎣0⎦⎣8⎦⎣8⎦⎣0⎦⎣4⎦⎣8⎦ cm²

1b. Round your answer to the nearest tenth.

Area _____58.1_____ cm²

2a. Draw a circle with a radius of 2.5 cm anywhere inside of the circle above.

2b. Shade the circle you drew.

2c. Calculate the area of the part that is *not* shaded. Show your work.

2.5 x² × π = 19.634954 cm²

58.088048 cm² − 19.634954 cm² = 38.453094 cm²

Area ⎣3⎦⎣8⎦.⎣5⎦ cm²
R to the nearest tenth.

3a. Estimate the area of the shaded part at the right.

Estimate ____14 - 18____ cm²

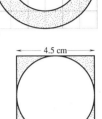

3b. The shaded part is built from two circles. Calculate the area of the shaded part. Show your work.

3 x² × π − 2 x² × π =

Area ⎣1⎦⎣5⎦.⎣7⎦⎣0⎦⎣7⎦⎣9⎦⎣6⎦⎣3⎦ cm²

4. A square is built around a circle at the right. Find the area of the shaded region. Show your work.

4.5 ÷ 2 = 2.25 cm

4.5 x² − 2.25 x² × π =

←———— 4.5 cm ————→

Area ⎣4⎦.⎣3⎦⎣5⎦ cm²
R to the nearest hundredth.

[If you cannot solve Problem 4 within a few minutes, open the HINT below. If you open the HINT and solve Problem 4, you will receive partial credit.]

H-I-N-T

- -

4a. What is the area of the square? ____20.25____ cm²

4b. How long is the diameter of the circle? ____4.5____ cm

4c. How long is the radius of the circle? ____2.25____ cm

4d. What is the area of the circle? ⎣1⎦⎣5⎦.⎣9⎦⎣0⎦⎣4⎦⎣3⎦⎣1⎦⎣3⎦ cm²

4e. What is the area of the shaded region? ⎣4⎦.⎣3⎦⎣5⎦ cm²
R to the nearest hundredth.

Name _____ Date _____ Class _____ *1*

Chapter 7 Quiz

1. Josh shaded and cut two congruent, right triangles from a circle in the sketch at the right. Find the area of the paper left over using the following steps.

←— 40 cm —→

1a. Area of circle ⎣5⎦⎣0⎦⎣2⎦⎣6⎦.⎣5⎦⎣4⎦⎣8⎦⎣2⎦ cm²

1b. Total area of both triangles ____1,600____ cm²

1c. Area of paper left over ⎣3⎦⎣4⎦⎣2⎦⎣6⎦.⎣5⎦⎣4⎦⎣8⎦⎣2⎦ cm²

2. The diameter of the large circle at the right is 6.4 cm. Each quarter-circle has a radius of 2 cm. Find the area of the unshaded part. Show your work.

3.2 x² × π = 32.169909 cm²
2 x² × π ÷ 2 = 6.2831853 cm²
32.169909 cm² − 6.2831853 cm² =

Area ⎣2⎦⎣5⎦.⎣8⎦⎣8⎦⎣6⎦⎣7⎦⎣2⎦⎣3⎦ cm²
or 25.886724

3a. The right triangle has a sector hole in the sketch at the right. The radius of the sector is 30 cm. Calculate the area of the shaded part.

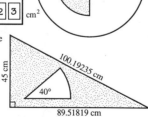

45 cm   100.19235 cm

40°

89.51819 cm

Area ____1,700____ cm²
You'll know.

3b. List your keystrokes. Draw in your own keystroke boxes.

⎡45⎤ ⎡×⎤ ⎡89.51819⎤ ⎡÷⎤ ⎡2⎤ ⎡−⎤ ⎡30⎤
⎡x²⎤ ⎡×⎤ ⎡π⎤ ⎡÷⎤ ⎡360⎤ ⎡×⎤ ⎡40⎤ ⎡=⎤

---

4. The circle at the right has a radius of 4 cm. The hole is built from 3 different sectors with radii of 2.5 cm, 1.5 cm, and 3.5 cm. Calculate the area of the shaded part. Show your work.

2.5 x² × π ÷ 360° × 23° = STO
1.5 x² × π ÷ 360° × 125° = SUM
3.5 x² × π ÷ 360° × 32° = SUM
4 x² × π = − RCL =

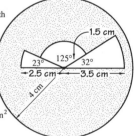

1.5 cm

23°   125°   32°
←2.5 cm→ ←3.5 cm→
4 cm

Area ⎣4⎦⎣3⎦.⎣1⎦⎣3⎦⎣5⎦⎣8⎦⎣1⎦⎣2⎦ cm²

[If you cannot solve Problem 4 within a few minutes, open the HINT below. If you open the HINT and solve Problem 4, you will receive partial credit.]

H-I-N-T

. . . .

4a. Measure and label the radius of each sector in the figure above.

4b. Calculate the area of each sector. Use the calculator's memory.

Area of 23° sector ____1.2544554____ cm²   ⎡STO⎤
Copy window.

Area of 125° sector ____2.4543693____ cm²   ⎡SUM⎤
Copy window.

Area of 32° sector ____3.4208453____ cm²   ⎡SUM⎤
Copy window.

4c. Calculate the area of the circle.

Area of circle ⎣5⎦⎣0⎦.⎣2⎦⎣6⎦⎣5⎦⎣4⎦⎣8⎦⎣2⎦ cm²

4d. Calculate the area of the shaded part.

Area of shaded part ⎣4⎦⎣3⎦.⎣1⎦⎣3⎦⎣5⎦⎣8⎦⎣1⎦⎣2⎦ cm²

Name _____ Date _____ Class _____ *1*

Mid-Chapter 8 Quiz

 1. Calculate the perimeter of the quarter-circle at the right. Show your work.

$$4.5 \times 2 \times \pi \div 4 + 4.5 \times 2 =$$

Perimeter | 1 | 6 | . | 0 | 6 | 8 | 5 | 8 | 3 | cm

4.5 cm

2a. The following figure is built from two quarter-circles and a square. Draw in lines to show the quarter-circles and the square.

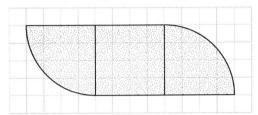

2b. Estimate the perimeter of the figure.

Estimated perimeter ____ 26 - 30 ____ cm

3. Use the following steps to calculate the perimeter of the figure above.

3a. Length of both curved parts | 1 | 2 | . | 5 | 6 | 6 | 3 | 7 | 1 | cm

3b. Length of straight parts ____ 16 ____ cm

3c. Perimeter | 2 | 8 | . | 6 | cm
R to the nearest tenth.

4a. The following figure is built from two quarter-circles. Calculate the perimeter of the figure.

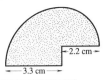
←— 3.3 cm —→
2.2 cm

Perimeter | 1 | 5 | . | 2 | 3 | 9 | 3 | 8 | cm

4b. List the keystrokes you used to find the perimeter of the figure. Draw in your own keystroke boxes.

| 2.2 | × | 2 | × | π | ÷ | 4 | = | STO | 3.3 | × | 2 |

| × | π | ÷ | 4 | = | SUM | 2.2 | SUM | 3.3 | SUM | 1.1 | SUM | EXC |

5a. The following figure is built from a square and two semicircles. The area of the square is 23.642 cm². Calculate the side length of the square.

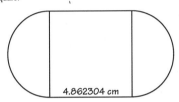
4.862304 cm

Side length ____ 4.862304 ____ cm
Copy window.
Label the figure.

5b. Calculate the perimeter of the figure.

Perimeter ____ 25 ____ cm
R to the nearest whole number.

Name _____ Date _____ Class _____ *1*

Chapter 8 Quiz

 1. Use the following steps to calculate the perimeter of the shaded half-strip at the right.

$$3 \times 2 \times \pi \div 2 + 2 \times 2 \times \pi \div 2 + 1 + 1 =$$

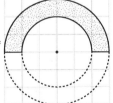

1a. Length of large curve | 9 | . | 4 | 2 | 4 | 7 | 7 | 8 | cm
$3 \times 2 \times \pi \div 2 =$

1b. Length of small curve | 6 | . | 2 | 8 | 3 | 1 | 8 | 5 | 3 | cm
$2 \times 2 \times \pi \div 2 =$

1c. Length of straight parts ____ 2 ____ cm

1d. Perimeter | 1 | 7 | . | 7 | 0 | 7 | 9 | 6 | 3 | cm
Problems 1a + 1b + 1c

2. The sketch at the right is built from four semicircles and a square. The semicircles are built along the sides of the square.

2a. Draw in lines on the figure to show the semicircles and square.

 2b. The area of the square is 100 cm². Calculate the perimeter of the figure.

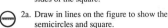
10 cm

Perimeter | 6 | 2 | . | 8 | 3 | cm
R to the nearest hundredth.

---

3. Calculate the perimeter of the quarter-strip at the right. Show your work.

$$4.5 \times 2 \times \pi \div 4 = \boxed{STO}$$
$$3 \times 2 \times \pi \div 4 = \boxed{SUM}$$
$$1.5 \times 2 = \boxed{SUM}\boxed{RCL}$$

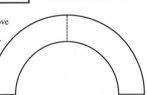
4.5 cm
3 cm

Perimeter | 1 | 4 | . | 7 | 8 | 0 | 9 | 7 | 2 | cm

4a. Ali used two of the quarter-strips above to build the half-strip at the right. Ali said, "Since I know the perimeter of one quarter-strip, I'll multiply by 2 to find the perimeter of the half-strip."

What was Ali's mistake? He counted the dashed line as part of the perimeter. He should have subtracted 3 from his answer.

4b. What is the perimeter of the half-strip?

Perimeter ____ 26.561945 ____ cm   or 26.561944 cm
Copy window.

5. The figure at the right is built from two congruent semicircles. Calculate the perimeter of the figure. The dotted lines are not part of the perimeter. Show your work.

$$6 \times \pi + 2 + 2 =$$

2 cm
2 cm

Perimeter | 2 | 2 | . | 8 | 4 | 9 | 5 | 5 | 6 | cm

Mid-Chapter 9 Quiz

Show your work when you use a calculator.

 1a. The circle at the right has a radius of 2.1 cm. Chord *AB* is the hypotenuse of the right triangle. Measure the length of Chord *AB* to the nearest 0.1 cm.

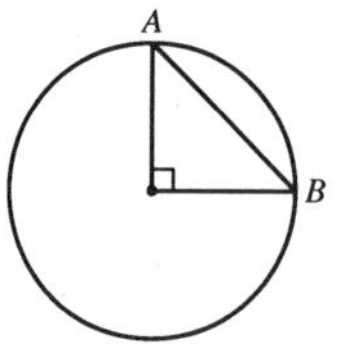

Measured length __2.9, 3.0, 3.1__ cm

1b. Calculate the length of Chord *AB*.

Chord *AB* | 2 | . | 9 | 6 | 9 | 8 | 4 | 8 | 5 | cm

Compare with your measurement in Problem 1a.

$2.1\ x^2 + 2.1\ x^2 = \sqrt{x}$ or
$2.1\ x^2 \times 2 = \sqrt{x}$

2. In the following figure, a circle is built around a square. The diameter of the circle cuts the square into two right triangles.

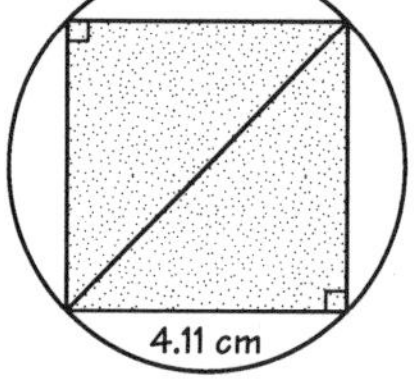

4.11 cm

2a. The perimeter of the square is 16.44 cm. Find the side length of the square and label the side length on the figure.

Side length ___4.11___ cm $16.44 \div 4 =$

2b. Calculate the diameter of the circle.

Diameter | 5 | . | 8 | 1 | 2 | 4 | 1 | 7 | 7 | cm $4.11\ x^2 \times 2 = \sqrt{x}$

---

3. The sketch at the right is built from a right triangle and a semicircle. Calculate the area of the figure.

$4.8\ x^2 + 7.3\ x^2 = \sqrt{x} \div 2 =$
$x^2 \times \pi \div 2 = + 4.8 \times 7.3 \div 2 =$

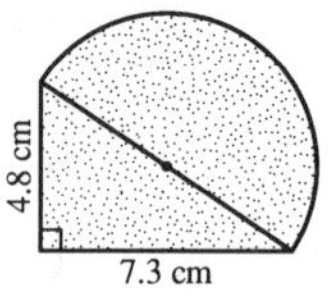

Area of figure | 4 | 7 | . | 4 | 9 | 4 | 7 | 2 | 1 | cm^2

[If you cannot solve Problem 3 within a few minutes, open the HINT below. If you open the HINT and solve Problem 3, you will receive partial credit.]

H-I-N-T

3a. Area of triangle | 1 | 7 | . | 5 | 2 | cm^2 $4.8 \times 7.3 \div 2 =$

3b. Diameter of semicircle | 8 | . | 7 | 3 | 6 | 7 | 0 | 4 | 2 | cm $4.8\ x^2 + 7.3\ x^2 = \sqrt{x}$

3c. Area of semicircle | 2 | 9 | . | 9 | 7 | 4 | 7 | 2 | 1 | cm^2

3d. Area of figure | 4 | 7 | . | 4 | 9 | 4 | 7 | 2 | 1 | cm^2 **Problem 3a + 3c**

Chapter 9 Quiz

Show your work when you use a calculator.

 1. A right triangle is built on the diameter of a semicircle at the right. Use the following steps to calculate the perimeter of the semicircle.

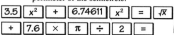

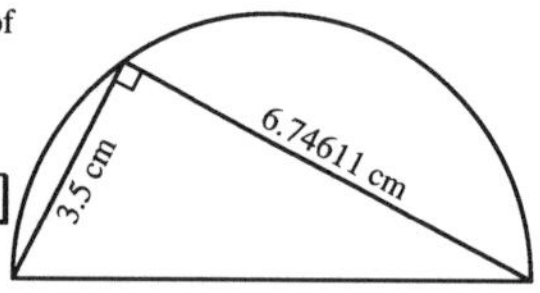

| 3.5 | x² | + | 6.74611 | x² | = | √x |
| + | 7.6 | × | π | ÷ | 2 | = |

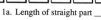

1a. Length of straight part ___7.6___ cm

1b. Length of curve | 1 | 1 | . | 9 | 3 | 8 | 0 | 5 | 2 | cm

1c. Perimeter ___19.5___ cm
R to the nearest tenth.

2a. The shaded figure at the right is built from a quarter-circle and a right triangle. Calculate the perimeter of the shaded figure. Label each part as you go.

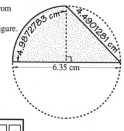

6.35 cm

Perimeter | 1 | 5 | . | 8 | 2 | 7 | 4 | 0 | 6 | cm

2b. List your keystrokes. Draw your own keystroke boxes.

| 6.35 | STO | ÷ | 2 | = | x² | × | 2 | = |
| √x | SUM | 6.35 | × | π | ÷ | 4 | = | SUM | EXC |

---

3. The following shaded semicircle fits along the hypotenuse of a right triangle as shown below. Calculate the perimeter of the shaded semicircle.

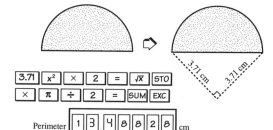

3.71 cm   3.71 cm

| 3.71 | x² | × | 2 | = | √x | STO |
| × | π | ÷ | 2 | = | SUM | EXC |

Perimeter | 1 | 3 | . | 4 | 8 | 8 | 2 | 8 | cm

4. Semicircles are built along the sides of a right triangle in the figure at the right. Find the perimeter of the figure.

2.5 cm   2.5 cm

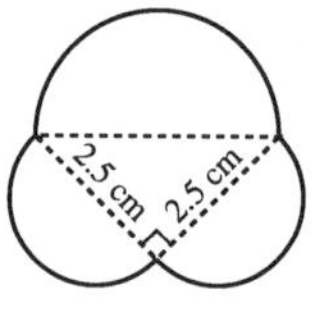

| 2.5 | x² | × | 2 | = | √x | × | π | ÷ |
| 2 | = | STO | 2.5 | × | π | = | SUM | EXC |

Perimeter | 1 | 3 | . | 4 | 0 | 7 | 5 | 8 | 5 | cm

5. Two congruent right triangles are built along the diameter of a semicircle in the sketch at the right. Calculate the perimeter of the figure.

30 cm
45 cm

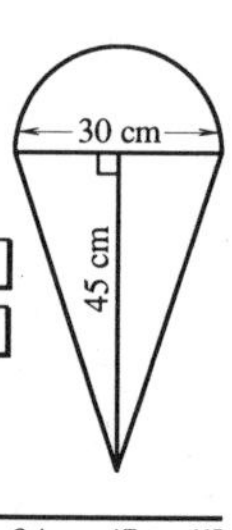

| 30 | ÷ | 2 | = | x² | + | 45 | x² | = | √x | × |
| 2 | = | STO | 30 | × | π | ÷ | 2 | = | SUM | EXC |

Perimeter | 1 | 4 | 1 | . | 9 | 9 | 2 | 2 | 2 | cm

Mid-Chapter 10 Quiz

1. A goat is tied to the corner of a barn in the sketch at the right. The shaded region shows the area the goat can graze. Calculate the grazing area.

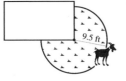

Area $\boxed{2}\boxed{1}\boxed{2}.\boxed{6}\boxed{5}$ ft^2

R to the nearest hundredth.

2. A goat is tied to a doghouse with a 5-foot tether in the following sketch. Draw and shade the goat's grazing region.

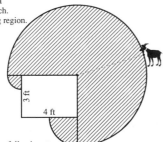

3 ft
4 ft

3. Calculate the grazing area using the following steps.

3a. Area of three-quarter circle $\boxed{5}\boxed{8}.\boxed{9}\boxed{0}\boxed{4}\boxed{8}\boxed{6}\boxed{2}$ ft^2

3b. Area of smaller quarter-circle $\boxed{0}.\boxed{7}\boxed{8}\boxed{5}\boxed{3}\boxed{9}\boxed{8}\boxed{2}$ ft^2

3c. Area of larger quarter-circle $\boxed{3}.\boxed{1}\boxed{4}\boxed{1}\boxed{5}\boxed{9}\boxed{2}\boxed{7}$ ft^2

3d. Total grazing area _____62.83_____ ft^2

R to the nearest hundredth.

---

4. A goat is tethered to a diamond-shaped barn. Each wall is 10 feet long. The goat's tether is also 10 feet long. The following sketch shows the region the goat can graze. Calculate the area of the shaded region. Show your work.

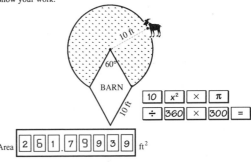

60°
BARN
10 ft

$\boxed{10}$ $\boxed{x^2}$ $\boxed{\times}$ $\boxed{\pi}$
$\boxed{\div}$ $\boxed{360}$ $\boxed{\times}$ $\boxed{300}$ $\boxed{=}$

Area $\boxed{2}\boxed{6}\boxed{1}.\boxed{7}\boxed{9}\boxed{9}\boxed{3}\boxed{9}$ ft^2

[If you cannot solve Problem 4 within a few minutes, open the HINT below. If you open the HINT and solve Problem 4, you will receive partial credit.]

H-I-N-T

4a. Find the area of the whole circle with a radius of 10 feet.

Area _____314.15927_____ ft^2
Copy window.

4b. Look at the shaded sector. What is the central angle of this shaded sector? Remember, a complete circle is 360°.

Central angle _____300_____ °

4c. Calculate the area of the shaded region.

Area $\boxed{2}\boxed{6}\boxed{1}.\boxed{7}\boxed{9}\boxed{9}\boxed{3}\boxed{9}$ ft^2

Test C

Show your work when you use a calculator.

1. In the following circle, two right triangles build a rectangle. The two triangles share a hypotenuse, which is also the diameter of the circle.

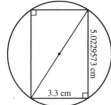

5.0229573 cm
3.3 cm

1a. Calculate the diameter of the circle.

Diameter _____6.01_____ cm

$\boxed{3.3}$ $\boxed{x^2}$ $\boxed{+}$ $\boxed{5.0229573}$
$\boxed{x^2}$ $\boxed{=}$ $\boxed{\sqrt{x}}$

1b. Calculate the circumference of the circle.

Circumference $\boxed{1}\boxed{8}.\boxed{8}\boxed{8}\boxed{0}\boxed{9}\boxed{7}\boxed{2}$ cm

$\boxed{6.01}$ $\boxed{\times}$ $\boxed{\pi}$ $\boxed{=}$

2. The shaded ring below is built from two circles. Calculate the area of the shaded ring.

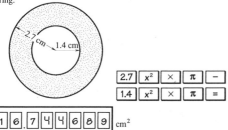

2.7 cm 1.4 cm

$\boxed{2.7}$ $\boxed{x^2}$ $\boxed{\times}$ $\boxed{\pi}$ $\boxed{-}$
$\boxed{1.4}$ $\boxed{x^2}$ $\boxed{\times}$ $\boxed{\pi}$ $\boxed{=}$

Area $\boxed{1}\boxed{6}.\boxed{7}\boxed{4}\boxed{4}\boxed{6}\boxed{8}\boxed{9}$ cm^2

---

3. A circular hole is cut out of a 78° sector in the following figure. Calculate the area of the shaded region.

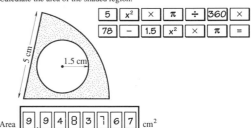

5 cm
1.5 cm

$\boxed{5}$ $\boxed{x^2}$ $\boxed{\times}$ $\boxed{\pi}$ $\boxed{\div}$ $\boxed{360}$ $\boxed{\times}$
$\boxed{78}$ $\boxed{-}$ $\boxed{1.5}$ $\boxed{x^2}$ $\boxed{\times}$ $\boxed{\pi}$ $\boxed{=}$

Area $\boxed{9}.\boxed{9}\boxed{4}\boxed{8}\boxed{3}\boxed{7}\boxed{6}\boxed{7}$ cm^2

4. A right triangle is built inside a quarter-circle in the figure at the right. The radius of the quarter-circle is 3.5 cm. Calculate the area of the shaded part. Show your work.

$\boxed{3.5}$ $\boxed{x^2}$ $\boxed{\times}$ $\boxed{\pi}$ $\boxed{\div}$ $\boxed{4}$ $\boxed{=}$
$\boxed{-}$ $\boxed{3.5}$ $\boxed{x^2}$ $\boxed{\div}$ $\boxed{2}$ $\boxed{=}$

Area $\boxed{3}.\boxed{4}\boxed{9}\boxed{6}\boxed{1}\boxed{2}\boxed{7}\boxed{5}$ cm^2

5. The sketch at the right is built from two congruent quarter-circles and two right triangles. Calculate the perimeter of the figure.

22.1 cm

$\boxed{22.1}$ $\boxed{x^2}$ $\boxed{\times}$ $\boxed{2}$ $\boxed{=}$ $\boxed{\sqrt{x}}$ $\boxed{\times}$ $\boxed{2}$ $\boxed{=}$ $\boxed{STO}$
$\boxed{22.1}$ $\boxed{\times}$ $\boxed{2}$ $\boxed{\times}$ $\boxed{\pi}$ $\boxed{\div}$ $\boxed{2}$ $\boxed{=}$ $\boxed{SUM}$ $\boxed{EXC}$

Perimeter $\boxed{1}\boxed{3}\boxed{1}.\boxed{9}\boxed{3}\boxed{7}\boxed{4}\boxed{4}$ cm

6a. A goat is tethered to a rectangular barn in the following sketch.
Draw and shade in the region that the goat is able to graze.
Remember to extend the sides when necessary.

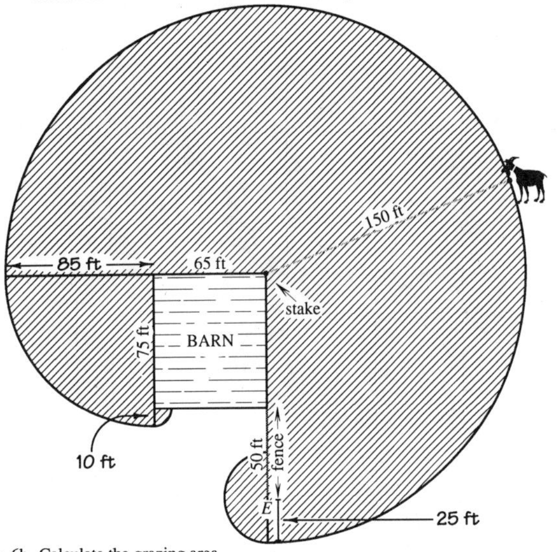

150 ft

85 ft   65 ft

stake

75 ft

BARN

10 ft

50 ft
fence

E

25 ft

6b. Calculate the grazing area.

| 150 | x^2 | × | π | ÷ | 4 | × | 3 | = | STO |

| 85 | x^2 | × | π | ÷ | 4 | = | SUM |

| 10 | x^2 | × | π | ÷ | 4 | = | SUM |

| 25 | x^2 | × | π | ÷ | 2 | = | SUM | EXC |

Grazing area | 5 | 9 | 7 | 4 | 9 | . | 1 | 6 | 5 | ft^2

Student Lab Book Answer Key

Accept ± 0.1 cm on straight linear measurements.
Accept a larger range for curved lengths.

Name _____ Date _____ Class _____ 1

1. Circumnavigate a Circle

1. Place a check below each *circle* in the following figure.

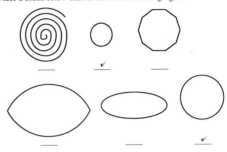

Figure A

2. How would you describe a circle? Make your description clear so that the other figures do not qualify.   **Answers will vary.**

   A closed figure. All points are the same distance from a

   center point.   .

3. The distance from the *center* of a circle to its *rim* is called a *radius*.
   Measure each radius to the nearest 0.1 cm in the following figure.

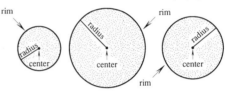

Figure B

   <u>1.1, 1.2, 1.3</u> cm   <u>2.1, 2.2, 2.3</u> cm   <u>1.6, 1.7, 1.8</u> cm

© David A. Page   *Maneuvers with Circles*

---

2   Chapter 1

4. A radius is drawn in the circle at the right.
   Draw another radius and label it "Radius B."
   Draw a third radius and label it "Radius C."
   Measure each radius to the nearest 0.1 cm.

   4a. Radius A <u>2.4, 2.5, 2.6</u> cm

   4b. Radius B <u>2.4, 2.5, 2.6</u> cm

   4c. Radius C <u>2.4, 2.5, 2.6</u> cm

   4d. What do you notice about your three measurements?   Figure C
       <u>They are the same length.</u>

5. The plural of radius is *radii* (pronounced "ray-dee-eye").
   How many radii could you draw in Figure C?

   Answer **Answers will vary.**
          infinite/lots/many

6a. Pablo drew a radius in the
    circle in Figure D. Measure
    Pablo's radius to the nearest
    0.1 cm.

    Radius <u>1.9, 2.0, 2.1</u> cm

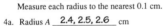

Figure D

6b. Pablo then drew a second radius next to
    the first radius. Without measuring, what
    is the distance straight across his circle?

    Distance <u>3.8, 4.0, 4.2</u> cm

The distance straight across
a circle and through the
center is called its *diameter*.
A diameter is built from two
radii. Notice that the end
points of a diameter lie
directly on the rim of the
circle.

Figure E

Figure F

Maneuvers with Circles   © David A. Page

Circumnavigate a Circle   3

7a. Place a check mark next to each circle which has a diameter drawn in it.

    Doesn't go
    through the
    center.

    Not straight
    across.

    This is only
    the radius.

Figure G

7b. Look at the circles you did not check above.
    Underneath those circles, explain why
    the line or lines are not diameters.

8a. How many diameters are drawn in the
    circle at the right?

    Answer _____2_____

8b. How many radii are drawn?

    Answer _____5_____

Figure H

8c. Measure the diameter to the
    nearest 0.1 cm.

    Diameter <u>4.7, 4.8, 4.9 cm</u>
             Put in units.

8d. Measure the radius to the nearest
    0.1 cm.

    Radius <u>2.3, 2.4, 2.5</u> cm

8e. How would you now describe a circle?   **Answers will vary.**

    A round closed shape where all

    points are the same distance from the center.

© David A. Page   *Maneuvers with Circles*

Student Lab Book Answer Key 135

9a. Cut out the circle at the bottom of the page.

9b. Fold the circle in half. Your circle will look like this:

9c. Fold the circle again. Your circle will look like this:

9d. Unfold your circle. The center of the circle is the point where the folds meet. Draw a dot there.

10a. Draw three radii in the circle you cut out. Measure each radius to the nearest whole centimeter. Label the measurements on the circle.

10b. What can you say about all the radii in a circle? **They are all the same length.**

11a. Draw three diameters and measure each one.

11b. What can you say about all the diameters in a circle? **All diameters in a circle are the same length.**

12. Can you draw a straight line in the circle that is longer than the diameter?

Answer _____**No**_____
          Yes or No

Why or why not? **The diameter is the longest line.**

- - - - - - - - Cut along line. - - - - - - - - -

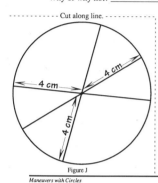

4 cm, 4 cm, 4 cm

Figure J

A *compass* is a tool used to draw circles. The sharp point on the compass is the center of the circle.

Compass

point →

13. Draw a circle below using the following steps.

   a. Place the sharp point of the compass in the middle of the ┼. This will be the center of the circle.

   b. Keep the point on the center and open the compass until the pencil touches the center of the dot (•).

   c. Without lifting the point, turn the compass to draw the circle.

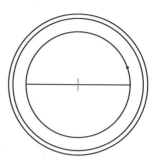

14. Draw a diameter in your circle. Measure it to the nearest 0.1 cm.

Answer __**5.9, 6.0, 6.1**__ cm

15. Without measuring, how long is the radius? __**2.95, 3, 3.05**__ cm

16a. Draw a different circle using the same center above, by opening or closing the compass.

16b. Measure the new diameter. **Answers will vary** cm

17a. Draw a third circle using the same center above.

17b. Measure the radius of your third circle. **Answers will vary** cm

18. Use the steps and sketches in the following table along with the center mark below to draw a circle with a radius of 4 cm.

		Steps	Sketches
	a.	Use your ruler to draw a dot 4 cm away from the center mark.	
	b.	Place the sharp point of the compass on the center mark. Then open the compass so that the sharp point is on the center and the pencil is on the dot you drew.	
	c.	Without lifting the point, turn the compass to draw the circle.	

19a. Draw a radius in the circle you drew below.

19b. Measure the radius to check.

First radius __**3.9, 4.0, 4.1**__ cm

19c. Draw and measure a different radius.

Second radius __**3.9, 4.0, 4.1**__ cm

19d. How long is the diameter?

Diameter __**7.8, 8.0, 8.2**__ cm

19e. Draw and measure a diameter.

Diameter __**7.9, 8.0, 8.1**__ cm

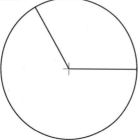

20a. Draw a circle with a radius of 2.4 cm.

20b. Draw a diameter.

20c. Without measuring, what is the length of the diameter?

Diameter __**4.8 cm**__
                Put in units.

20d. How did you find the length of the diameter?
Multiplied the radius by 2.

21a. Draw a circle with a diameter of 5.6 cm. Measure the diameter to check.

21b. Draw a radius.

21c. Without measuring, what is the length of the radius?

Radius __**2.8**__ cm

21d. How did you find the length of the radius? **Divided the diameter by 2.**

22. Figure K is a sketch. What is its radius?

Radius __**13.275**__ cm

23. A different circle has a radius of 617,283.5 cm. What is the diameter of this circle?

Diameter __**1,234,567**__ cm
                You'll know.

24. Jenna's pool has a diameter of 114 cm. What is the radius of her pool?

Radius __**57**__ cm

26.55 cm

Figure K

Perimeter and Circumference

A *polygon* is a closed shape which has three or more straight sides. Figure L shows three examples of polygons.

Figure L

1. Measure each side of the polygons in Figure L to the nearest 0.1 cm and label them on the figure.

The following shapes are special polygons called *regular polygons*.

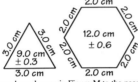

2. Measure each side of the regular polygons in Figure M to the nearest 0.1 cm and label them on the figure.

3. What is special about a regular polygon? __All the sides are the same length. All the angles are the same.__

The distance around the outside of a shape is called the *perimeter*. Imagine a bug crawling around the outside of the polygon at the right. The perimeter is the distance the bug crawls to get all the way back to the point where it started.

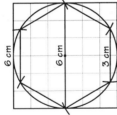

Start Here

Figure N

4. What is the perimeter of this polygon?

   Perimeter ____12____ cm

5. Find the perimeter of each polygon in Figure L and Figure M. Write the perimeter inside each polygon.

Unlike polygons, the distance around a circle is called its *circumference*. The circumference is the distance the bug crawls to get all the way back to the point where it started.

If you draw a circle on the sidewalk with chalk and walk around it, you are walking on the circle's circumference.

Alfredo drew the following circle with his compass. The distance his pencil traveled to form the circle is the circumference.

Figure P

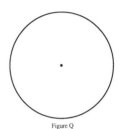

← Circumference

6. Michelle and Sandor wrapped a piece of string around the circle in Figure Q and then measured the string to find its circumference. What other way could you find the circumference of the circle at the right?

   __Bend a ruler.__

   __Bend a pipe cleaner and__
   __measure the pipe cleaner.__

   __Bend a piece of paper.__

   _____

   _____

Figure Q

Ervin said, "A good way to estimate the circumference of a circle is to build a square around it and use the square's perimeter as an estimate."

7. Estimate the circumference of the circle using the following steps.

   7a. Use the center point to draw a circle with a radius of 3 cm on the centimeter grid below.

   7b. Trace a square around the circle.

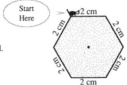

Figure R

   7c. Draw a diameter and label its length. Your drawing should look like the sketch in Figure S.

   7d. Label the side length of the square.

   7e. What do you notice about the length of the *diameter* and the *side length* of the square?

   __The diameter and the side length of the square are equal.__

Figure S

   7f. Find the perimeter of the square. ____24____ cm

   Notice that four diameters of the circle form the perimeter of the square. The perimeter of the square built around a circle is one estimate for the circumference of the circle.

8. Is the circle's circumference smaller or larger than the perimeter of the square?

   Answer ___Smaller___
          Smaller or Larger

Lance said, "To find another estimate for the circumference of a circle, draw a *regular hexagon* inside of it." A regular hexagon is a polygon with six equal sides.

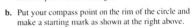

9. Use the following steps to draw a regular hexagon inside the circle on page 10.

   a. Set your compass for the length of the radius, 3 cm. Once you set that distance, make sure the compass doesn't change.

   b. Put your compass point on the rim of the circle and make a starting mark as shown at the right above.

   c. Place your compass point on the starting mark and make a new mark along the rim.

   d. Continue this until you get back to where you started.

   e. Place a dot where each mark touches the rim.

   f. Connect the dots with straight lines to form a regular hexagon like the sketch in Figure T. Label the length of one side.

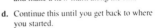

Figure T

10. Find the perimeter of the regular hexagon. ____18____ cm

   Notice that 6 radii, which is also the same as 3 diameters, build the perimeter of the regular hexagon. The perimeter of the hexagon is another estimate for the circumference of the circle.

11. Is the circle's circumference smaller or larger than the perimeter of the regular hexagon?

   Answer ___Larger___
          Smaller or Larger

The circumference of a circle is smaller than the square's perimeter and larger than the hexagon's perimeter. Consider the circle with a radius of 3 cm.

12. The circumference of the circle is between ___18___ and ___24___.

13. Estimate the circumference of the circle. ___18 - 24___ cm

14. Measure the circumference of the circle. ___18.5 - 19.5___ cm

15. Estimate the circumference of the circle at the right using the following steps.

15a. Measure the perimeter of the square around the circle.

Answer __21.2, 21.6, 22.0__ cm

15b. Measure the perimeter of the regular hexagon inside the circle.

Answer __15.6, 16.2, 16.8__ cm

Figure U

15c. Estimate the circumference of the circle.

Answer _____16 - 20_____ cm

15d. Elijah said, "I didn't use the six radii to estimate the circumference of the circle. I used the diameter of the circle instead."

How did Elijah estimate the circumference of the circle? __He estimated__

__with 3 diameters instead of 6 radii.__

Complete the following steps to collect data that will show a relationship between the diameter of a circle and its circumference.

16a. As a class, gather five different cylinders. For example, you can use a coffee can, an oatmeal carton, and a frozen orange juice can. Label the cylinders "1", "2", "3", "4", and "5". Divide into teams. Each team will work with one cylinder.

16b. Draw the diameter on the circle of each cylinder. Be sure you run across the center to get a diameter and not a shorter line.

Not a Diameter

Diameter

17. If the center of the circle is not marked, how do you draw a diameter?

__Measure the longest distance across the circle.__

---

18. Measure the diameter of your team's cylinder to the nearest 0.1 cm.
Diameter __Answers will vary.__ cm

19. Use a measuring tape to find the circumference of your team's cylinder.
Circumference __Answers will vary.__ cm

20a. Collect the data from your classmates and complete the following table.

Cylinder	Measured Diameter *Put in units.*	Measured Circumference *Put in units.*
1		
2		
3		
4		
5		

Answers will vary.

20b. Compare the diameter and circumference columns. For each cylinder, about how many diameters equal the circumference?

Answer _____about 3_____

21. Liz measured the diameter on her cylinder. Then she cut pieces of string that equaled the diameter. Liz taped the pieces of string along the circumference as shown in the following picture.

Diameter

Diameter

Diameter

Diameter

Diameter

Figure V

21a. Use string and Liz's method on one of your cylinders.

21b. Is the circumference built from three diameters? ____No____
Yes or No

Explain. __The circumference is built from a little more than three diameters.__

Using measurements, Circumference ÷ Diameter is a little more than 3. To do careful work with circles, you must work with the number π, which is spelled *pi* (pronounced "pie"). Press $\boxed{\pi}$ on your calculator.

Window: $\boxed{3}.\boxed{1}\boxed{4}\boxed{1}\boxed{5}\boxed{9}\boxed{2}\boxed{7}$

Notice that π is a little more than 3.

You do not need to memorize π because your calculator knows π to 7 decimal places.

For every circle: Circumference ÷ Diameter = π

To *estimate* the circumference of a circle, multiply the diameter by 3.
To *calculate* the circumference of a circle, multiply the diameter by π.

22a. Jenny drew a circle with a diameter of 5 cm. To estimate the circumference of the circle, she multiplied 5 cm by 3.

Jenny's estimate _____15_____ cm

22b. To calculate the circumference of her circle, Jenny pressed:

$\boxed{5}\ \boxed{\times}\ \boxed{\pi}\ \boxed{=}$

Circumference __15.707963__ cm
Copy window.
Compare with Jenny's estimate.

23. A circle has a diameter of 8.2 cm. Calculate the circle's circumference.

Circumference _____25.8_____ cm
R to the nearest tenth.

24a. A circle has a radius of 3 cm. Estimate the circumference. Be careful! You are given the length of the radius.

Estimate _____18 - 20_____ cm

24b. Calculate the circumference.

Circumference $\boxed{1}\boxed{8}.\boxed{8}\boxed{4}\boxed{9}\boxed{5}\boxed{5}\boxed{6}$ cm

---

Homework 1: Circumnavigate a Circle

1a. Draw a circle with a radius of 3.1 cm using the center at the right.

1b. Measure the circumference to the nearest 0.1 cm.

Circumference __18.5 - 20.5__ cm

2a. Draw a circle with a diameter of 7.8 cm below.

2b. Measure the circumference to the nearest 0.1 cm.

Circumference __23.5 - 25.5__ cm

3. A compact disc has a radius of 6 cm. Circle the best estimate for the circumference of the compact disc.

6 cm   12 cm   18 cm   24 cm   (36 cm)   50 cm

4. Calculate the circumference of the compact disc.

Circumference __37.699112__ cm
Copy window.

5. A circle has a diameter of 12.2 cm. Calculate its circumference.

Circumference __38.32743__ cm
Copy window.

6. Complete the following table. Remember to include the units.
List the keystrokes you used to find the circumference.

	Radius	Diameter	Circumference *Copy window.*	Keystrokes
a.	2.75 cm	5.5 cm	17.27876 cm	2.75 × 2 × π =
b.	5.5 cm	11 cm	34.557519 cm	11 × π =
c.	11 cm	22 cm	69.115038 cm	11 × 2 × π =
d.	22 cm	44 cm	138.23008 cm	44 × π =
e.	44 cm	88 cm	276.46015 cm	44 × 2 × π =

7a. In the table above, what happens to the length of the radius?

The radius is doubled each time.

7b. What happens to the length of the diameter?

The diameter is doubled each time.

7c. What happens to the circumference?

The circumference is doubled each time.

8a. The Ridge Street Block Club is planting a circular garden in an empty lot.
The diameter of the garden will be 40 ft. A fence around the garden will
protect it from visiting creatures (rabbits) during the night. How many
feet of fence is needed?

Length | 1 | 2 | 5 | . | 6 | 6 | 3 | 7 | 1 | ft

8b. The store only sells fence by the whole foot. How many whole feet
should the Ridge Street Block Club buy?

Answer _____ 126 _____ feet

8c. The fence costs $2.50 per foot. How much will the garden fence cost?

Answer $ _____ 315 _____

Maneuvers with Circles   © *David A. Page*

---

2. What's Inside?

1. Figure A shows 9 squares.
Each of the squares has a
side length of 1 centimeter.
Measure one of these squares
with your ruler.

The **area** of, or space covered
by, one of these centimeter
squares is **1 square centimeter**
and can be written as **1 cm²**.

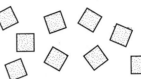

Figure A

These nine squares can be put together to make the larger
square in Figure B. The area of the larger square is 9 cm².

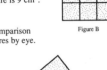

Figure B

2. Use the 9 cm² square in Figure B as a comparison
to estimate the area of the following figures by eye.

Estimate _____ 10 - 15 _____ cm²   Estimate _____ 9 - 18 _____ cm²

Estimate _____ 18 - 27 _____ cm²   Estimate _____ 7 - 10 _____ cm²

Figure C

© *David A. Page*   *Maneuvers with Circles*

---

3. Now count square centimeters and pieces of square centimeters to get a
better estimate. Compare your answers with Problem 2.

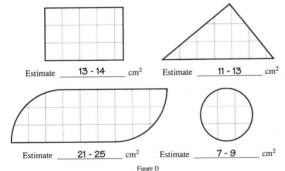

Estimate _____ 13 - 14 _____ cm²   Estimate _____ 11 - 13 _____ cm²

Estimate _____ 21 - 25 _____ cm²   Estimate _____ 7 - 9 _____ cm²

Figure D

4a. Draw a circle that has a radius of 5 cm using the center mark below.

4b. Use the following **25 cm² stamp**
to estimate the area of the circle.

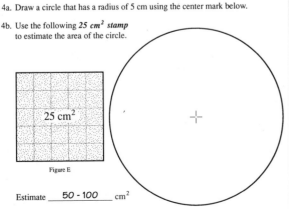

25 cm²

Figure E

Estimate _____ 50 - 100 _____ cm²

Maneuvers with Circles   © *David A. Page*

---

5. A circle with a radius of 5 cm is placed in a square below.
Use the following steps to find the area of the square.

5a. How many square centimeters are in one row? _____ 10 _____

5b. How many rows are there in the entire square? _____ 10 _____

5c. To find the area of the square, multiply the number of square centimeters
in one row by the number of rows.

Answer _____ 100 _____ cm²

To find the area of a square, multiply its side length by itself.

6a. Estimate the area of the circle in Figure F.

Estimate _____ 75 - 100 _____ cm²

6b. Explain how you estimated the area in Problem 6a. **Answers will vary. I counted**

number of squares in the circle. Or I counted the number of

shaded squares and subtracted it from 100.

6c. Is your estimate more or less than the estimate in Problem 4b? **More or Less**

More or Less

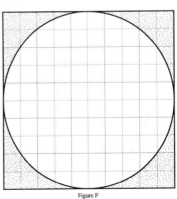

Figure F

© *David A. Page*   *Maneuvers with Circles*

The radius of the following circle is 6 cm. A shaded square is built along the radius. Notice that the side length of the square is the same length as the radius.

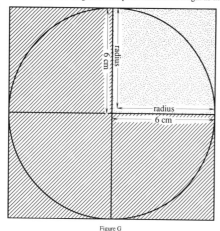

Figure G

Radius × Radius = Area of One Square Built on Radius

 7. What is the area of the shaded square above? ___**36 cm²**___
Put in units.

8. Build and shade three more squares on the radii of the circle above. Figure G should look like the sketch at the right.

Figure H

Radius × Radius × 4 = Area of Four Squares Built on Radius

9a. What is the area of four squares? ____**144**____ cm²

9b. Is the area of four squares more or less than the area of the circle?

Answer ___**More**___
More or Less

Since the area of four squares is too big, let's see how three of these squares compare to the area of the circle.

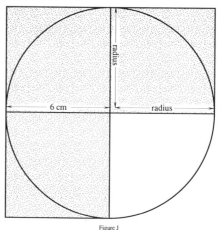

Figure J

Radius × Radius × 3 = Area of Three Squares
‾‾‾‾‾‾‾‾‾‾‾‾‾‾‾‾‾‾‾
Area of One Square

10a. What is the area of one square? ____**36**____ cm²

10b. What is the area of three squares? ____**108**____ cm²

10c. Do you think the area of three squares is more, less, or equal to the area of the circle?

Answer ___**More, Less, or Equal**___   *Accept all 3. It is too close to*
More, Less, or Equal   *tell for sure.*

10d. Why? ___**Answers will vary. For example: The overlaps (3) look**___
___**smaller than the last ¼ circle.**___

The following sketch shows another way to think about the area of a circle. Take the three outside pieces from the squares and see if they fit into the fourth part of the circle.

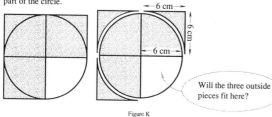

Will the three outside pieces fit here?

Figure K

This method is shown for a circle with a radius of 6 cm. The three outside corners were cut and placed into the fourth part. If you want to try it, copy and cut out Figure J on page 21.

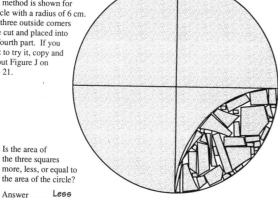

Figure L

11a. Is the area of the three squares more, less, or equal to the area of the circle?

Answer ___**Less**___
More, Less, or Equal
Compare with your guess in Problem 10c.

11b. Why? ___**There are spaces between the pieces.**___

---

12. You estimated the area of the circle using the following methods.

| 6 | × | 6 | × | 4 | = | ____**144**____ cm² is too big!
Area of 1 square   *Area of 4 squares*

| 6 | × | 6 | × | 3 | = | ____**108**____ cm² is too small!
Area of 1 square   *Area of 3 squares*

> The area of a circle is a little more than the area of three squares built on the radii. Remember, π is a little more than 3.
> The area of a circle is π × the area of one square built on the radius.
> To **estimate** the area of a circle, multiply: Radius × Radius × 3.
> To **calculate** the area of a circle, multiply: Radius × Radius × π.

13. To calculate the area of a circle with a radius of 6 cm, use the following keystrokes.

| 6 | × | 6 | × | π | = | ____**113.09734**____ cm²
Area of 1 square   *Copy window.*

14a. The circle at the right has a radius of 3 cm. Find the area of the square built on the radius.

Area of square ____**9**____ cm²

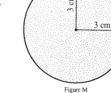

Figure M

> Multiplying a number by itself is called **squaring** the number. Instead of multiplying 3 × 3, you can use x^2, a special key called **x-squared**.

14b. To find the area of the square in Figure M, press | 3 | x^2 |.
Window ____**9**____ cm²
Compare with Problem 14a.

14c. Estimate the area of the circle in Figure M. ____**27**____ cm²

15. Calculate the area of the circle in Figure M. List your keystrokes.

| 3 | x^2 | × | π | = | | | |
You do not need to use all the keystroke boxes.

Area ___**28.274334**___ cm²
Copy window.

16a. Look at the circle at the right.
Estimate the area of the square
built on the radius.
Hint: Think about the length of the radius
rounded to the nearest whole number.

Estimate _____9_____ cm^2

16b. Estimate the area of the circle.

Estimate _____27_____ cm^2

16c. Calculate the area of the circle.

Area _____30_____ cm^2
You'll know.

16d. List the keystrokes you used.

| 3.0901936 | x^2 | × | π | = | |

17. A circle has a radius of 3.9894228 cm.

17a. Estimate the area of the square built on the radius.

Estimate ___16 cm^2___
Put in units.

17b. Estimate the area of the circle.

Estimate ___48 cm^2___
Put in units.

17c. Calculate the area of the circle.

Area _____50_____ cm^2
You'll know.

18. Calculate the area of the circle in the sketch
at the right.

Area | 1 | 6 | 4 | 2 | 2 | . | 0 | 1 | 6 | cm^2

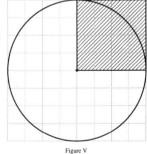

72.3 cm

Figure P

19a. What is the radius of the circle in Figure Q?

Radius _____2.4_____ cm

19b. Calculate the area of this circle.

Area _____18.1_____ cm^2
R to the nearest tenth.

19c. Ramena's answer is 72.4 cm^2.
What did she do wrong? __Ramena used the__
__diameter instead of the radius.__

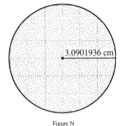

4.8 cm

Figure Q

20a. The circle in Figure R has a diameter of 5.56 cm. Draw a diameter.

20b. The following keystrokes were used by
different students to calculate the area of
the circle in Figure R. Only one set of
keystrokes is correct. Check the correct set
of keystrokes.

_____ | 5.56 | x^2 | × | π | = |

_____ | 5.56 | ÷ | 2 | x^2 | × | π | = |

✔ | 5.56 | ÷ | 2 | = | x^2 | × | π | = |

Figure R

20c. Calculate the area of the circle.

Area | 2 | 4 | . | 2 | 7 | 9 | 4 | 8 | 5 | cm^2

21. A sketch of a square picture frame is
shown at the right. The frame creates a
circular window for the picture. Find the
area of the circular window using
the following steps.

27 cm

21a. What is the radius of the circle?

Radius _____13.5_____ cm

21b. Area | 5 | 7 | 2 | . | 5 | 5 | 5 | 2 | 6 | cm^2

Figure S

---

22. The circle at the right has a radius of
1 cm. What is the area of the square
built on the radius?

Area of square _____1_____ cm^2

Figure T

23. The length of the radius was doubled in the circle at the
right. What is the area of the square built on the radius?

Area of square _____4_____ cm^2

Figure U

24a. The length of the radius was doubled again in
Figure V. Build a square on the radius.
Shade the square.

24b. What is the area built on the radius?

Area of square _____16_____ cm^2

25. Mitchell thought, "If I double
the radius of a circle, the area of the
circle will also double."
Do you agree with Mitchell?

Answer _____No_____
Yes or No

26a. Complete the following table.
Multiply the area of the square built
on the radius by 3 to find the
estimated area of the circle.

Figure V

Radius	Area of Square Built on Radius	Estimated Area of Circle
1 cm	1 cm^2	3 × 1 cm^2 = 3 cm^2
2 cm	4 cm^2	3 × 4 cm^2 = 12 cm^2
4 cm	16 cm^2	3 × 16 cm^2 = 48 cm^2
8 cm	64 cm^2	3 × 64 cm^2 = 192 cm^2

26b. When the radius is doubled, what happens to the area of the circle?
__The area of the circle quadruples (× 4).__

Name _____ Date _____ Class _____ 27

Homework 2: What's Inside?

1a. The figure at the right is a sketch. Find the area of
the square built on the radius.

Area of square _____25_____ cm^2

1b. Estimate the area of the circle. _____75_____ cm^2

1c. Calculate the area of the circle. __78.539816__ cm^2
Compare with your estimate on page 19.

5 cm

Figure W

2. Draw a square along the radius of each circle in the following sketches.
Write the area of each square on the figure. Then estimate the area of
each circle.

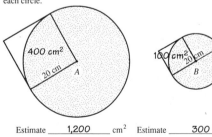

400 cm^2

20 cm   A

100 cm^2 20 cm

B

Estimate ___1,200___ cm^2 Estimate ___300___ cm^2

Figure X

3. Calculate the area the circles in Figure X. List your keystrokes.

3a. Area of Circle A | 1 | 2 | 5 | 6 | . | 6 | 3 | 7 | 1 | cm^2

| 20 | x^2 | × | π | = | | |
You do not need to use all the keystroke boxes.

3b. Area of Circle B | 3 | 1 | 4 | . | 1 | 5 | 9 | 2 | 7 | cm^2

| 20 | ÷ | 2 | = | x^2 | × | π | = | |
You do not need to use all the keystroke boxes.

Student Lab Book Answer Key   141

4. The shaded figure at the right is built from identical circles. Three lines are drawn through the centers of the circles. The length of each line is 6.45 cm. Use the following steps to find the area of the figure.

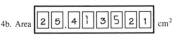

4a. What is the diameter of one circle?

Diameter ____2.15____ cm

4b. Area ⎹2⎸5⎸.⎸4⎸1⎸3⎸5⎸2⎸1⎸ cm²

5a. Calculate the area of a circle with a radius of 5,000 cm.

Area __78,539,816__ cm²
Copy window.

5b. Would this circle fit in your classroom? Why or why not? __No. A circle with a radius of 5,000 cm would have a diameter of 10,000 cm or 100 meters. This circle would not even fit in a football field.__

6. The Jardine House is a building in Hong Kong that was specially designed with large circular windows. The Jardine House has 52 floors because there are 52 weeks in a year. Only 45 of the floors have circular windows. On these 45 floors, there are 7 windows on the east side, 7 windows on the west side, 12 windows on the north side, and 12 windows on the south side.

6a. How many circular windows does the Jardine House have? Show your work.   There are 38 windows on each floor.
7 + 7 + 12 + 12 = 38

Answer ____1,710____ windows   38 × 45 = 1,710

6b. The diameter of each circular window is 70 inches. Calculate the area of one window.

Area ⎹3⎸8⎸4⎸8⎸.⎸4⎸5⎸1⎸ in.²

6c. Calculate the area of all the circular windows.

Area ⎹6⎸5⎸8⎸0⎸8⎸5⎸1⎸.⎸2⎸ in.²

Figure Y

Maneuvers with Circles   © David A. Page

---

3. In and About

1. Complete the following table. Put in units.

	Radius	Diameter	Circumference _R to the nearest hundredth._	Area _R to the nearest hundredth._
a.	0.25 cm	0.5 cm	1.57 cm	0.20 cm²
b.	0.5 cm	1 cm	3.14 cm	0.79 cm²
c.	1 cm	2 cm	6.28 cm	3.14 cm²
d.	2 cm	4 cm	12.57 cm	12.57 cm²
e.	4 cm	8 cm	25.13 cm	50.27 cm²
f.	8 cm	16 cm	50.27 cm	201.06 cm²
g.	16 cm	32 cm	100.53 cm	804.25 cm²

2a. Draw a circle with a radius of 3 cm at the right.

2b. Look at the table and predict its circumference.

Prediction ____13 - 25____ cm

2c. Look at the table and predict its area.

Prediction ____13 - 50____ cm²

2d. Calculate the circumference of this circle.

Circumference ____18.85____ cm
R to the nearest hundredth.

2e. Calculate the area of this circle.

Area ____28.27____ cm²
R to the nearest hundredth.

2f. Compare your calculated answers with your predictions.

3. A circle has an area of 100 cm². Predict its circumference.

Prediction ____26 - 50____ cm

The diameter must be greater than 8 cm and less than 16 cm.

© David A. Page   _Maneuvers with Circles_

---

4. The square in the sketch at the right has a side length of 5 cm. What is the area of the square?

Area ____25____ cm²

5. The following sketch shows a square built around a circle. The area of the square is 49 cm².

5a. All the sides of a square are the same length. To find the side length of the square, Leo thought, "What number times itself gives me 49?" Answer Leo's question to find the side length of the square.

Side length ____7____ cm
Label the figure.

5b. Notice that the side length of the square is the same length as the diameter of the circle. What is the diameter of the circle above?

Diameter ____7____ cm
Label the figure.

6a. The area of the square in the sketch at the right is 81 cm². Find the diameter of the circle.

Diameter ____9____ cm

6b. Draw and label the length of a diameter on Figure C.

6c. What length did you find first, before the diameter?

Answer __Side length of square__

|← 5 cm →|

Figure A

7 cm
← Side Length →

Diameter
• 7 cm

Figure B

9 cm

Figure C

Maneuvers with Circles   © David A. Page

7a. The area of the square in the sketch at the right is 70.56 cm². Circle the best estimate for the side length of the square.

6 cm   (8 cm)   10 cm   12 cm

7b. Robyn uses trial and error to find the side length of the square. Her first estimate is too big. Complete Robyn's table. (Hint: Use [x²] to help.)

Side Length	Area _You want 70.56 cm²._
9 cm	81 cm² _Too big._
8 cm _What's your next try?_	64 cm² _Too big or (too small)?_
8.5 cm _What's your next try?_	72.25 cm² _(Too big) or too small?_
8.4 cm _What's your next try?_	70.56 cm² _Too big or too small?_
cm _What's your next try?_	cm² _Too big or too small?_

← Side Length →

Diameter

Figure D

Answers will vary.

7c. Side length of square or diameter of circle ____8.4____ cm

8a. The square in the following sketch has an area of 136.89 cm². Find the diameter of the circle (side of the square) using trial and error.

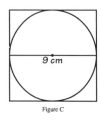

11.7 cm

Figure E

8b. Diameter ____11.7____ cm
Label the figure.

Side Length	Area _You want 136.89 cm²._
11 cm	121 cm² _Too small._
12 cm	144 cm² _Too big._
11.5 cm _What's your next try?_	132.25 cm² _Too big or (too small)?_
11.6 cm _What's your next try?_	134.56 cm² _Too big or (too small)?_
11.7 cm _What's your next try?_	136.89 cm² _Too big or too small?_
cm _What's your next try?_	cm² _Too big or too small?_

Answers in table will vary.

© David A. Page   _Maneuvers with Circles_

---

9. Use trial and error to find the side length of a square whose area is 299.29 cm². Use the following tables to keep track of your trials. Don't forget to fill in the missing units.

Answers will vary.

Side Length	Area You want 299.29 cm²	Side Length	Area You want 299.29 cm²
20 cm	400 cm² Too big	17.3 cm	299.29 cm²
15 cm	225 cm² Too small		
16 cm	256 cm² Too small		
18 cm	324 cm² Too big		
17 cm	289 cm² Too small		
17.5 cm	306.25 cm² Too big		
17.4 cm	302.76 cm² Too big		

Side length ___17.3___ cm

There is a faster way to find the side length of a square when you know its area. Find $\sqrt{x}$ on the calculator. This is called the *square root of x*. If you know the area of a *square*, use the square root key to find its side length.

For example, the area of a square is 81 cm². To find the side length, press [81] [√x]. (On some calculators, you need to press a shift key to get $\sqrt{x}$.)

$\sqrt{81}$ = 9, since 9 × 9 = 81. A square with an area of 81 cm² has sides that are 9 cm long.

What number times itself equals 169? ___13___

What is the square root of 144? ___12___

What is the square root of 299.29? ___17.3___
Compare with the table in Problem 9.

$\sqrt{324}$ = ___18___ $\sqrt{400}$ = ___20___

$\sqrt{325}$ = ___18.03___ $\sqrt{410}$ = ___20.25___
R to the nearest hundredth.   R to the nearest hundredth.

---

10. The area of the square at the right is 10 cm². Estimate the side length of the square. Think: What number squared is close to 10?

Estimate ___3___ cm

Figure F

11a. Use the square root key to calculate the side length of the square.

Press: [10] [√x]

Side length ___3.1622777___ cm
Copy window.

11b. How long is the diameter of the circle?

Diameter ___3.2___ cm
R to the nearest tenth.

12. In the sketch at the right, a square is built on the radius of a circle. The area of the square is 100 cm². Notice the side length of the square is also the radius of the circle. What is the length of the radius?

Radius ___10___ cm

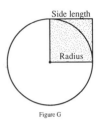
Figure G

13. A square is built on the radius of the circle in the sketch at the right. The square has an area of 107.5369 cm².

13a. Use the answer to Problem 12 to help estimate the length of the radius.

Estimate ___10___ cm

13b. Find the length of the radius using [√x].

Radius ___10.37___ cm

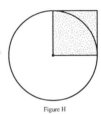
Figure H

---

14. A square is built on the radius in the following circle.

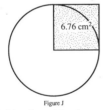
6.76 cm²

Figure J

14a. Trisha found the circle's radius and then the area of the circle using the following keystrokes.

Radius

Press: [6.76] [√x] [x²] [×] [π] [=] ___21.237166___ cm²
Copy window.

Area of Square
Built on Radius

14b. Tedda said, "You took the square root and then you squared. The area of the square built on the radius is 6.76 cm². Since I already know the area of the square, I can use pi (π) to find the area of the circle." Tedda used the following keystrokes.

Press: [6.76] [×] [π] [=] ___21.237166___ cm²
Copy window.
Compare with Problem 14a.

15. Three squares are built on the radius of the circle in the sketch at the right. The total area of all three squares is 223.45354 cm². This is a good estimate for the area of the circle.

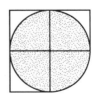
Figure K

15a. Find the area of one square built on the radius.

Area of one square [7][4].[4][8][4][5][1][3] cm²

15b. Calculate the area of the circle using π. Compare your answer with the total area of the three squares.

Area ___234___ cm²
You'll know.

16a. The circle in the sketch at the right has an area of 90 cm². Tammy estimated the area of the square built on the radius. She said, "The area of the circle is almost equal to the area of three squares built on the radius. I only want the area of one square."

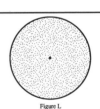
Figure L

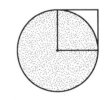

90 cm² ÷ 3 = ___30___ cm²
Area of
Circle   Estimated Area
of One Square

Figure M

16b. Shannon said, "Dividing by 3 is a good estimate, but I can find the *accurate* area of the square on the calculator." Complete Shannon's keystrokes to calculate the area of one square built on the radius.

Press: [90] [÷] [π] [=] ___28.64789___ cm²
Area of
Circle   Special Number of
Squares in Circle   Area of Square
Compare with Tammy's estimate.

16c. The side length of the square equals the length of the radius. Take the square root to find the length of the radius.

Radius ___5.4___ cm
R to the nearest tenth.

17a. The following circle has an area of 60.821234 cm². Estimate the area of the square built on the radius.

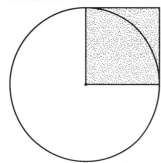

Figure N

Estimate _____20_____ cm²

17b. Estimate the side length.

Estimate _____4 - 5_____ cm

18a. Calculate the area of the square built on the radius in Figure N.

Area of square _____19.36_____ cm²
Compare with Problem 17a.

18b. List the keystrokes for Problem 18a.

[60.821234] [÷] [π] [=] [ ]

18c. Use [√x̄] to calculate the radius.

Radius _____4.4_____ cm   or 4.4045431
Compare with Problem 17b.

18d. Measure the radius to the nearest 0.1 cm.

Radius ___4.3, 4.4, 4.5___ cm
Compare with Problem 18c.

19a. Measure the radius at the right to the nearest 0.1 cm.

Measured radius ___2.4, 2.5, 2.6___ cm

19b. The area of the circle is 20 cm². What is the area of the square built on the radius?

Area of square _____6.3661977_____ cm²
Copy window.

19c. What is the radius of the circle? _____2.5_____ cm
R to the nearest tenth.
Compare with Problem 19a.

Figure P

19d. List the keystrokes that find the length of the radius.

[20] [÷] [π] [=] [√x̄] [ ] [ ] [ ]
You do not need to use all the keystroke boxes.

20. The area of the circle in the sketch at the right is 706.85835 cm². Use the following steps to calculate the circumference of the circle.

20a. What is the radius? _____15_____ cm
You'll know.

20b. What is the diameter? _____30_____ cm

Figure Q

20c. Calculate the circumference.

Circumference [9][4][.][2][4][7][7][8] cm

20d. List your keystrokes to find the circumference of the circle in one run.

[706.85835] [÷] [π] [=] [√x̄] [×] [2] [×] [π] [=] [ ]
Area of Circle

21. The area of a circle is 500 cm². List the keystrokes and calculate the circumference of this circle.

[500] [÷] [π] [=] [√x̄] [×] [2] [×] [π] [=] [ ]

Circumference [7][9][.][2][6][6][5][4][6] cm

---

22. Measure the diameter of the circle in Figure R to the nearest 0.1 cm.

Measured diameter ___7.5, 7.6, 7.7___ cm

23a. About how many diameters fit along the circumference of a circle?

Answer _____3_____

23b. The circumference of the circle is 24 cm. What is the exact number of diameters that fit on the circumference?

Answer _____π_____

Figure R

23c. Complete the following keystrokes to calculate the diameter of Figure R.

Press: [24] [÷] [π] [=]
Circumference

23d. What is the length of the diameter of the circle?

Diameter _____7.6394373_____ cm
Copy window.
Compare with Problem 22.

24. A circle has a circumference of 188.49556 cm.

24a. Calculate the diameter of the circle.

Diameter _____60_____ cm
You'll know.

24b. What is the radius of the circle?

Radius _____30_____ cm

24c. List the keystrokes you used to find the radius.

[188.49556] [÷] [π] [÷] [2] [=] [ ] [ ]

---

25. Estimate the area of the following circle.

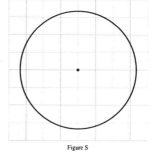

Figure S

Estimate ___27 - 35___ cm²   Answers will vary.

26. The circumference of the circle in Figure S is 21 cm. Use the following steps to calculate the area of the circle.

26a. What is the diameter of the circle? ___6.6845076___ cm
Copy window.

26b. Calculate the radius of the circle.

Radius [3][.][3][4][2][2][5][3][8] cm

26c. Find the area of the circle.

Area [3][5][.][0][9][3][6][6][5] cm²
Compare with Problem 25.

27. The circumference of a circle is 83.512488 cm. List the keystrokes to calculate the area of this circle in one run.

[83.512488] [÷] [π] [÷] [2] [=] [x²] [×] [π] [=] [ ]

Area _____555_____ cm²
You'll know.

28. The General Sherman Tree in Sequoia National Park, California has a circumference of 114.7 feet near its base. It is not a perfect circle, but assume it is here. Calculate the diameter of this tree.

Diameter $\boxed{3\;6\;.\;5\;1}$ ft

R to the nearest hundredth.

29. A European chestnut tree was cut down leaving a stump. The area of the circle on the top of the stump was reported at 2,219.3 ft². Calculate the circumference of the tree.

Circumference $\boxed{1\;6\;7\;.\;0}$ ft

R to the nearest tenth.

30a. Near Oaxaca, Mexico, stands an ancient cypress tree that scientists think may be 3,000 years old. The tree is about 113 feet in circumference and about 130 feet high. Calculate the diameter of this tree.

Diameter $\boxed{3\;5\;.\;9\;7}$ ft

R to the nearest hundredth.

30b. If this tree were cut, what would be the area on top of the stump?

Area $\boxed{1\;0\;1\;6\;.\;2}$ ft²   or 1,016.1

R to the nearest tenth.

31. Which tree in Problems 28, 29, and 30, has the largest diameter?

Answer _____29_____

32a. Measure the circumference of a tree to the nearest whole centimeter.

Circumference _____ cm   **Answers will vary.**

32b. Calculate the diameter of the tree you measured. _____ cm

32c. How does this tree compare to the trees above?

It is smaller.

Homework 3: In and About

1a. Yolanda's watch face has a circumference of approximately 12 cm. Estimate the diameter of her watch face.

Estimate _____4_____ cm

1b. Calculate the diameter of the watch.

Diameter $\boxed{3\;.\;8\;1\;9\;7\;1\;8\;6}$ cm

2. The circumference of Elaine's pool is 48 feet. The area of Pam's pool is 255 ft². Calculate the diameter of each pool to find out which pool is larger. List the keystrokes.

2a. Diameter of Elaine's pool $\boxed{1\;5\;.\;2\;8}$ ft

R to the nearest hundredth.

2b. $\boxed{48}\;\boxed{\div}\;\boxed{\pi}\;\boxed{=}\;\boxed{}\;\boxed{}\;\boxed{}$

You do not need to use all the keystroke boxes.

2c. Diameter of Pam's pool $\boxed{1\;8\;.\;0\;2}$ ft

R to the nearest hundredth.

2d. $\boxed{255}\;\boxed{\div}\;\boxed{\pi}\;\boxed{=}\;\boxed{\sqrt{x}}\;\boxed{\times}\;\boxed{2}\;\boxed{=}$

You do not need to use all the keystroke boxes.

2e. Who has the larger pool? _____Pam_____

Elaine or Pam

2f. Average the diameters in Problems 2a and 2c.

Average diameter _____16.65_____ ft

2g. Calculate the area of this average pool.

Area $\boxed{2\;1\;7\;.\;7\;3}$ ft²   or 217.70

R to the nearest hundredth.

---

3. Marjorie's backyard is a square. The largest pool she can fit in her yard has a circumference of 40.84 ft.

3a. What is the side length of her backyard?

Length _____13.0_____ ft

R to the nearest tenth.

3b. What is the area of her backyard?

Area _____169.0_____ ft²

R to the nearest tenth.

3c. Draw a sketch of Marjorie's backyard. Label the sketch with the side length and area.

13 ft   169 ft²   13 ft

4a. The following rectangle is a sketch of a blackboard. Draw the largest circle within the boundaries of the rectangle.

75 cm   height   width

Figure T

4b. The largest circle that can be drawn on the blackboard in Ms. Carter's class is a circle with an area of 17,671.459 cm². With this information, which can you find, the height or the width of the blackboard?

Answer _____Height_____

Height or Width

4c. Calculate this distance for the sketch above. Label the sketch.

Length _____75_____ cm

R to the nearest whole number.

5a. How many whole circles with a circumference of 94.24778 cm could be drawn along the height of Ms. Carter's blackboard in Problem 4?

Answer _____2_____ circles

5b. Sketch the circles in Figure U.

height   width

Figure U

6. The area of the square in Figure V is 38.5641 cm². Two identical circles fit inside the square. Circle an estimate for the total area of the circles.

5 cm²

(15 cm²)

20 cm²

25 cm²

30 cm²

Figure V

7. Find the area of the two circles in Problem 6 using the following steps.

7a. Side length of square $\boxed{6\;.\;2\;1}$ cm

Measure to check.

7b. Diameter of one circle _____3.105_____ cm

Copy window.

7c. Radius of one circle $\boxed{1\;.\;5\;5\;2\;5}$ cm

Measure to check.

7d. Area of two circles $\boxed{1\;5\;.\;1\;4\;4\;0\;8\;7}$ cm²

Compare with Problem 6.

8. In the following figure, the diameter of one small circle equals the radius of the large circle. The area of the large circle is 28.652582 cm². Calculate the area of the shaded part using the following steps.

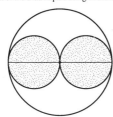

Figure W

8a. Radius of large circle ___3.02___ cm
Measure to check.

8b. Radius of small circle ___1.51___ cm
Measure to check.

8c. Area of shaded part [1][4].[3][2][6][2][9][1] cm²

9. The diameter of the circle at the right is the same length as the side of the square. The area of the circle is 14.186254 cm².

9a. Measure the side length of the square.

Measured side length ___4.2, 4.3, 4.4___ cm

9b. Calculate the side length of the square.

Side length ___4.25___ cm
Compare with Problem 9a.

9c. Calculate the area of the square.

Area of square [1][8].[0][6][2][5] cm²

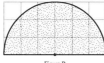

Figure X

---

4. Pieces of Circles

1. Cut out the circle below. Fold the circle in half. Cut along the fold.

   This circle is cut into two equal pieces or two half circles. A half circle is also called a *semicircle*.

   Since two pieces like make a whole circle,

   the area of equals the area of the circle

   divided by two.

2. Glue or tape one of your semicircles at the right.

3. The area of the *entire* circle you cut out is 40 cm². What is the area of one of the semicircles?

   Area of semicircle ___20 cm²___
   Put in units.

Save the other semicircle for Problem 11.

- - - - - - - - - - - - Cut below this line. - - - - - - - - - - - -

Figure A

---

4. Count shaded square centimeters to estimate the area of the semicircle at the right.

   Estimate ___12 - 16 cm²___
   Put in units.

Figure B

5. Use the following steps to calculate the area of the semicircle.

5a. Imagine the entire circle as shown in Figure C. Count centimeters to find the radius of the circle. ___3___ cm

5b. Calculate the area of the *whole* circle using the following keystrokes. Keep the answer in the window.

Press: [3] [x²] [×] [π] [=]

Answer ___28.274334___ cm²
Copy window.

5c. Calculate the area of the semicircle.

Area of semicircle ___14___ cm²
R to the nearest whole number. Compare with your estimate in Problem 4.

5d. List the keystrokes that calculate the area of a semicircle with a radius of 3 cm.

[3] [x²] [×] [π] [=] [÷] [2] [=] [ ] [ ] [ ]
You do not need to use all the keystroke boxes.

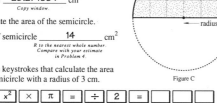

radius

Figure C

6a. Measure the radius of the semicircle at the right to the nearest whole centimeter.

Radius ___5 cm___
Put in units.

6b. Calculate the area of a circle with this radius. Keep the answer in the window.

Area [7][8].[5][3][9][8][1][6] cm²

6c. Calculate the area of the semicircle.

Area [3][9].[2][6][9][9][0][8] cm²

6d. Round your answer to the nearest tenth.

Area ___39.3 cm²___
Put in units.

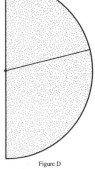

Figure D

7. The radius of the following semicircle is 4 cm. Calculate the area of the semicircle. List your keystrokes.

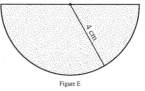

Figure E

Area of semicircle [2][5].[1][3][2][7][4][1] cm²

[4] [x²] [×] [π] [=] [÷] [2] [=] [ ]

8. The diameter of the semicircle at the right is 7.4 cm.

8a. How long is the radius?

Radius ___3.7___ cm
_Measure to check
your answer._

Figure F

8b. Is the radius smaller or larger than the radius in Problem 7?

Answer ___Smaller___
Smaller or Larger

8c. Estimate the area of the semicircle.

Estimate ___15 - 24___ cm^2

8d. Now calculate the area of the semicircle.

Area [2][1].[5][0][4][2][0][2] cm^2
Compare with your estimate.

9. The semicircle in the sketch at the right has a diameter of 18 cm.

9a. How long is the radius? ___9 cm___
Put in units.

18 cm
Figure G

9b. Calculate the area of the semicircle.

Area of semicircle [1][2][7].[2][3][4][5] cm^2

9c. List your keystrokes.

[18] [÷] [2] [=] [x^2] [×]
[π] [=] [÷] [2] [=]
You do not need to use all the keystroke boxes.

10. The diameter of a semicircle is 17.697936 cm. Calculate the area of the semicircle.

Area of semicircle ___123___ cm^2
The sum of the digits is 6.

11a. Take your other semicircle from page 45. Fold the semicircle in half. Cut along the fold.

Since four pieces like ⌂ make a whole circle,

the area of ⌂ equals the area of the circle divided by four.

⌂ is called a *quarter-circle*.

11b. The area of the entire circle from page 45 is 40 cm^2. What is the area of one quarter-circle?

Area of quarter-circle ___10 cm^2___
Put in units.

12. Estimate the area of the quarter-circle at the right.

Estimate ___3 - 3$\frac{1}{2}$___ cm^2

2 cm
Figure H

13. Use the following steps to calculate the area of the shaded quarter-circle.

13a. Calculate the area of the whole circle in Figure H. Keep the answer in the window.

Area of circle ___12.566371___ cm^2
Copy window.

13b. Four quarter-circles build the circle. The quarter-circle is one piece out of four. What should you do to find the area of the quarter-circle?

Answer ___Divide the area of the circle by 4.___

13c. Calculate the area of the quarter-circle.

Area of quarter-circle ___3.1415927___ cm^2
_Copy window.
Compare with your estimate
in Problem 12._

14a. The circle in the sketch at the right has a radius of 3.8 cm. Calculate the area of the *whole* circle.

Area [4][5].[3][6][4][5][9][8] cm^2

3.8 cm
Figure J

14b. Calculate the area of the shaded quarter-circle.

Area of quarter-circle [1][1].[3][4] cm^2
R to the nearest hundredth.

15a. Draw a circle with a radius of 3.5 cm at the right.

15b. Draw two diameters to divide the circle into quarter-circles. Shade one of the quarter-circles.

15c. Is the area of this quarter-circle smaller or larger than the one in Problem 14?

Answer ___Smaller___
Smaller or Larger

15d. Calculate the area of the shaded quarter-circle.

Area of quarter-circle [9].[6][2] cm^2
R to the nearest hundredth.

16. The radius of the quarter-circle at the right is 3.3 cm.

16a. Compare the quarter-circles in Problems 14, 15, and 16. Estimate the area of the quarter-circle in Figure K.

Estimate ___5 - 9 cm^2___
Put in units.

3.3 cm
Figure K

16b. Calculate the area of the quarter-circle.

Area [8].[5][5][2][9][8][6] cm^2

16c. List your keystrokes.

[3.3] [x^2] [×] [π] [=] [÷] [4] [=]

Pieces Put Together

1. Three quarter-circles are put together to build the shaded figure at the right. Count to estimate the area of the shaded figure.

Estimate ___7 - 12 cm^2___
Put in units.

Figure L

2. Calculate the area of the shaded figure using the following steps.

2a. Calculate the area of the circle. Do not clear the window.

Area of circle [1][2].[5][6][6][3][7][1] cm^2

2b. Calculate the area of one quarter-circle. Do not clear the window.

Area of quarter-circle [3].[1][4][1][5][9][2][7] cm^2

2c. Since there are three quarter-circles, multiply by 3 to find the area of the shaded figure.

Area of shaded figure ___9.424778___ cm^2 or 9.4247781
_Copy window.
Compare with Problem 1._

2d. List the keystrokes to find the area of the shaded figure in one run.

[2] [x^2] [×] [π] [÷] [4] [×] [3] [=] [ ] [ ] [ ]

3. Kendra used a different method and pressed the following keystrokes.

[2] [x^2] [×] [π] [−] [2] [x^2] [×] [π] [÷] [4] [=]

3a. Put a loop around the keystrokes that find the area of the whole circle.

3b. Put a box around the keystrokes that find the area of one quarter-circle.

3c. Explain Kendra's method. ___Kendra found the area of the entire___
___circle first. She subtracted a quarter-circle because three___
quarter-circles make up the shaded region. It's like a quarter-
circle was cut out.

4. The figure at the right is built from 3 quarter-circles.

4a. Draw in radii to show the 3 quarter-circles.

4b. Estimate the area of the ▨ shading.

Estimate _18 - 24 cm²_
Put in units.

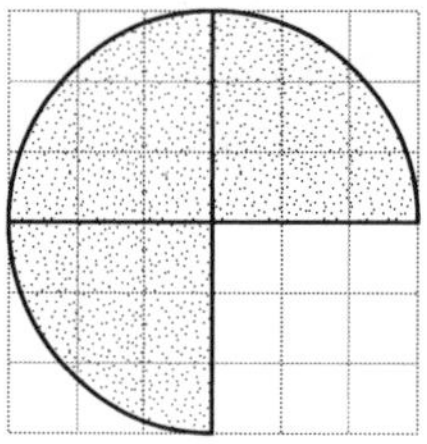

5a. Calculate the area of the ▨ shading.

Area _____21_____ cm²
R to the nearest whole number.
Compare with your estimate.

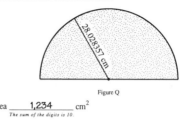

Figure M

5b. List your keystrokes for Problem 5a.

| 3 | x^2 | × | π | = | ÷ | 4 |
| × | 3 | = | | | | |

You do not need to use all the keystroke boxes.

6. The figure at the right is built from quarter-circles. Calculate its area. Show your work.

| 2.5 | x^2 | × | π | = | ÷ | 4 | × | 3 | = |

Area | 1 | 4 | . | 7 | 2 | 6 | 2 | 1 | 6 | cm²

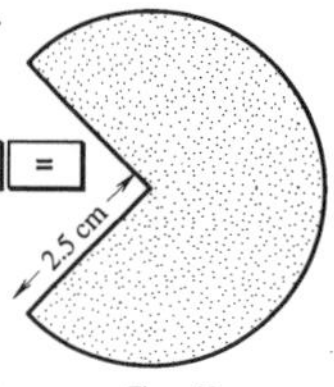

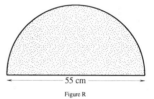

Figure N

7. The sketch at the right is built from quarter-circles. The diameter is 16 cm. Calculate the area of the figure.

Area | 1 | 5 | 0 | . | 8 | 0 | cm²
R to the nearest hundredth.

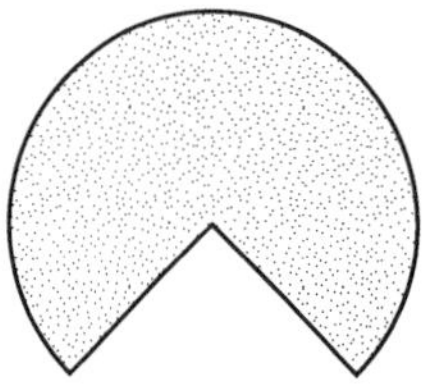

Figure P

Homework 4: Pieces of Circles

1. The semicircle in the following sketch has a radius of 28.028357 cm. Calculate the area of the semicircle.

Figure Q

Area _____1,234_____ cm²
The sum of the digits is 10.

2. The semicircle in the following sketch has a diameter of 55 cm.

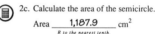

├─── 55 cm ───┤

Figure R

2a. Is the area of this semicircle smaller or larger than the area in Problem 1?

Answer ___Smaller___
Smaller or Larger

2b. Explain your answer. **The radius in Figure R is smaller so its area is smaller.**

2c. Calculate the area of the semicircle.

Area _____1,187.9_____ cm²
R to the nearest tenth.

---

3. Calculate the area of the quarter-circle at the right. List your keystrokes. Draw your own keystroke boxes.

| 2.7 | x^2 | × | π | = | ÷ | 4 | = |

Area _____5.7_____ cm²
R to the nearest tenth.

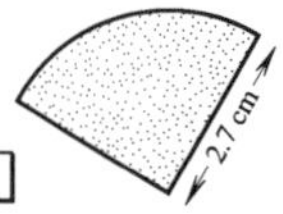

Figure S

4. The radius in the sketch at the right is 6.5147002 cm. Calculate its area. Show your work.

| 6.5147002 | x^2 | × | π | ÷ | 4 | × | 3 | = |

Area _____100_____ cm²
You'll know.

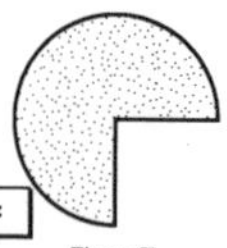

Figure T

5. Look at the shaded area in Figure U. Notice that the shaded region is built from identical quarter-circles.

5a. What is the area of the big square in Figure U?

Area _____36_____ cm²

5b. Is the shaded area smaller or larger than the area of the square?

Answer ___Smaller___
Smaller or Larger

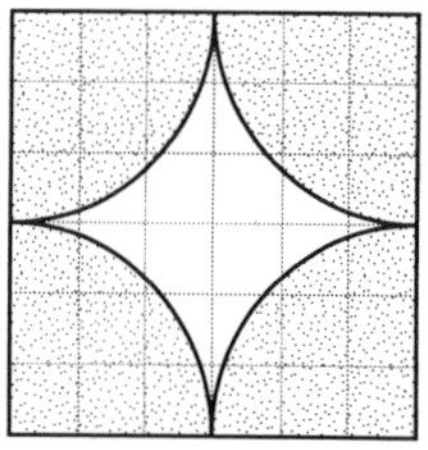

Figure U

5c. Why? **The shaded part does not fill in the entire square. The white space is left over.**

6. Calculate the area of the shaded region in Figure U. Hint: How many quarter-circles are there?

Area | 2 | 8 | . | 2 | 7 | 4 | 3 | 3 | 4 | cm²

---

5. Remember That Number

1. The circle at the right has a diameter of 6.3661978 cm.

1a. Calculate the circumference of the circle. List your keystrokes.

| 6.3661978 | × | π | = | |

Circumference _____20_____ cm
You'll know.

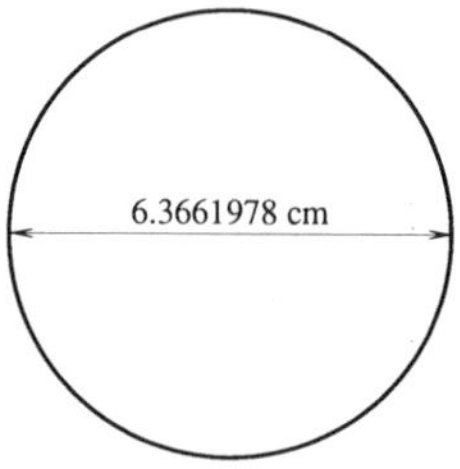

1b. Calculate the area of the circle. List your keystrokes.

| 6.3661978 | ÷ | 2 | = | |
| x^2 | × | π | = | |

Area | 3 | 1 | . | 8 | 3 | 0 | 9 | 8 | 9 | cm²

6.3661978 cm

Figure A

In the problems above, 6.3661978 was pressed twice. Instead of pressing a messy number twice, use the calculator's scratch pad (called **memory**) to save a number. Memory is very helpful with complicated problems.

On the TI-30 SLR+™, the four keys at the bottom left run the memory.

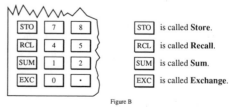

STO	is called **Store**.
RCL	is called **Recall**.
SUM	is called **Sum**.
EXC	is called **Exchange**.

Figure B

The following pages describe how to use these four keys.

STO Key

One way to activate your calculator's memory is to use the STO key. Put the year you were born into your calculator. For example, if you were born in 1980, press 1980. Now press STO. The year you were born is now in the calculator's memory.

> STO takes a copy of the number in the window and puts it into the memory. Any number that was in memory before is now gone.

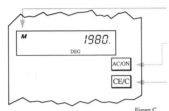

The **M** in the window means you have a number in **M**emory.

WARNING! If you press this, it will erase the number in the window **and** the memory!

USE THIS INSTEAD. This key clears the window but not the memory.

Figure C

EXC Key

The EXC key exchanges the number in the window with the number in the memory.

2. Figures D and E are sketches of a circle and a semicircle.

 2a. Predict which shape has the larger area.

Answer <u>Circle or Semicircle</u>
       Circle or Semicircle

 2b. Use the calculator's memory to compare their areas. Calculate the area of the *circle*.

Area of circle <u> 124 </u> cm²
           You'll know.

Press STO. Do not press AC/ON.

6.2825493 cm

Figure D

2c. Calculate the area of the *semicircle*.

Area of semicircle <u> 125 </u> cm²
         You'll know.
         Not 250.

8.9206206 cm

Figure E

Press EXC to see the circle's area.

You EXChanged two numbers. The number in the memory went into the window. The number that was in the window went into the memory.

2d. Which area is larger? <u>Semicircle</u>
       Circle or Semicircle

2e. Press EXC again. Now the semicircle's area is in the window and the circle's area is in memory. Press AC/ON. You just cleared the window and the memory. The **M** is gone. "0" is in the window and memory. Press EXC to check.

> Some people call EXC the "swap key." One important use of EXC is to take a peek at the memory without losing the number in the window. Press EXC once to peek at what is in memory. Press EXC again to get the numbers back the way they were.

Complete the tables in Problems 3 through 6. After you press each key, fill out what is in the window and memory.

3.

Press:	AC/ON	27	STO	5
Window	0	27	27	5
Memory	0	0	27	27

4.

Press:	AC/ON	88	STO	121	EXC
Window	0	88	88	121	88
Memory	0	0	88	88	121

5.

Press:	AC/ON	53	STO	47	STO
Window	0	53	53	47	47
Memory	0	0	53	53	47

6.

Press:	AC/ON	8.741	STO	7	EXC	EXC	EXC
Window	0	8.741	8.741	7	8.741	7	8.741
Memory	0	0	8.741	8.741	7	8.741	7

Do the following problems using STO and EXC.

7. Press: AC/ON 125 STO + 25 =

7a. What do you see in the window? <u> 150 </u>

7b. What number is in memory? <u> 125 </u>
          Peek to check.

8. Press: AC/ON 73 × EXC =

8a. What do you see in the window? <u> 0 </u>

8b. What number is in memory? <u> 73 </u>

9. Fill in the following boxes to create your own problem using STO and EXC. **Answers will vary.**

Press: AC/ON 21 × 5 STO 7 EXC =

9a. What number do you see in the window? <u> 105 </u>

9b. What number is in memory? <u> 7 </u>

RCL Key

10a. The circle at the right has a diameter of 7.0028175 cm. Store the diameter in memory.

Press: 7.0028175 STO

10b. The diameter is now in the window and in the memory. Calculate the circumference of the circle.

Press: × π =

Circumference <u> 22 </u> cm
         You'll know.

10c. Find the radius of the circle.

Press: RCL ÷ 2 =

Radius <u>3.5014088</u> cm
     Copy window.

10d. When you pressed RCL, what number came to the window? <u>7.0028175</u>

7.0028175 cm

Figure F

> RCL (Recall) takes a copy of the number in memory and puts it in the window. The number that used to be in the window is gone.

Complete the following tables.

11.

Press:	AC/ON	100	STO	23	RCL
Window	0	100	100	23	100
Memory	0	0	100	100	100

12.

Press:	AC/ON	103	STO	406	RCL
Window	0	103	103	406	103
Memory	0	0	103	103	103

13. Press: [AC/ON] [20] [STO] [65] [+] [35] [=] [×] [RCL] [=]

13a. What do you see in the window? **2,000**

13b. What is in memory? **20**

14. Press: [AC/ON] [20] [STO]

14a. What is in memory? **20**
Don't clear your calculator.

14b. Press: [180] [+] [RCL] [+] [RCL] [+] [RCL] [=]

Window: [M 2 4 0.]

14c. What number is being added to the window every time you press [+] [RCL] in Problem 14b?

Answer **20**

[RCL] vs. [EXC]

15. Fill in the following tables. Press [EXC] twice to peek into memory.

15a.

Press:	25	STO	30	EXC
Window	25	25	30	25
Memory	0	25	25	30

15b.

Press:	25	STO	30	RCL
Window	25	25	30	25
Memory	0	25	25	25

15c. The keystrokes in the two tables above only differ by the last keystroke. What is the difference between [EXC] and [RCL]? **Answers will vary. When you press RCL, you lose the number in the window. or EXC puts a new number in memory.**

16. Press: [2] [x²] [×] [π] [=] [STO]
[2.8] [x²] [×] [π] [÷] [2] [=]

16a. The top row finds the area for which shape? **Circle**
Circle or Semicircle

16b. The bottom row finds the area for which shape? **Semicircle**
Circle or Semicircle

16c. Is the answer to the top row in the window or memory? **Memory**
Window or Memory

16d. If you want to compare the two areas, you don't want to lose either one. Which key do you press, [EXC] or [RCL]? **EXC**

16e. Which area is larger? **Circle**

[SUM] Key

Each time you press [SUM], it takes the number that is in the window and adds it to the number in memory.

17. Press: [AC/ON] [10] [STO] [20] [SUM] [EXC]
(10 is stored in memory.) (20 is added to the 10 in memory.) (See 30 in the window.)

17a. What is in the window? **30**

17b. What is in memory? **20**

18. Press the keystrokes listed in the following table.
(395 is stored in memory.) (5 is added to memory each time [SUM] is pressed.)

Press:	AC/ON	395	STO	5	SUM	SUM	SUM	EXC
Window	0	395	395	5	5	5	5	410
Memory	0	0	395	395	400	405	410	5

Each table below has a series of keystrokes.

a. First predict what will be in the window and memory at the end of each series. Write your predictions next to each table.

b. Then use your calculator to complete the tables.

Predictions will vary.

19.

Press:	AC/ON	91	STO	9	SUM
Window	0	91	91	9	9
Memory	0	0	91	91	100

20.

Press:	AC/ON	91	STO	3	SUM	SUM	SUM
Window	0	91	91	3	3	3	3
Memory	0	0	91	91	94	97	100

21.

Press:	AC/ON	91	STO	3	SUM	CE/C	EXC
Window	0	91	91	3	3	0	94
Memory	0	0	91	91	94	94	0

22.

Press:	AC/ON	91	STO	3	SUM	AC/ON	6	EXC	RCL
Window	0	91	91	3	3	0	6	0	6
Memory	0	0	91	91	94	0	0	6	6

* 23.

Press:	AC/ON	91	STO	3	SUM	SUM	RCL	SUM	RCL
Window	0	91	91	3	3	3	97	97	194
Memory	0	0	91	91	94	97	97	194	194

Try It Out!

1. Use your calculator's memory to calculate the circumference and area of the circle in the sketch at the right.

1a. Complete the following keystrokes to calculate the circumference of the circle.

[74.17323] [STO] [×] [π] [=] [ ]

Circumference [2 3 3 . 0 2 2 0 7] cm

74.17323 cm

Figure G

1b. The diameter of the circle is in the memory. [RCL] (Recall) the diameter to calculate the area of the circle. List your keystrokes.

[RCL] [÷] [2] [=] [x²] [×] [π] [=] [ ]

Area **4,321** cm²
You'll know.

2. Estimate the area and circumference of the circle below.

2a. Estimated area **27 - 48** cm²

2b. Estimated circumference **18 - 25** cm

3. The circle at the right has a 3.7424103 cm radius. Use the calculator's memory to calculate the area and circumference of the circle. Then compare your answers to your estimates. List your keystrokes.

[3.7424103] [STO] [x²] [×] [π] [=]
[RCL] [×] [2] [×] [π] [=]

3a. Area **44** cm²
You'll know.

3b. Circumference **23.514257** cm
Copy window.

Figure H

4. Two quarter-circles with different radii are put together in the following
   figure. Use the calculator's memory to calculate the area of the figure.

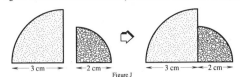

Figure J

4a. Area of one quarter-circle. __7.0685835__ cm²   Press: [STO]
                                Copy window.   or 3.1415927

4b. Area of the other quarter-circle. __3.1415927__ cm²   Press: [SUM]
                                      Copy window.   or 7.0685835

4c. To see the final answer, press [RCL].

    Area | 1 | 0 | . | 2 | 1 | 0 | 1 | 7 | 6 | cm²

5. Two quarter-circles are put together in the sketch below. Use the
   following steps to calculate the area of the entire figure.

5a. Calculate the area of the larger quarter-circle.

    Area __95.033178__ cm²
         Copy window.

    Press: [STO]

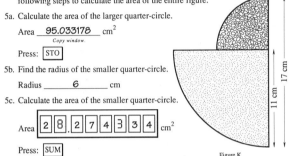

5b. Find the radius of the smaller quarter-circle.

    Radius _____6_____ cm

5c. Calculate the area of the smaller quarter-circle.

    Area | 2 | 8 | . | 2 | 7 | 4 | 3 | 3 | 4 | cm²

    Press: [SUM]   Figure K

5d. Press [RCL] to find the total area. __123.3__ cm²
                                         R to the nearest tenth.

6. The figure at the right is built from
   four quarter-circles of different sizes.
   Count square centimeters to estimate
   the area of the entire shaded figure.

   Estimate __21 - 25__ cm²

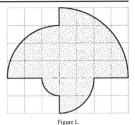

Figure L

7. Using the steps below as a guide,
   calculate the area of the shaded
   quarter-circles. After each quarter-
   circle, fill in the missing calculator
   memory keystroke.

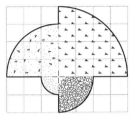

Figure M

7a. Area of ⠄⠄⠄⠄ shading __12.566371__ cm²   Press: [STO]
                          Copy window.

7b. Area of ⠄⠄⠄⠄ shading __7.0685835__ cm²   Press: [SUM]
                          Copy window.

7c. Area of 🟰 shading __3.1415927__ cm²   Press: [SUM]
                       Copy window.

7d. Area of ⠄⠄ shading __0.7853982__ cm²   Press: [SUM]
                       Copy window.

7e. Now find the total area of the shaded figure.   Press: [RCL] or [EXC]

    Area | 2 | 3 | . | 5 | 6 | 1 | 9 | 4 | 5 | cm²
                   Compare with Problem 6.

Homework 5: Remember That Number

1. Press the keystrokes in the table. For each keystroke, write the number
   that is in the window and the number that is in memory.

Press:	AC/ON	74.63	STO	48.37	SUM	EXC	RCL
Window	0	74.63	74.63	48.37	48.37	123	48.37
Memory	0	0	74.63	74.63	123	48.37	48.37

2. Use [STO], [SUM], and [RCL] to do the problem
   at the right. Do not use [+]. Write the memory
   keys next to each number.

   Calculator's answer __1,000__
                        You'll know.

3.6589741	STO
845.26981	SUM
51.07521	SUM
+ 99.996006	SUM
	RCL

3. The sketch at the right
   is built from quarter-circles
   and a square. Calculate the
   area of the entire figure using
   memory. Show your work.

   A = 27 x^2 × π ÷ 4 = STO

   B = 27 x^2 SUM

   C = 27 x^2 × π ÷ 4 = SUM

   D = 34 x^2 × π ÷ 4 = SUM

   E = 54.2 x^2 × π ÷ 4 = SUM
                         RCL or EXC

   Area __5,089.25__ cm²
        R to the nearest hundredth.

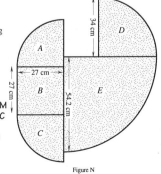

Figure N

4. Use your calculator's memory to find the area and
   circumference of the circle at the right.

4a. Area __15.7__ cm²
         R to the nearest tenth.

4b. Circumference __14.1__ cm
                  R to the nearest tenth.

4c. List your keystrokes so that you key in the
    messy radius only once. Finish up with area in
    the memory and circumference in the window.

    | 2.2379 | STO | x^2 | × | π | = | |
    | EXC | × | 2 | × | π | = | |

2.2379 cm

Figure P

5. The following figure is built from five different circles.

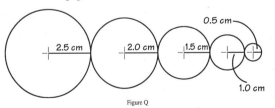

Figure Q

5a. Measure the radius of each circle to the nearest 0.5 cm. Label the radii
    with your measurements.

5b. Use the calculator's memory to calculate the area of the figure.

    Area | 4 | 3 | . | 1 | 9 | 6 | 8 | 9 | 9 | cm²

5c. List your keystrokes in one run.

2.5	x^2	×	π	=	STO	2.0	x^2	×	π	=	SUM
1.5	x^2	×	π	=	SUM	1.0	x^2	×	π	=	SUM
0.5	x^2	×	π	=	SUM	RCL					

6. Figure R is built from quarter-circles with radii of 1.5 cm, 2.5 cm, 3.5 cm, and 4.5 cm. Draw and label each radius. Then calculate the area of the shaded region using memory. Show your work.

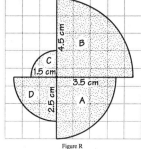

A = 3.5 x^2 × π ÷ 4 = STO

B = 4.5 x^2 × π ÷ 4 = SUM

C = 1.5 x^2 × π ÷ 4 = SUM

D = 2.5 x^2 × π ÷ 4 = SUM

RCL or EXC

Figure R

Area of shaded region | 3 | 2 | . | 2 | 0 | 1 | 3 | 2 | 5 | cm²

7a. The following figure is built from semicircles. Count square centimeters to estimate the area of the entire figure.

Estimate   **51 - 58**   cm²

7b. Calculate its area using memory.

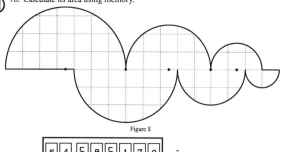

Figure S

Area | 5 | 4 | . | 5 | 8 | 5 | 1 | 7 | 2 | cm²

Maneuvers with Circles   © *David A. Page*

Accept ± 0.1 cm on linear measurements.
Accept ± 1° on angle measurements.

Name _____ Date _____ Class _____ 69

6. Circles, Sectors, and Angles

A circle can be built from *sectors*. The following circles are cut into sectors.

Figure A

Semicircles and quarter-circles are just two examples of sectors.

A sector is built from a curve called an *arc* and two straight sides that meet at the *vertex*.

The straight sides of a sector are radii of the circle. Notice that the vertex of the sector is also the center of the circle.

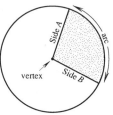

Figure B

1. Look at the shaded part in Figure C. Explain why the shaded part is not a sector.

Figure C

The shaded part is not a sector because its vertex is not at the center of the circle. or The sides are not the same length.

© *David A. Page*   *Maneuvers with Circles*

Imagine the circle is a clock. The amount of turning from start to finish shows the *central angle*.

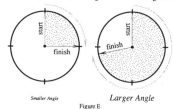

Figure D

The more you turn the clock hand, the larger the central angle becomes.

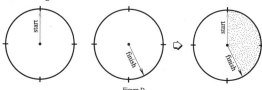

Smaller Angle   *Larger Angle*

Figure E

The following figure shows examples of sectors.

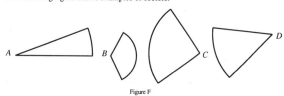

Figure F

2. Compare the amount of turning in each sector above. List the central angles from smallest to largest. Write "*A*," "*B*," "*C*," or "*D*" on the lines.

   A   **D**   **C**   **B**

   Smallest   *Largest*

Maneuvers with Circles   © *David A. Page*

Circles, Sectors, and Angles   71

3. Is the following central angle small or large? Remember, think of the amount of turning.

E •———————————————————————

Figure G

Answer   **Small**

     Small or Large

We measure central angles in a special unit called *degrees*. The sector above has a small central angle that measures one degree. This can be written as 1°.

Figure H shows three examples of central angles and their measurements.

A 30° angle is built from thirty 1° angles.   A 60° angle is built from sixty 1° angles.   A 110° angle is built from one hundred ten 1° angles.

Figure H

Larger angles have larger degree measures.

You don't always know the degree measure of a central angle. But there are some angles you can easily recognize. A 90° angle is called a *right angle*. Look at the following examples of right angles. Sometimes a "box" is drawn at the vertex to show a 90° angle.

The corner of a sheet of paper is 90°.   A quarter-circle has a central angle of 90° and is built from ninety 1° sectors.

Figure J

© *David A. Page*   *Maneuvers with Circles*

When two **congruent** sectors with a central angle of 90° (two quarter-circles) are put together, a semicircle is formed.

90°   90°   90° 90°   180°

Figure K

A semicircle has a central angle of 180°.

When four congruent sectors with central angles of 90° or two sectors with a central angle of 180° are put together, a whole circle is formed.

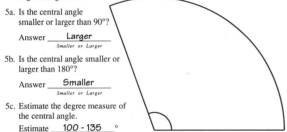

90° 90°   180°
90° 90°   180°

Figure L

4. How many 1° sectors are in a circle? ___360___

5. Use the following steps to estimate the degree measure of the central angle in Figure M.

5a. Is the central angle smaller or larger than 90°?

Answer ___Larger___
Smaller or Larger

5b. Is the central angle smaller or larger than 180°?

Answer ___Smaller___
Smaller or Larger

5c. Estimate the degree measure of the central angle.

Estimate ___100 - 135___ °

Figure M

You can find the degree measure of a sector's angle using a **protractor**.

Chelsea uses Steps **a** through **d** to measure the following central angle.

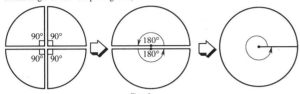

stop here

start here

Figure N

a. Chelsea knows the angle measurement is between 90° and 180°.

b. Chelsea places the center of the protractor over the vertex of the sector.

c. She lines up one side of the sector with the 0° mark. She begins at 0° and reads the degree marks until she reaches the other side.

d. The side of the sector goes through both the 60° and 120° mark on the protractor. Since the central angle is between 90° and 180°, Chelsea knows that the central angle measures 120°.

6. Use Chelsea's method to measure the central angle in Problem 5.

Measurement ___109, 110, 111___ °
Compare with your estimate
in Problem 5c.

---

7. A protractor is placed on the sector in Figure P. Notice there is a 0° mark on both the left and right side of the protractor, but only the left side lines up with the sector's side. Use the following steps to find the measurement of the central angle.

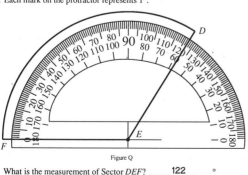

A
B
C

Figure P

7a. Is the central angle smaller than or larger than 90°? ___Smaller___
Smaller or Larger

7b. What is the measurement of the central angle? ___80___ °

8. Each mark on the protractor represents 1°.

D
E
F

Figure Q

What is the measurement of Sector *DEF*? ___122___ °

9. Sylvia's answer for Problem 8 was 118°. What did Sylvia do wrong?

She didn't read the protractor from the left. The numbers are going up from left to right.

The following figure shows Melanie's paper. She plans to measure the central angle. First she decides the central angle is smaller than 90°.

NAME: *Melanie*

Figure R

To make it easier to measure, she turns the sheet of paper as shown at the right. Melanie places the center of the protractor on the vertex and notices the sides are too short to reach the degree marks on the protractor.

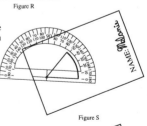

Figure S

Melanie decides to make the sides longer. This is called "**extending the sides**." Once Melanie extends the sides, she can then measure the central angle. Extending the sides does not change the measurement of the central angle.

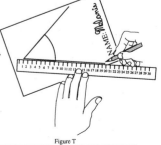

Figure T

10. Use Melanie's method to extend the sides in Figure U.
Measure the sector's angle.

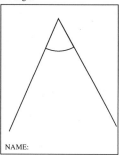

NAME:

Figure U

Measurement __53, 54, 55__ °

11a. Is the sector in Figure V more or less than 90°?

Answer __Less__

More or Less

11b. Estimate the measurement of the sector in Figure V.

Estimate __50 - 70__ °

Figure V

11c. Now extend the sides and measure the angle.

Measurement __56, 57, 58__ °

Compare with your estimate.

12a. Is the angle in Figure W more or less than 90°?

Answer __More__

More or Less

12b. Estimate the measurement.

Estimate __140 - 170__ °

Figure W

12c. Measure the central angle in Figure W.

Measurement __164, 165, 166__ °

Area of Sectors

The sector or quarter-circle at the right
has a central angle of 90° and a radius of 3 cm.

Find the area of the 90° sector using
the following steps.

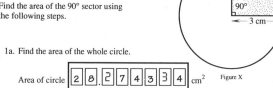

90°

← 3 cm →

Figure X

1a. Find the area of the whole circle.

Area of circle | 2 | 8 | . | 2 | 7 | 4 | 3 | 3 | 4 | cm²

Keep this number in your window.

1b. How many 90° sectors are in a circle? _____4_____

1c. Divide the area of the circle by the number of 90° sectors in the circle to
find the area of one sector.

Area of 90° sector | 7 | 0 | . | 0 | 6 | 8 | 5 | 8 | 3 | 5 | cm²

Keep this number in your window.

2. A 270° sector is built from three 90° sectors. Calculate the area of the
following 270° sector.

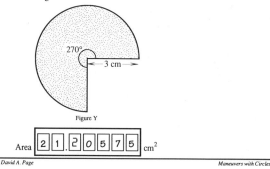

270°

← 3 cm →

Figure Y

Area | 2 | 1 | . | 2 | 0 | 5 | 7 | 5 | cm²

---

3. Use the following steps to find the number
of 60° sectors in the circle below.

3a. Cut out the 60° sector in Figure BB.

3b. Place the vertex of the sector on the
center of the circle in Figure CC.
Trace the sector as shown at the right.

60°

Figure Z

3c. Trace another sector next to the first
sector as shown in Figure AA.

3d. Continue drawing 60° sectors until no more fit.

3e. How many 60° sectors fit in the circle?

Answer _____6_____

60° 60°

Figure AA

Save your sector.

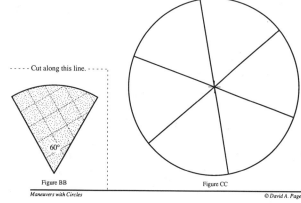

- - - - - Cut along this line. - - - - -

60°

Figure BB   Figure CC

---

4. Glue your 60° sector
in the space at the right.

60°

5. Count the square centimeters in the 60° sector above to estimate the area.
Circle the best estimate.

1 cm²   5 cm²   (10 cm²)   60 cm²

6. Calculate the area of the 60° sector using the following steps.

6a. The radius of the circle in Figure CC is 5 cm. Calculate the circle's area.

Area of circle | 7 | 8 | . | 5 | 4 | cm²

R to the nearest hundredth.

6b. How many 60° sectors fit in the circle? _____6_____

6c. Divide the area of the circle by the number of 60° sectors in the circle to
find the area of one 60° sector.

Area of 60° sector | 1 | 3 | . | 1 | cm²

R to the nearest tenth.

7a. Terry started to trace 45° sectors in the circle below. Draw in the other radii to show the number of 45° sectors in a circle.

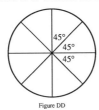

Figure DD

7b. How many 45° sectors build a circle? _____**8**_____

8a. Joline did the same thing as Terry but with 30° sectors. Finish drawing in radii below to show the number of 30° sectors in a circle.

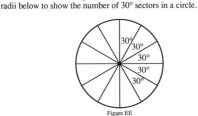

Figure EE

8b. How many 30° sectors build a circle? _____**12**_____

9. Julie started to draw 12° sectors in the circle at the right. Instead, she used a faster way to find the number of 12° sectors in a circle. Julie knew a circle has 360°, so she divided it into 12° parts.

9a. 360° ÷ 12° = _____**30**_____

9b. There are _____**30**_____ 12° sectors in a circle.

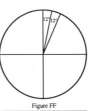

Figure FF

---

10. The circle in the sketch at the right has a radius of 8 cm. Calculate the area of the circle.

Area _____**201.06**_____ cm²
R to the nearest hundredth.

Figure GG

11. Complete the table to find the area of each sector with an 8 cm radius.

Degrees in Whole Circle	Central Angle	Number of Sectors in Circle	Area of Sector with Radius of 8 cm *R to the nearest hundredth.*
a.	360°	60°	6	201.06 cm² ÷ 6 = 33.51 cm² *Area of Whole Number of Sectors Area of One*
b.	360°	45°	8	201.06 cm² ÷ **8** = **25.13** cm²
c.	**360°**	30°	12	201.06 cm² ÷ 12 = 16.76 cm²
d.	**360°**	15°	24	201.06 cm² ÷ 24 = 8.38 cm²
e.	**360°**	12°	30	201.06 cm² ÷ 30 = 6.70 cm²
f.	**360°**	11°	32.727273 *Copy window.*	201.06 cm² ÷ 32.727273 = 6.14 cm²
g.	**360°**	10°	36	201.06 cm² ÷ 36 = 5.59 cm²

12. The radius of each sector in the table is 8 cm. When the radius is the same, what happens to the area of the sector as the central angle gets smaller?

  The area of the sector gets smaller.

---

13. The 120° sector at the right has a radius of 3 cm.

13a. How many 120° sectors are there in a circle?

  Answer _____**3**_____

13b. Calculate the area of the sector. Remember, find the area of a full circle with a radius of 3 cm first. Show your work.

  $3\ x^2 \times \pi \div 3 =$

  Area of 120° sector _____**9.4**_____ cm²
        R to the nearest tenth.

Figure HH

14. The following 1° sector has a radius of 11 cm. Calculate its area using the steps below.

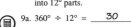

Figure JJ

14a. Calculate the area of a circle with a radius of 11 cm.

  Area | 3 | 8 | 0 | . | 1 | 3 | 2 | 7 | 1 | cm²

14b. How many 1° sectors build a circle? _____**360**_____

14c. Calculate the area of the 1° sector. | 1 | . | 0 | 6 | cm²
         R to the nearest hundredth.

15. Five of the 1° sectors from Problem 14 are put together to make the following 5° sector. Calculate the area of the 5° sector.

Figure KK

  Area of 5° sector _____**5.3**_____ cm²
         R to the nearest tenth.

---

16. Estimate the area of the 50° sector at the right.

  Estimate _____**5 - 7**_____ cm²

17a. Use the following keystrokes to find the area of a 1° sector with a 3.5 cm radius.

  Press: | 3.5 | | x^2 | | × | | π | | ÷ | | 360 | | = |
      Area of circle

  Answer _____**0.1069014**_____ cm²
      Copy window.

Figure LL

17b. Now multiply your answer by 50 to find the area of the 50° sector.

  Area of 50° sector _____**5.3**_____ cm²
       R to the nearest tenth.
       Compare with Problem 16.

18. The radius of the sector at the right is 4 cm. Calculate the area of the 100° sector using the following steps.

18a. Calculate the area of a circle with a radius of 4 cm.

  Area of circle | 5 | 0 | . | 2 | 6 | 5 | 4 | 8 | 2 | cm²

Figure MM

18b. Divide by 360 to find the area of a 1° sector with a radius of 4 cm.

  Area of 1° sector | 0 | . | 1 | 3 | 9 | 6 | 2 | 6 | 3 | cm²

18c. Multiply by 100 to find the area of the 100° sector.

  Area of 100° sector | 1 | 3 | . | 9 | 6 | 2 | 6 | 3 | 4 | cm²

18d. List the keystrokes you used to find the area of the 100° sector.

  | 4 | | x^2 | | × | | π | | ÷ | | 360 | | × | | 100 | | = | | | | |
    You do not need to use all the keystroke boxes.

19. Calculate the area of the sector at the right using the following steps.

19a. Measure the angle of the sector to the nearest degree. Label the angle measure on the sector.

Angle _**64, 65, 66**_ °

19b. Measure the radius to the nearest 0.1 cm. Label the length of the radius on the sector.

Radius _**6.4, 6.5, 6.6**_ cm

19c. Calculate the area of the circle.

Area of circle _**128.67964 - 136.84778**_ cm²
Copy window.

19d. Calculate the area of the sector.

Area of sector _**22.9 - 25.1**_ cm²
R to the nearest tenth.

65°

6.5 cm

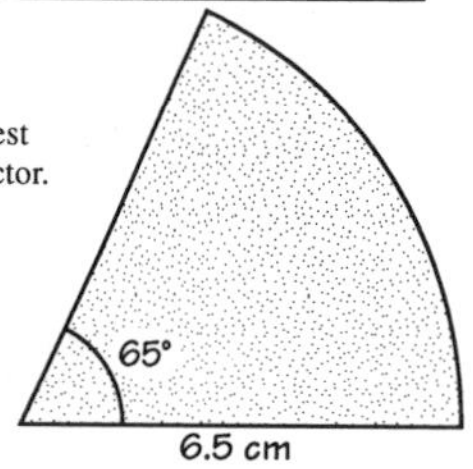

Figure NN

20. Measure the central angle and radius of the sector in Figure PP.

20a. Angle _**126, 127, 128**_ °

20b. Radius _**3.4, 3.5, 3.6**_ cm

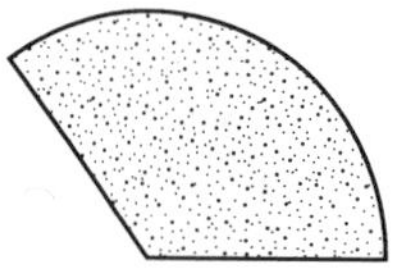

Figure PP

21. Calculate the area of the sector in Figure PP.

Area _**12.7 - 14.5**_ cm²
R to the nearest tenth.

22. Each of the sectors in the figure at the right has a central angle of 60°. Measure the radius of each sector to the nearest half cm. Write your measurements on the figure.

23. Calculate the area of Figure QQ using the calculator's memory.

Area of Figure QQ [2][6][.][0][5] cm²
R to the nearest hundredth.

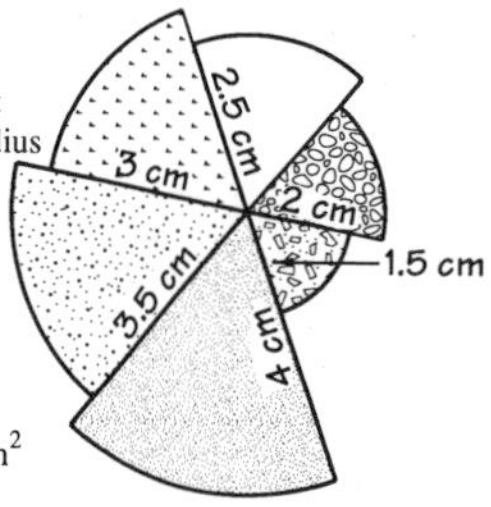

2.5 cm
3 cm
2 cm
3.5 cm
4 cm
1.5 cm

Figure QQ

Homework 6: Circles, Sectors, and Angles

1. Write "could be" or "crazy" after each statement.

∠A is a right angle. _**Crazy**_

∠A is 175°. _**Crazy**_

∠A is smaller than ∠B. _**Crazy**_

∠B is smaller than 180°. _**Could be**_

∠B is larger than 90°. _**Crazy**_

∠B is 10°. _**Could be**_

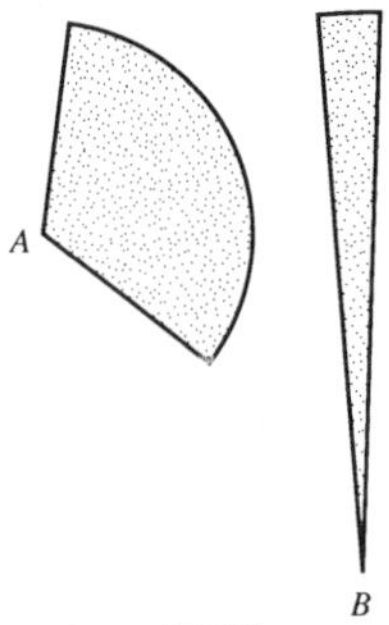

A

B

Figure RR

2a. Look at the angles in the figure below. Write an "S" on the sector with the smallest central angle. Write an "L" on the sector with the largest central angle.

2b. Measure each central angle. Don't forget to extend the sides. Write the measurement next to each angle.

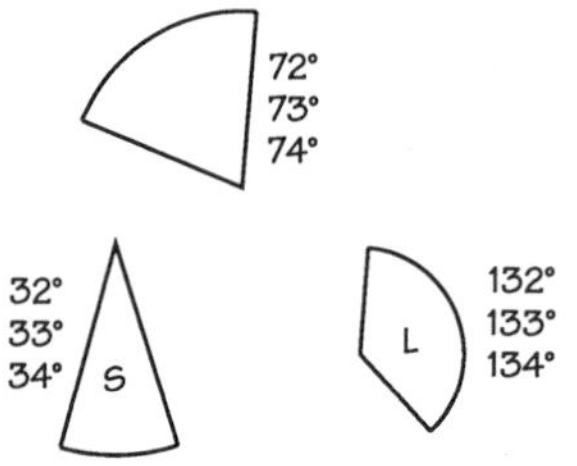

72°
73°
74°

32°
33°
34° S

132°
133°
134° L

Figure SS

---

3. Find the number of degrees in the sector with the ▨ shading at the right. Show your work.

137° + 84° = 221°
360° − 221° = 139°
Answer _**139**_ °

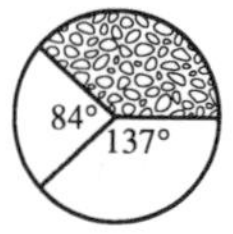

84°
137°

Figure TT

4. The circle at the right is cut into five sectors. The sectors with the ▨ shading are the same size. Find the number of degrees in one ▨ sector using the following steps.

4a. Find the total number of degrees in the sectors that are not shaded with ▨.

Answer _**120**_ °

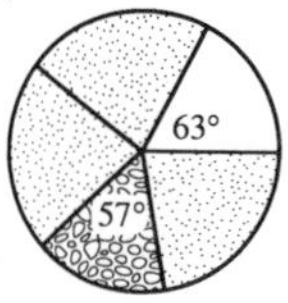

4b. Find the total number of degrees in the three ▨ sectors.

Answer _**240**_ °

4c. Find the number of degrees in one ▨ sector.

Answer _**80**_ °

63°
57°

Figure UU

5. Find the number of 72° sectors that fit in a circle. Show your work.

360 ÷ 72° = 5

Answer _**5**_

72°
3.2 cm

6. Calculate the area of the 72° sector in Figure VV. Show your work.

3.2 x² × π ÷ 5 = or
3.2 x² × π ÷ 360 × 72 =

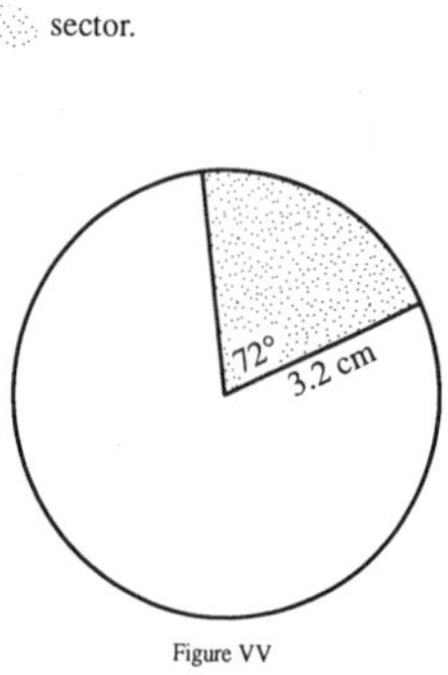

Area of 72° sector _**6.4**_ cm²
R to the nearest tenth.

Figure VV

---

7. Calculate the area of the 18° sector in Figure WW. Show your work.

3.9 x² × π ÷ 360 × 18 = or
3.9 x² × π ÷ 20 =

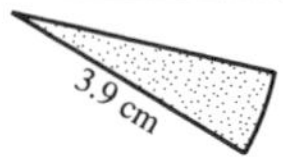

Area of sector _**2.4**_ cm²
R to the nearest tenth.

3.9 cm
Figure WW

8. A sector has a central angle of 32° and a radius of 4.4 cm. Calculate the area of this 32° sector.

Area of sector _**5.4**_ cm²
R to the nearest tenth.

9a. Calculate the area of the 300° sector in the sketch at the right.

Area of sector [8][4][8][.][2] cm²
R to the nearest tenth.

9b. List the keystrokes you used to calculate the area of the sector.

[18] [x²] [×] [π] [÷] [360]
[×] [300] [=] [ ] [ ] [ ]
You do not need to use all the keystroke boxes.

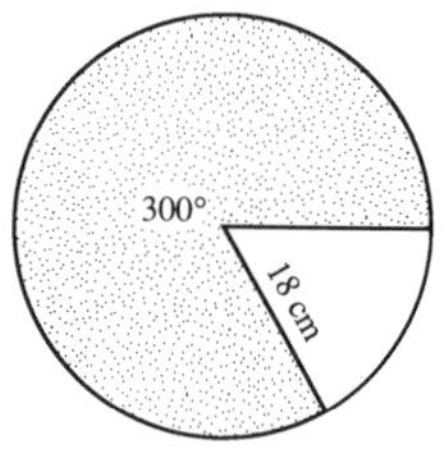

300°
18 cm

Figure XX

10. Twelve of the sectors at the right fit in a circle.

10a. Without measuring, what is the degree measure of the sector?
Answer _**30**_ °

10b. Calculate the area of the sector. Show your work.

4.8 x² × π ÷ 12 =

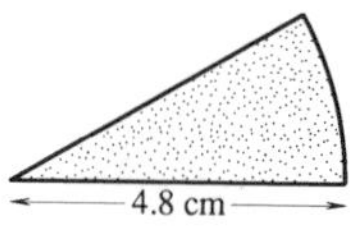

Area of sector _**6.0**_ cm²
R to the nearest tenth.

4.8 cm
Figure YY

---

11. Find the area of the following sector using the steps below.

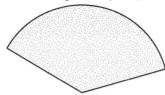

Figure ZZ

11a. Measure the radius of the circle to the nearest 0.1 cm.

Radius __4.9, 5.0, 5.1__ cm

11b. Measure the central angle of the sector to the nearest degree.

Answer __133, 134, 135__ °

11c. Calculate the area of the sector.
Show your work. __4.9 x² × π ÷ 360 × 133 =__

Area of sector __27.9 - 30.6__ cm²
R to the nearest tenth.

12a. Without measuring, which sector at the right
has the larger central angle, A or B?

Answer __B__
A or B

12b. Predict which sector has the larger area.

Answer __A or B__
A or B

A

44°, 45°, 46°
5.9 cm, 6.0 cm, 6.1 cm

13. Make the necessary measurements and find
the area of Sector A and Sector B.

13a. Area of Sector A __13.36608 - 14.937051__ cm²
Copy window.

13b. Area of Sector B __10.935273 - 12.663324__ cm²
Copy window.

13c. Were your answers to 12a and 12b correct?

Answer __Yes or No__
Yes or No

B

149°, 150°, 151°
2.9 cm, 3.0 cm, 3.1 cm

Figure AAA

---

7. Circles with Holes

1. Draw a circle with a radius of 2 cm anywhere inside the circle below.

2a. Cut out the large circle at the bottom of the page.

2b. Fold it in half to find a diameter of the circle. Measure the diameter to the
nearest whole cm.

Diameter __8__ cm

2c. How long is the radius? __4__ cm

2d. Calculate the area of the large circle.

Area of large circle __50.3__ cm²
R to the nearest tenth.

3. Calculate the area of the smaller circle.

Area of smaller circle __12.6__ cm²
R to the nearest tenth.

4. Cut out the smaller circle. You will have a circle with a hole in it.

- - - - - - - - - - - - - - - Cut below this line. - - - - - - - - - - - - - - -

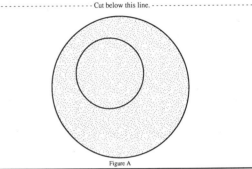

Figure A

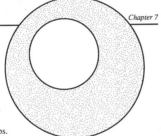

5. Glue or tape the circle with
the hole at the right. This is
the part left over.

6. Find the area of the part left
over using the following steps.

Area of large circle − Area of small circle = Area of circle with hole

__50.3 cm²__ − __12.6 cm²__ = __37.7__ cm²
Copy answer from   *Copy answer from*
Problem 2d.   *Problem 3.*

7. Did everyone draw the small circle in the same place? __No__
Yes or No

8a. When the small circle is in a different place, is the area left over the same?

Answer __Yes__
Yes or No

8b. Why or why not? __The areas of both circles stay the same. It does
not matter where the small circle is placed.__

---

9. Use the centimeter grid to estimate the area
of the shaded part in Figure B.

Estimate __23 - 28__ cm²

10. Calculate the area of the shaded part in
Figure B using the following steps.

10a. How long is the radius of the larger circle?

Radius of larger circle __3 cm__
Put in units.

10b. Calculate the area of the larger circle.

Area of larger circle __28.27__ cm²
R to the nearest hundredth.

Figure B

10c. How long is the radius of the white circle? __1__ cm

10d. What is the area of the white circle? __3.14__ cm²
R to the nearest hundredth.

10e. Subtract to find the area of the shaded part.

Area of shaded part __25.1__ cm²
R to the nearest tenth.
Compare with your estimate
in Problem 9.

11a. Draw a radius for the white circle
in Figure C. Measure and label the radius
to the nearest 0.1 cm. __0.9, 1, or 1.1 cm__

11b. Calculate the area of the white circle.

Area of white circle __3.1415927__ cm²
2.54469 or 3.8013271   *Copy window.*

11c. Calculate the area of the larger circle.

Area of larger circle __19.634954__ cm²
Copy window.

1 cm   2.5 cm

Figure C

11d. Calculate the area of the shaded part.

Area of shaded part __16.5__ cm²   or 17.1 or 15.8
R to the nearest tenth.

12. The radius of the white circle in the sketch at the right is 2.3 cm. The radius of the large circle is 9.45 cm. Calculate the area of the shaded part. List your keystrokes. Draw in your own keystroke boxes. Hint: Use the calculator's memory.

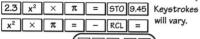

| 2.3 | x^2 | × | π | = | STO | 9.45 | Keystrokes |

| x^2 | × | π | = | – | RCL | = | will vary. |

Area of shaded part | 2 | 6 | 3 | . | 9 | 3 | cm^2
R to the nearest hundredth.

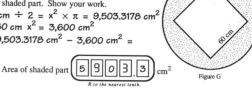
Figure D

13a. The *diameter* of the white circle in Figure E is 48.585623 cm. The diameter of the large circle is 100 cm. Draw and label the diameters. Calculate the area of the shaded part.

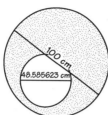

Area of shaded part ___6,000___ cm^2
You'll know.

13b. Is Figure E a sketch? ___Yes___
Yes or No

Figure E

14. The radius of the circle at the right is 3.2 cm. Draw and label the radius of the circle. The side length of the square hole is 3 cm. Label the side length of the square. Find the area of the shaded part using the following steps.

14a. Calculate the area of the circle.

Area of circle | 3 | 2 | . | 1 | 7 | cm^2
R to the nearest hundredth.

14b. Calculate the area of the square.

Area of square ___9 cm^2___
Put in units.

14c. Calculate the area of the shaded part.

Area of shaded part ___23.2___ cm^2
R to the nearest tenth.

Figure F

---

15. The sketch at the right shows a circle with a square hole. The diameter of the circle is 110 cm. Calculate the area of the shaded part. Show your work.

110 cm ÷ 2 = x^2 × π = 9,503.3178 cm^2
60 cm x^2 = 3,600 cm^2
9,503.3178 cm^2 – 3,600 cm^2 =

Area of shaded part | 5 | 9 | 0 | 3 | . | 3 | cm^2
R to the nearest tenth.

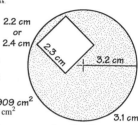
Figure G

16. The hole in Figure H is a square. Make the necessary measurements to calculate the area of the shaded part. Measure to the nearest 0.1 cm. Label your measurements on the figure and show your work.

 2.2 cm
 or
 2.4 cm

3.2 cm x^2 × π = 32.169909 cm^2
2.3 cm x^2 = 5.29 cm^2
32.169909 cm^2 – 5.29 cm^2 = 26.879909 cm^2
Area of shaded part ___26.9___ cm^2
R to the nearest tenth.

Answers can range between 24.4 cm^2 and 29.4 cm^2.

3.1 cm
or
3.3 cm
Figure H

17. There are two square holes in the figure at the right. Calculate the area of the shaded part. Show your work.

4 cm x^2 × π = 50.265482 cm^2
1.4 cm x^2 × 2 = 3.92 cm^2
50.265482 cm^2 – 3.92 cm^2 =
46.345482 cm^2

Area of shaded part | 4 | 6 | . | 3 | cm^2
R to the nearest tenth.

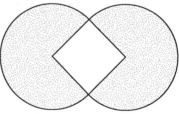
Figure J

---

18. The area of the square in the sketch at the right is 600 cm^2. Calculate the area of the shaded part using the steps below.

24.494897 cm
12.247449 cm

Figure K

18a. Use $\sqrt{x}$ to calculate the side length of the square. Label its length on the figure.

Side length | 2 | 4 | . | 4 | 9 | 4 | 8 | 9 | 7 | cm

18b. Calculate the length of the radius. Label it on the figure.

Radius | 1 | 2 | . | 2 | 4 | 7 | 4 | 4 | 9 | cm

18c. What is the area of the circle? ___471.2389___ cm^2 or 471.23892
Copy window.

18d. Describe in words what you subtract to find the area of the shaded part.

___Area of the square___ – ___Area of the circle___ = Shaded Area

18e. Calculate the area of the shaded part above.

Area ___128.8___ cm^2
R to the nearest tenth.

19. The area of the square in the following sketch is 573.15446 cm^2. Calculate the area of the shaded part. Show your work. Use your calculator's memory so you only have to key in the messy number once.

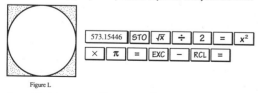

| 573.15446 | STO | $\sqrt{x}$ | ÷ | 2 | = | x^2 |

| × | π | = | EXC | – | RCL | = |

Figure L

Area of shaded part ___123___ cm^2
You'll know.

---

20. The area of the square at the right is 10 cm^2. The area of the shading is 20 cm^2. Label the figure. What is the area of the circle?

Area of circle ___30 cm^2___
Put in units.

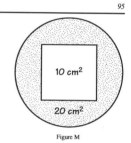
Figure M

★ 21. The area of the square in the following figure is 9 cm^2. Calculate the area of the shading. Two of the corners of the square are at the centers of the circles. Show your work.

Figure N

| 9 | $\sqrt{x}$ | x^2 | × | π | = | ÷ | 4 | × | 3 | × | 2 | = |
or
| 9 | $\sqrt{x}$ | x^2 | × | π | = | ÷ | 4 | × | 6 | = |
or
| 9 | × | π | = | ÷ | 4 | × | 6 | = |

Area of shading | 4 | 2 | . | 4 | 1 | 1 | 5 | 0 | 1 | cm^2

Right Triangles

1. A triangle with a right angle is called a ***right triangle***. The following figure shows examples of right triangles. The "box" drawn in the right angle shows that the triangle is a right triangle.

Figure P

1a. The longest side of a right triangle is called the ***hypotenuse***. Write "hypotenuse" along the longest side of each right triangle above.

1b. Notice the hypotenuse is always across from the right angle. We usually say ***opposite to*** the right angle. The other two sides of a right triangle are called the ***legs***. Write "leg" along the legs of each right triangle above.

2a. Draw a box for the right angle in the following triangle.

Figure Q

2b. How did you find the right angle? __It was across from the longest side (hypotenuse). or I used a corner of a piece of paper.__

2c. Write "hypotenuse" and "leg" in the correct places in Figure Q.

A rectangle can be cut into two ***congruent*** (same size and shape) right triangles.

Figure R

Two congruent right triangles build a rectangle.

Figure S

To calculate the area of a right triangle, build a rectangle from the two legs as shown in the figure at the right.

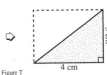

Figure T

3a. What is the area of the rectangle in Figure T? ____12____ cm²

3b. The rectangle is built from two triangles.
Find the area of one of the triangles. ____6____ cm²

4. Draw the rectangle made from the legs of each triangle below. Find the area of each triangle.

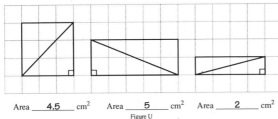

Area ___4.5___ cm²   Area ___5___ cm²   Area ___2___ cm²

Figure U

5. Cut out the circle at the bottom of the page.

- - - - - - - - - - - - - - - - - Cut along this line. - - - - - - - - - - - - - - - - -

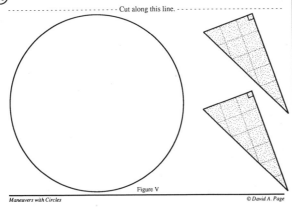

Figure V

---

6. Make the necessary measurements to calculate the area of the circle.

Area of circle ____78.5____ cm²   R to the nearest tenth.   **Answers may range between 77.0 and 80.1 cm².**

7. Cut out the right triangles. Compare the triangles with each other. What do you notice? __They are congruent.__

8. Place the triangles in the rectangle at the right. The triangles make a rectangle 6 cm by 3 cm. Find the area of the rectangle.
Area of rectangle ____18____ cm²

Figure W

9. The area of the rectangle is equal to the area of 2 triangles.
What is the area of one of the triangles? ____9____ cm²

10. Trace one of the triangles inside the circle. Then cut out the triangle.

11. Glue the circle with the triangular hole here.

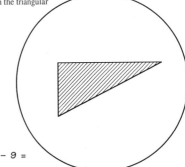

$$10 \div 2 = x^2 \times \pi - 9 =$$

12. Calculate the area of the part left over. Show your work.

Area ____69.5____ cm²   R to the nearest tenth.   **Answers may range between 68.0 cm² and 71.1 cm².**

13. The diameter of the circle in the sketch at the right is 8 cm.

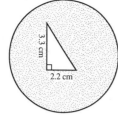

Figure X

3.3 cm
2.2 cm

13a. Calculate the area of the circle.

Area __50.265482__ cm²
Copy window.

13b. Calculate the area of the triangle.

Area of triangle __3.63__ cm²

13c. Calculate the area of the shaded part.

Area of shaded part | 4 | 6 | . | 6 | 3 | 5 | 4 | 8 | 2 | cm²

14a. Draw a right triangle with legs of 6 cm and 2 cm inside the circle at the right.

14b. Find the area of your triangle and write your answer inside the triangle.

14c. Shade the area outside the triangle.

14d. The shaded area is 38 cm². What is the area of the circle?

Area of circle __44 cm²__
Put in units.

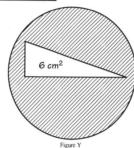

6 cm²

Figure Y

15. Calculate the area of the white part in the sketch at the right. The diameter of the circle is 9.2 cm. Show your work.

6.5904402 cm × 5 ÷ 2 = 16.476101 cm²
9.2 cm ÷ 2 = x² × π = 66.476101 cm²
66.476101 cm² − 16.476101 cm² =
Area of white part __50__ cm²
You'll know.

6.5904402 cm
5 cm

Figure Z

---

16. Estimate the area of the shaded part in Figure AA at the right.

Estimate __22 – 28 cm²__
Put in units.

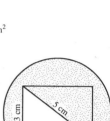

Figure AA

17a. The diameter of the circle at the right is 5.81 cm. Calculate the area of the circle.

Area of circle | 2 | 6 | . | 5 | 1 | cm²
R to the nearest hundredth.

17b. One leg of the triangle is 2.37 cm. The other leg is 1.75 cm. Calculate the area of the right triangle.

Area of triangle __2.07__ cm²
R to the nearest hundredth.

17c. Calculate the area of the shaded part.

Area of shaded part __24.4__ cm²
R to the nearest tenth.
Compare with your estimate.

18. Find the area of the circle in Figure BB using the following steps.

18a. Build a rectangle from the two legs.

18b. Which numbers should you use to find the area of the triangle?

Answers __3__ and __4__

18c. What is the area of the triangle?

Area __6 cm²__
Put in units.

18d. The area of the shaded part is 24 cm². What is the area of the circle?

Area __30 cm²__
Put in units.

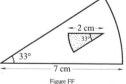

3 cm
5 cm
4 cm

Figure BB

---

19. The diameter of the following circle is 5.5 cm. Calculate the area of the shaded part using the steps below.

2 cm

Figure CC

19a. Area of circle __23.758294__ cm²
Copy window.

19b. Area of quarter-circle | 3 | . | 1 | 4 | 1 | 5 | 9 | 2 | 7 | cm²

19c. Area of shaded part __20.6__ cm²
R to the nearest tenth.

20. The hole in the following sector is a square with a side length of 1 cm. Calculate the area of the shaded part. Show your work.

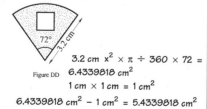

72°
3.2 cm

Figure DD

3.2 cm x² × π ÷ 360 × 72 =
6.4339818 cm²
1 cm × 1 cm = 1 cm²
6.4339818 cm² − 1 cm² = 5.4339818 cm²

Area of shaded part | 5 | . | 4 | 3 | 3 | 9 | 8 | 1 | 8 | cm²

---

21. Calculate the area of the shaded part in the figure at the right. List your keystrokes using the calculator's memory.

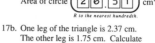

1.7 cm
60°
5 cm

Figure EE

21a. Area of white circle __2.2698007__ cm²
Copy window.

21b. Area of 60° sector __13.089969__ cm²
Copy window.

21c. Area of shaded part __10.820169__ cm²
Copy window. or 10.820168

| 1.7 | ÷ | 2 | = | x² | × | π | = | STO | 5 | x² |
| × | π | ÷ | 360 | × | 60 | = | − | RCL | = |

22. Calculate the area of the white part in the figure at the right. Show your work.

7 cm x² × π ÷ 360 × 33 −
2 cm x² × π ÷ 360 × 33 =

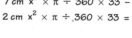

2 cm
33°
33°
7 cm

Figure FF

Area of white part | 1 | 2 | . | 9 | 6 | cm²
R to the nearest hundredth.

23. The diameter of the circle at the right is 7 cm. Calculate the shaded area. Show your work.

360° − 60° = 300°
7 ÷ 2 = x² × π = ÷ 360 × 300 =

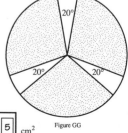

20°
20°
20°

Figure GG

Shaded area | 3 | 2 | . | 0 | 7 | 0 | 4 | 2 | 5 | cm²

Homework 7: Circles with Holes

The following figures can be thought of as circles with holes in them.

button   record   ring   paper towel roll

Figure HH

1. List three other objects that are circles with holes in them.

   ___life saver___   ___tire___   ___donut___

 2. Calculate the area of the shaded region in the following sketch.

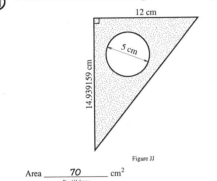

12 cm

5 cm

14.939159 cm

Figure JJ

Area ____70____ cm²
You'll know.

---

 3. All the circles in the following figure have a diameter of 2.5 cm.
Calculate the area of the shaded part. Use the calculator's memory.

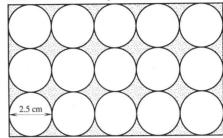

2.5 cm

Figure KK

Area of shaded part $\boxed{2\ 0\ .\ 1\ 1\ 8\ 9\ 2\ 2}$ cm²

✱ 4. There are two different-sized circles in the rectangle below.
Calculate the area of the shaded part. Use the calculator's memory.

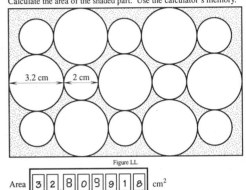

3.2 cm   2 cm

Figure LL

Area $\boxed{3\ 2\ .\ 8\ 0\ 9\ 9\ 1\ 8}$ cm²

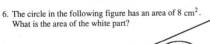 5a. The diameter of the white circle
in the sketch at the right is 25.7 cm.
What is the area of the white circle?
Area __518.74763__ cm²
Copy window.

5b. The area of the large circle is twice
the area of the white circle.
What is the area of the large circle?
Area __1,037.4953__ cm²
Copy window.

Figure MM

5c. Calculate the area of the shaded part.
Area of shaded part ____518.7____ cm²
R to the nearest tenth.

6. The circle in the following figure has an area of 8 cm².
What is the area of the white part?

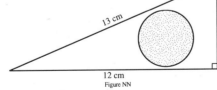

13 cm   5 cm

12 cm
Figure NN

Area ___22 cm²___
Put in units.

7a. The figure at the right is on a centimeter grid.
The curves are quarter-circles. Estimate the
area of the shading.
Estimate ____6 - 8____ cm²

7b. Calculate the area of the shading.
Show your work.

$4\ cm^2 + 1\ x^2 \times \pi =$

Figure PP

Area $\boxed{7\ .\ 1\ 4\ 1\ 5\ 9\ 2\ 7}$ cm²

---

8. The area of the shading in the figure at the right
is 35 cm². The area of the circle is 80 cm².
Use the following steps to calculate the
side length of the square.

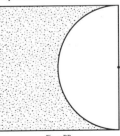

8a. What is the area of the square?
Area of square ____45____ cm²

8b. Calculate the side length of the square.

Figure QQ

Side length of square $\boxed{6\ .\ 7\ 0\ 8\ 2\ 0\ 3\ 9}$ cm
Put in units.

9. The area of the following square is 49.39804 cm². The semicircle built
along its side is cut out of the square. Calculate the area of the shaded
region using the steps below.

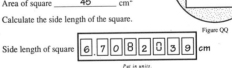

Figure RR

9a. Length of square ___7.0283739___ cm

9b. Radius of semicircle ___3.514187___ cm

9c. Area of semicircle ___19.398565___ cm²

9d. Area of shaded part ____30____ cm²
R to the nearest whole number.

10. The big circle below has a diameter of 15 cm. Calculate the area of the shaded part.

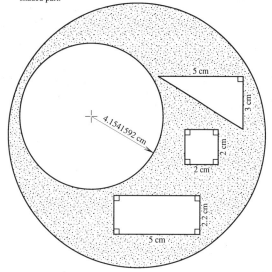

4.1541592 cm

5 cm

3 cm

2 cm
2 cm

2.2 cm

5 cm

Figure SS

Area of shaded part _____100_____ cm²
You'll know.

11. The diameter of the semicircle at the right is 6 cm. Calculate the area of the shading.

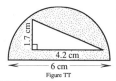

1.7 cm

4.2 cm

6 cm

Figure TT

Area of shading | 1 | 0 | . | 5 | 6 | 7 | 1 | 6 | 7 | cm²

---

8. Perimeter of Pieces

1. The circle at the right has a radius of 3 cm. Use the following steps to calculate the circumference of the circle.

1a. What is the diameter of the circle?

   Diameter _____6_____ cm

1b. Calculate the circumference of the circle in Figure A.

   Circumference | 1 | 8 | . | 8 | cm
   R to the nearest tenth.

Figure A

1c. List your keystrokes.

   | 3 | × | 2 | × | π | = | |
   You do not need to use all the keystroke boxes.

2. The semicircle in Figure B also has a radius of 3 cm. Measure the perimeter of the semicircle to the nearest 0.1 cm. Remember, the perimeter is the distance all the way around a shape.

   Measured perimeter ___15.1 - 15.7___ cm

Diameter

Figure B

3. Calculate the perimeter of the semicircle in Figure B using the following steps.

3a. What is the length of the curved part? | 9 | . | 4 | 2 | 4 | 7 | 7 | 8 | cm

3b. What is the length of the straight part? _____6_____ cm

3c. What is the perimeter? ___15.4___ cm
R to the nearest tenth.
Compare with Problem 2.

4a. To calculate the perimeter of Figure B, Andy used the following keystrokes. Calculate Andy's answer.

   | 3 | × | 2 | × | π | ÷ | 2 | = | **9.424778**
   Copy window.
   Compare with Problem 3c.

4b. What did Andy actually calculate? **Just ½ of the circumference. Just the curved part of the perimeter.**

5a. The semicircle in the following sketch has a diameter of 18 cm. Calculate the perimeter of the semicircle.

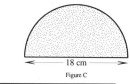

18 cm

Figure C

Perimeter | 4 | 6 | . | 2 | 7 | 4 | 3 | 3 | 4 | cm

5b. List your keystrokes for Problem 5a.   **Keystrokes may vary.**

   | 18 | × | π | ÷ | 2 | + | 18 | = | | | |
   You do not need to use all the keystroke boxes.
   18 STO × π ÷ 2 = SUM RCL

6. The figure at the right is built from a square and four semicircles with diameters of 3 cm. Calculate the perimeter of the figure. Show your work.

   3 × π × 2 =
        or
   3 × π ÷ 2 × 4 =

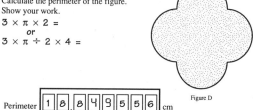

Figure D

Perimeter | 1 | 8 | . | 8 | 4 | 9 | 5 | 5 | 6 | cm

---

7. The sketch at the right is built from four semicircles and a rectangle. The rectangle is 10 cm by 2.7323954 cm.

   Calculate the perimeter (around the outside of the figure) using the following steps and the calculator's memory.

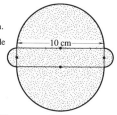

10 cm

Figure E

7a. Calculate the total length of the large curves.

   Length of large curves | 3 | 1 | . | 4 | 1 | 5 | 9 | 2 | 7 | cm [STO]

7b. Calculate the total length of the small curves.

   Length of small curves ___8.5840733___ cm [SUM]
   Copy window.

7c. Press [RCL] to find the perimeter of the entire figure.

   Answer _____40_____ cm
   You'll know.

8. Calculate the perimeter of the quarter-circle in Figure F using the following steps.

2 cm

Figure F

8a. What is the diameter of the circle?

   Diameter _____4_____ cm

8b. Calculate the length of the curved part. Remember, four quarter-circles build a circle.

   Length of curved part | 3 | . | 1 | 4 | 1 | 5 | 9 | 2 | 7 | cm

8c. What is the total length of both straight parts? _____4_____ cm

8d. What is the perimeter of the quarter-circle? ___7.1___ cm
R to the nearest tenth.

9a. A circle has a radius of 3.2 cm. Draw the circle at the right.

9b. Draw two diameters in your circle to divide it into quarter-circles.

9c. Shade one of the quarter-circles.

9d. Calculate the perimeter of your shaded quarter-circle. Remember to include the two straight parts.

Perimeter [1 1 . 4 2 6 5 4 8] cm

10a. The radius of the quarter-circle in Figure G is 3.3 cm. Will the perimeter be smaller or larger than the quarter-circle in Problem 9d?

Answer ___Larger___
_{Smaller or Larger}

← 3.3 cm →

10b. Calculate the perimeter of this quarter-circle.

Perimeter __11.783628__ cm
_{Compare with Problem 9d.}

Figure G

10c. List your keystrokes for Problem 10b.

[3.3] [×] [2] [×] [π] [÷] [4] [+]   Answers will vary.
[3.3] [+] [3.3] [=] [ ] [ ] [ ]
_{You do not need to use all the keystroke boxes.}

11. Calculate the perimeter of the shaded figure at the right. Show your work.

6 × π ÷ 4 = 4.712389
4.712389 × 4 = 18.849556
or
6 × π = 18.849556

Perimeter [1 8 . 8] cm
_{R to the nearest tenth.}

Figure H

---

12. The figure at the right is built from four quarter-circles of different sizes. Estimate the perimeter of the figure.

Estimated perimeter ___19 - 23___ cm

13. Calculate the perimeter of Figure J using the following steps and the calculator's memory. First, calculate the length of each curve. Fill in the missing memory keystrokes.

Figure J

13a. Length of Curve A [1 . 5 7 0 7 9 6 3] cm [STO]

13b. Length of Curve B [4 . 7 1 2 3 8 9] cm [SUM]

13c. Length of Curve C [6 . 2 8 3 1 8 5 3] cm [SUM]

13d. Length of Curve D [3 . 1 4 1 5 9 2 7] cm [SUM]

13e. What is the total length of all the straight pieces?

Total length ___6___ cm [SUM]

13f. Press [RCL] to find the perimeter of the figure.

Perimeter [2 1 . 7 0 7 9 6 3] cm

13g. Round your answer to the nearest tenth.

Perimeter ___21.7___ cm
_{Compare with Problem 12.}

---

14. The diameter of the circle in the sketch at the right is 9 cm. Calculate the circumference of the circle.

Circumference __28.274334__ cm
_{Copy window.}

9 cm

Figure K

15. The sketch at the right is built from a semicircle and three smaller, congruent semicircles. The smaller semicircles lie on the diameter of the large semicircle. Use the following steps to calculate the perimeter of the figure.

9 cm

Figure L

15a. Find the length of the large curve.

Length of large curve [1 4 . 1 3 7 1 6 7] cm

15b. Calculate the total length of the small curves.

Length of three small curves [1 4 . 1 3 7 1 6 7] cm

15c. Perimeter of figure __28.274334__ cm
_{Copy window.}
_{Compare with Problem 14.}

16. Three different semicircles lie on the 9 cm diameter in the sketch below. Find the perimeter of the figure using the following steps.

16a. Length of large curve __14.137167__ cm
_{Copy window.}

16b. Length of small curve __3.9269908__ cm
_{Copy window.}

16c. Length of medium curve __10.210176__ cm
_{Copy window.}

← 6.5 cm →
9 cm

Figure M

16d. Perimeter of figure [2 8 . 2 7 4 3 3 4] cm
_{Compare with Problem 15c.}

Strips

1a. Draw a diameter in the large circle at the bottom of the page.

1b. Measure the diameter to the nearest whole cm. ___10___ cm

2a. Place the point of your compass on the center of the large circle. Draw a circle with a radius of 3 cm.

2b. What is the diameter of the small circle? ___6___ cm

3. Shade the part that is outside the small circle.

4a. Cut out the large circle and remove the small circle.

What do you have left? __a donut, a ring, a circle with a hole__

4b. Fold the shaded part in half and cut along the fold.

5. Each of the pieces is a "half-strip". Glue a half-strip in the circle on the next page. A place for the half-strip is drawn in the circle.

- - - - - - - - - - - - - - - - Cut below this line. - - - - - - - - - - - - - - - -

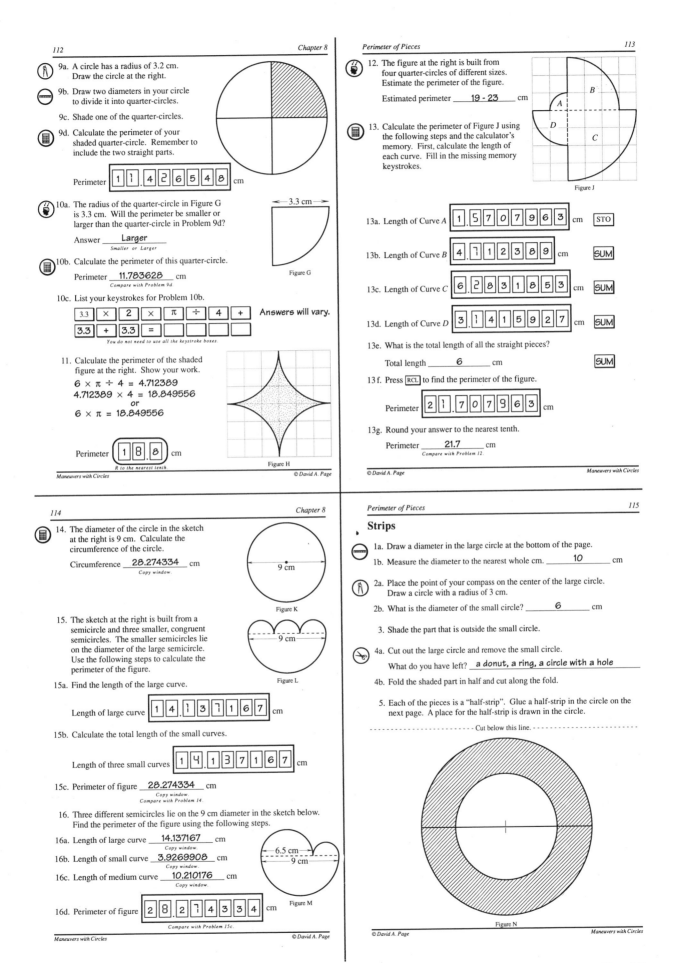

Figure N

6. Write the length of the diameter of each circle on the figure at the right.

 7. Measure the perimeter of the half-strip to the nearest 0.1 cm.

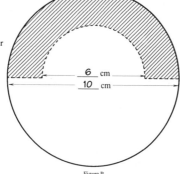

6 cm
10 cm

Figure P

Measured perimeter   __27.0 - 31.0__   cm

---

8. Calculate the perimeter of the half-strip in Figure P using the following steps.

8a. Length of both straight parts   __4__   cm

8b. Calculate the length of the large curve.

Length of large curve | 1 | 5 | . | 7 | 0 | 7 | 9 | 6 | 3 | cm

8c. Calculate the length of the small curve.

Length of small curve | 9 | . | 4 | 2 | 4 | 7 | 7 | 8 | cm

8d. Perimeter | 2 | 9 | . | 1 | 3 | 2 | 7 | 4 | 1 | cm

Compare with Problem 7.

9. Use the following steps to calculate the perimeter of the half-strip at the right.

9a. The large curve is part of a large circle. What is the diameter of the circle?

Diameter of large circle   __6__   cm

9b. Length of large curve | 9 | . | 4 | 2 | 4 | 7 | 7 | 8 | cm

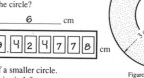

Figure Q

9c. The small curve is part of a smaller circle. What is the diameter of this circle?

Diameter of small circle   __3 cm__
Put in units.

9d. Length of small curve   __4.712389__   cm
Copy window.

9e. Length of both straight parts   __3__   cm

9f. Perimeter | 1 | 7 | . | 1 | 3 | 7 | 1 | 6 | 7 | cm

A half-strip is cut in half as shown below. One of these new pieces is called a quarter-strip.

Figure R

10. Use the following steps to find the perimeter of the quarter-strip.

10a. The large curve is part of the larger circle. What is the diameter of this circle?

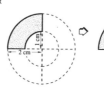

Figure S

Diameter   __4__   cm

10b. Four large curves build the circumference of the large circle. What is the length of the large curve?

Length of large curve | 3 | . | 1 | 4 | 1 | 5 | 9 | 2 | 7 | cm

10c. The small curve is part of a circle. What is the diameter of this circle?

Diameter   __2__   cm

10d. Find the length of the small curve. Remember, four of these curves build the circumference.

Length of small curve | 1 | . | 5 | 7 | 0 | 7 | 9 | 6 | 3 | cm

10e. Length of both straight parts   __2__   cm

10f. Perimeter of figure | 6 | . | 7 | 1 | 2 | 3 | 8 | 9 | cm

---

11. Estimate the perimeter of the following quarter-strip.

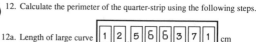

Figure T

Estimated perimeter   __24 - 28__   cm

12. Calculate the perimeter of the quarter-strip using the following steps.

12a. Length of large curve | 1 | 2 | . | 5 | 6 | 6 | 3 | 7 | 1 | cm

12b. Length of small curve | 7 | . | 8 | 5 | 3 | 9 | 8 | 1 | 6 | cm

12c. Length of both straight parts   __6__   cm

12d. Perimeter   __26.4__   cm
R to the nearest tenth.
Compare with your estimate.

Homework 8: Perimeter of Pieces

1a. The circumference of a circle is 24.4 cm.
A semicircle is cut from this circle as
shown in the sketch at the right.
Circle the best estimate for the
perimeter of this semicircle.

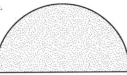

5 cm   10 cm   ⟨20 cm⟩   25 cm

Figure U

1b. How did you choose your estimate? **It could not be 5 cm or 10 cm**
because the curved part is 12.2 cm already. It could not be
25 cm because it is bigger than the circumference of the circle.

2. The following figure is built from two small, congruent semicircles and
two large, congruent semicircles. The diameter of the small semicircle
is 3 cm. The diameter of the large semicircle is 5 cm. Calculate the
perimeter of the figure using the steps below.

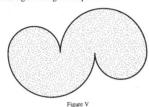

Figure V

2a. Total length of small curves | 9 | . | 4 | 2 | 4 | 7 | 7 | 8 | cm

2b. Total length of large curves | 1 | 5 | . | 7 | 0 | 7 | 9 | 6 | 3 | cm

2c. Perimeter | 2 | 5 | . | 1 | 3 | 2 | 7 | 4 | 1 | cm

Maneuvers with Circles   © *David A. Page*

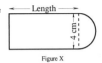

3. The sketch at the
right shows a
basketball key.
Calculate the
perimeter of the
basketball key.

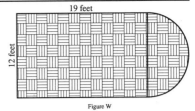

Figure W

Perimeter | 6 | 8 | . | 8 | 4 | 9 | 5 | 5 | 6 | ft

★ 4. The sketch at the right is built from a rectangle
and a semicircle. The perimeter of the entire
figure is 26.3 cm. Calculate the length of the
rectangle.

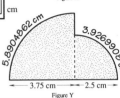

Figure X

Length | 8 | . | 0 | 0 | 8 | 4 | 0 | 7 | 3 | cm

5. The figure at the right is
built from two quarter-circles.
Find its perimeter using the
following steps. Label each
part as you go along.

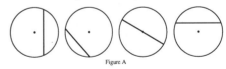

Figure Y

5a. Length of large curve | 5 | . | 8 | 9 | 0 | 4 | 8 | 6 | 2 | cm

5b. Length of small curve __3.9269908__ cm
    Copy window.

5c. Length of straight parts ____7.5____ cm

5d. Perimeter | 1 | 7 | . | 3 | 1 | 7 | 4 | 7 | 7 | cm

© *David A. Page*   *Maneuvers with Circles*

6a. Estimate the perimeter of the half-strip at the right.

Estimate ____15 - 19____ cm

6b. Calculate the perimeter of the half-strip.

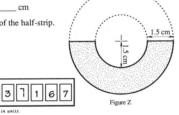

Figure Z

Perimeter | 1 | 7 | . | 1 | 3 | 7 | 1 | 6 | 7 | cm
Put in units.

7. Calculate the perimeter
of the quarter-strip at
the right.

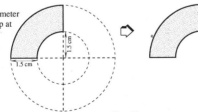

Figure AA

Perimeter | 1 | 0 | . | 0 | 6 | 8 | 5 | 8 | 3 | cm

8. The figure at the right is built from the figures
in Problems 6 and 7. Calculate the perimeter
of the figure.

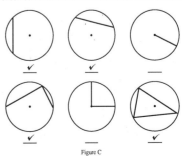

Perimeter | 2 | 4 | . | 2 | 0 | 5 | 7 | 5 | cm

Figure BB

Maneuvers with Circles   © *David A. Page*

---

9. Circles, Chords, and the Pythagorean Theorem

The lines in the circles in Figure A are *chords*.

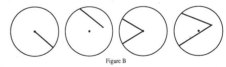

Figure A

The lines in the circles in Figure B are *not* chords.

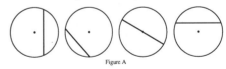

Figure B

1. Describe a chord. **A segment inside a circle that connects two**
points on the rim of the circle.

2. Place a check below each circle that has one or more chords drawn in it.

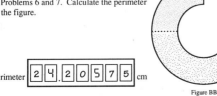

Figure C

© *David A. Page*   *Maneuvers with Circles*

3. Measure the length of the chord at the right to the nearest 0.1 cm.

Measured length   <u>4.6, 4.7, 4.8</u>   cm

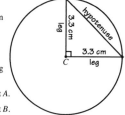

4. Point *C* is the center of the circle. Points *A* and *B* have been specially placed so that you can build a right triangle in the circle. Use the following steps to build Right Triangle *ACB*.

   a. Draw a line from the center to Point *A*.

   b. Draw a line from the center to Point *B*.

   c. With the corner of a sheet of paper, check that Angle *C* is a right angle. Draw a box in the 90° angle.

Figure D

5a. Label each side of the triangle in Figure D with either "leg" or "hypotenuse."

5b. The radius of the circle is 3.3 cm. Label the radii above. Notice the legs of the triangle are also radii of the circle, and the hypotenuse of the triangle is a chord of the circle.

6. How long is each leg of the triangle?

6a. Leg *AC* <u>3.3</u> cm

6b. Leg *CB* <u>3.3</u> cm

7. How long is the measured hypotenuse of the triangle in Figure D?

Hypotenuse <u>4.6, 4.7, 4.8</u> cm
<small>Should agree with Problem 3.</small>

Now let's look at how to calculate the actual length of a hypotenuse when the length of both legs are given.

8. The legs of Right Triangle *DEF* are 3 cm and 4 cm long. Measure the length of the hypotenuse to the nearest whole cm.

Measured hypotenuse <u>5</u> cm

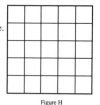

Figure E

Pythagoras, a famous Greek mathematician and philosopher, knew a way to calculate the hypotenuse of any right triangle if he knew the length of the two legs.

Pythagoras found the length of the hypotenuse by building squares along each of the sides of the triangle as shown at the right.

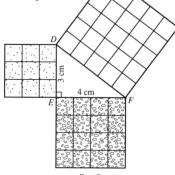

Figure F

Pythagoras noticed that the area of the square built along one leg plus the area of the square built along the other leg equaled the area of the square built along the hypotenuse. This is called the ***Pythagorean Theorem***.

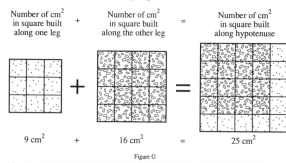

Number of cm² in square built along one leg	+	Number of cm² in square built along the other leg	=	Number of cm² in square built along hypotenuse
9 cm²	+	16 cm²	=	25 cm²

Figure G

---

9. The area of the large square built along the hypotenuse is 25 cm². The side length of the square is also the hypotenuse of the triangle. Press $\boxed{25}$ $\boxed{\sqrt{x}}$ to calculate the hypotenuse of Triangle *DEF*.

Hypotenuse *DF* <u>5</u> cm
<small>Compare with Problem 8.</small>

Figure H

10a. Triangle *GHJ* below is the same triangle you built in the circle on page 124. Use the following steps to calculate the length of *GJ*.

10b. To calculate the area of the square built on Leg *GH*, press $\boxed{3.3}$ $\boxed{x^2}$.

Area <u>10.89</u> cm²

10c. To calculate the area of the square built along Leg *HJ*, press $\boxed{3.3}$ $\boxed{x^2}$.

Area <u>10.89 cm²</u>
<small>Put in units.</small>

10d. Add the area of the two smaller squares to find the area of the large square.

Area of <u>21.78 cm²</u>
<small>Put in units.</small>

10e. Now take the square root to find the length of Hypotenuse *GJ*.

Hypotenuse *GJ* $\boxed{4}.\boxed{6}\boxed{6}\boxed{5}\boxed{9}\boxed{0}\boxed{4}\boxed{8}$ cm

10f. Hypotenuse *GJ* is the same length as Chord *AB* on page 124. Was your measurement on page 124 close to the calculated answer?

Answer <u>Yes</u>
<small>Yes or No</small>

Figure J

---

11. Show that the area of the squares built along the legs is equal to the area of the one large square built along the hypotenuse using the steps in Problems 11 and 12.

   a. Build a square along each leg of the right triangle below.

   b. Shade or color one of the squares.

   c. Cut out the triangle and the squares.

   d. Glue the triangle on a different piece of paper.

   e. Cut and arrange the squares to build a larger square along the hypotenuse of the triangle.

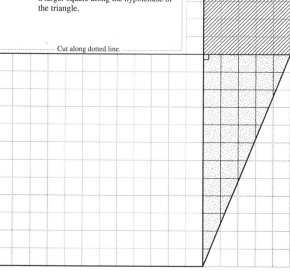

    ········· Cut along dotted line. ·········

Figure K

Use your figure from Problem 11 to complete the following problems.

12a. Area of square built on one leg _____25_____ cm²

12b. Area of square built on other leg ____144 cm²____
      Put in units.

12c. Area of square built on hypotenuse ____169 cm²____
      Put in units.

12d. Length of hypotenuse _____13_____ cm

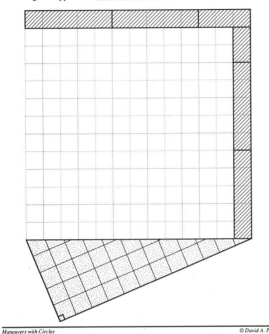

13. Measure Chord *KM* to the nearest 0.1 cm.

   Answer ____6.2, 6.3, 6.4____ cm

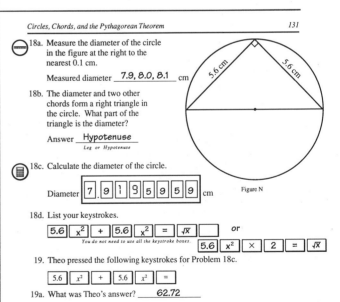

Figure L

14. Since Chord *KM* is also the hypotenuse of a right triangle, Dennis used the Pythagorean Theorem to calculate the length of Chord *KM*.

Dennis pressed the following keystrokes.

Area of Square Built along Hypotenuse

Side Length of Square
or
Length of Hypotenuse

14a. Put a loop around the keystrokes that give the area of the square built along one of the legs.

14b. Put a box around the keystrokes that give the area of the square built along the other leg.

14c. Use Dennis' keystrokes to calculate the length of Chord *KM*.

Chord *KM* [6].[3][6][3][9][6][1] cm
Compare with your measurement.

15a. Label each side of Triangle *RQP* below with either "leg" or "hypotenuse."

15b. Are the legs of the triangle also the radii of the circle? ____No____
     Yes or No

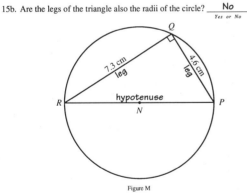

Figure M

15c. Hypotenuse *RP* is also a chord of the circle. What is special about this chord?

It is the diameter of the circle.

16. Measure Chord *RP* to the nearest 0.1 cm.

   Measured length __8.5, 8.6, 8.7 cm__
   Put in units.

17a. Fill in the keystrokes to find the length of Chord *RP* in one run.

17b. Use the Pythagorean Theorem to calculate the length of Chord *RP*.

   Chord *RP* ____8.6____ cm
   R to the nearest tenth.

18a. Measure the diameter of the circle in the figure at the right to the nearest 0.1 cm.

   Measured diameter ____7.9, 8.0, 8.1____ cm

18b. The diameter and two other chords form a right triangle in the circle. What part of the triangle is the diameter?

   Answer ____Hypotenuse____
   Leg or Hypotenuse

Figure N

18c. Calculate the diameter of the circle.

   Diameter [7].[9][1][9][5][9][5][9] cm

18d. List your keystrokes.

   [5.6][x²][+][5.6][x²][=][√x][ ]   or
   You do not need to use all the keystroke boxes.
                          [5.6][x²][×][2][=][√x]

19. Theo pressed the following keystrokes for Problem 18c.

   [5.6][x²][+][5.6][x²][=]

19a. What was Theo's answer? ____62.72____

19b. What did Theo forget to do? __Take the square root.__

20. Rodney pressed the following keystrokes for Problem 18c.

   [5.6][x²][+][5.6][x²][√x]

20a. What was Rodney's answer? ____5.6____

20b. What did Rodney forget to do? __He did not press [=] between__
    [x²] __and__ [√x].

Homework 9: Circles, Chords, and the Pythagorean Theorem

1a. Two radii of the circle and Chord *SU* form a right triangle in the sketch at the right. Calculate the length of Chord *SU*.

Answer ___**100**___ cm
<small>You'll know.</small>

1b. List your keystrokes.

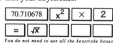

70.710678	x^2	×	2
=	√x		

<small>You do not need to use all the keystroke boxes.</small>

2a. Label the "legs" of Triangle *VWX* in the sketch below.

2b. Use the Pythagorean Theorem to calculate the length of Diameter *VX* in the sketch below. Point *Y* is the center of the circle.

Diameter | 8 | . | 1 | 7 | 8 | 0 | 5 | 5 | 4 | cm

2c. Find the radius of the circle.

Radius ___**4.1**___ cm
<small>R to the nearest tenth.</small>

2d. Label all the radii shown in Figure Q.

3a. Label the "hypotenuse" of Triangle *VYZ*.

3b. Calculate the length of Chord *VZ*.

Chord *VZ* ___**5.8**___ cm
<small>R to the nearest tenth.</small>

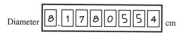
Figure P

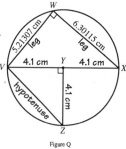
Figure Q

---

4. Triangles *GKJ* and *HKJ* are congruent in the sketch at the right. The length of Chord *GH* is 65 cm. Label the "legs" of the two smaller triangles. Use the Pythagorean Theorem to find the radius of the circle.

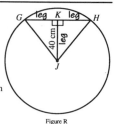
Figure R

Radius | 5 | 1 | . | 5 | 3 | 8 | 8 | 2 | cm

5a. Four chords build a square in the figure at the right. Measure each chord to the nearest 0.1 cm to find the perimeter.

Measured perimeter ___**16.4 cm - 17.2 cm**___
<small>Put in units.</small>

5b. Use the radii of the circle to calculate the perimeter of the square. Show your work.

$3 \ x^2 + 3 \ x^2 = $ √x
One chord is 4.2426407 cm
4.2426407 × 4 = 16.970563

Perimeter ___**17.0**___ cm
<small>R to the nearest tenth.
Compare with your measurement.</small>

Figure S

★ 6. The sketch at the right is built from a square and a circle. The radius of the circle is 78.488853 cm. Calculate the length of the square's diagonal. Show your work.

Diameter: 78.488853 × 2 = 156.97771 cm
156.97771 x^2 + 156.97771 x^2 = √x

Diagonal ___**222**___ cm
<small>You'll know.</small>

Figure T

---

7. The sketch at the right shows part of a baseball field. This part is built from a right triangle and a semicircle. The side length of the triangle is 120 feet. Calculate the perimeter using the following steps.

7a. Find the length of the dotted hypotenuse.

Answer ___**169.70563**___ ft
<small>Copy window.</small>

7b. Calculate the length of the curve.

Length | 2 | 6 | 6 | . | 5 | 7 | 2 | 9 | 8 | ft

7c. Length of straight sides ___**240**___ ft

7d. Calculate the perimeter.

Perimeter | 5 | 0 | 6 | . | 5 | 7 | 2 | 9 | 8 | ft

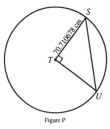
Figure U

8. The radius of the large circle below is 3.1 cm and Point *A* marks its center. The radius of the small circle is 1.8 cm and Point *C* marks its center. Use the Pythagorean Theorem and the following steps to find the lengths of Chords *ED* and *EB*.

8a. Label the radii in Figure V.

8b. Calculate the length of Chord *ED*.

Chord *ED* ___**2.5455844**___ cm
<small>Copy window.</small>

8c. Calculate the length of Chord *EB*.

Chord *EB* ___**4.384062**___ cm
<small>Copy window.</small>

9a. Is Line *BD* a chord of one of the circles? ___**No**___
<small>Yes or No</small>

Why or why not? ___**It does not connect 2 points on the rim of one circle.**___

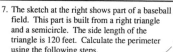
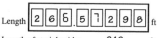
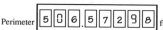
Figure V

9b. Find the length of Line *BD*.

Answer ___**1.8384776**___ cm
<small>Measure to check.</small>

---

10. Grazing Goats

A farmer tied his goat, Billy, to a stake so that the goat could graze. A long rope or *tether* was used to tie the goat to the stake. Two days later, the farmer noticed Billy had eaten all the grass within a circular region.

1. The sketch at the right shows the circular region of grass that Billy ate. Notice Billy's tether is 15 feet long. What is the area of this circular region in square feet (ft^2)?

Area | 7 | 0 | 6 | . | 8 | 5 | 8 | 3 | 5 | ft^2

Figure A

2. Since Billy ate all the grass in this circular region, the farmer moved him to a place with fresh grass. In the sketch at the right, Billy is tied to a fence post with the same tether. Billy can only graze on one side of the fence. His grazing region is a semicircle. What is the area of this semicircular region?

Area ___**353.42917**___ ft^2
<small>Copy window.</small>

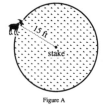
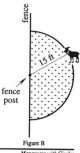
Figure B

---

3. The next day, the farmer moved Billy into a yard enclosed by a rectangular fence. He tied Billy to a stake in the corner of the yard (so he wouldn't eat the petunias).

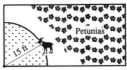

Figure C

3a. What part of a circle can Billy graze?

Answer __quarter-circle__   ($\frac{1}{4}$ of a circle)

 3b. Calculate the area of the grass Billy can graze.

Area __176.71459__ ft^2

Copy window.

3c. Compare your answers to Problems 1, 2, and 3b.

4. Billy is now tethered to the corner of a small rectangular barn. The following sketch shows the region that Billy can graze.

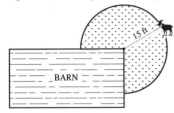

Figure D

4a. Circle the name of the largest region Billy can graze.

quarter-circle   semicircle   ($\frac{3}{4}$ circle)   full circle

4b. Calculate the area that Billy can graze.

Area | 5 | 3 | 0 | . | 1 | 4 | 3 | 7 | 6 | ft^2

---

5. Billy is attached to a stake at the corner of a barn in Figure E.

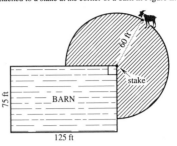

Figure E

When the tether is tight, it acts like a large compass. Use your compass and the following steps to draw a picture of the area where Billy can graze.

   a. Place the sharp point of your compass on the stake in Figure E.

b. Place the pencil on the end of the tether.

c. Draw the part of the circle where Billy can graze. (Beware! The tether cannot go inside the barn.)

d. Compare your drawing with the picture at the right.

6. Shade the region Billy can graze in Figure E.

7. Calculate the area that Billy can graze. Show your work.

$60 \ x^2 \times \pi \div 4 \times 3 =$

Area | 8 | 4 | 8 | 2 | . | 3 | ft^2

R to the nearest tenth.

So far, the tether has been shorter than the sides of the barn. The picture at the right shows what happens when the tether is longer than the side of the barn. When the goat turns the corner of the barn, the tether bends.

8. Now Billy's tether is attached to the barn at Point B. The sketch at the right shows the area that Billy can graze. Billy's tether is 100 feet. Notice that it is longer than one side of the barn. The length of CD is the radius of a quarter-circle. Find the length of CD using the steps below. Label CD on the figure.

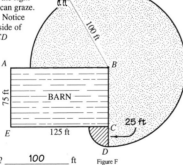

Figure F

8a. What is the length of BD? __100__ ft

8b. What is the length of BC? __75__ ft

8c. What is the length of CD? __25__ ft

Don't forget to show this length on the figure.

9a. Calculate the area of the region. __23,561.945__ ft^2

Copy window.

9b. Calculate the area of the ///////, region. __490.87385__ ft^2

Copy window.

9c. Add the two areas to find the total grazing area in Figure F.

Area | 2 | 4 | 0 | 5 | 2 | . | 8 | 1 | 9 | ft^2

---

10. Now Billy is on an even longer tether. The sketch at the right shows the area that Billy can graze. Billy's tether is 150 feet. Notice that it is longer than both sides of the barn.

The lengths of DE and AF are the radii of the quarter-circles. Find DE and AF using the following steps. Write these lengths on the figure.

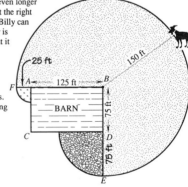

Figure G

10a. What is the length of BE? __150__ ft

10b. What is the length of DE? __75__ ft

10c. What is the length of BF? __150__ ft

10d. What is the length of AF? __25__ ft

11a. Calculate the area of the region. __53,014.376__ ft^2

Copy window.

11b. Calculate the area of the region. __4,417.8647__ ft^2

Copy window.

11c. Calculate the area of the region. __490.87385__ ft^2

Copy window.

11d. Add the three areas to find the total grazing area in Figure G.

Area | 5 | 7 | 9 | 2 | 3 | . | 1 | 1 | 5 | ft^2

12. Use the steps below to calculate Billy's grazing area in the sketch at the right. Don't press [ACQN] after you start or you will erase the memory.

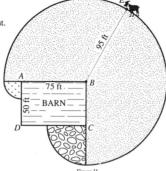

Figure H

12a. Calculate the area of the ░░░ region. __21,264.655__ ft² [STO]
Copy window.

12b. Calculate the area of the ∴·∴ region. __314.15927__ ft² [SUM]
Copy window.

12c. Calculate the area of the ◌◌ region. __1,590.4313__ ft² [SUM]
Copy window.

12d. What is the total area the goat can graze? Press [RCL].

Total area | 2 | 3 | 1 | 6 | 9 | . | 2 | 4 | 6 | ft²

13. Use your compass and the following steps to draw the area the goat can graze on the *next page*.

13a. Use your ruler to extend Side *AB* to the left of *A*. You can extend the side to any length.

```
        - - - - A       B
                D       C
```

13b. Now extend Side *BC* down below *C*.

```
        A     B
        D   C
            :
```

Figure J

13c. Put the compass point on *B* and the compass pencil on *E*. Draw three-fourths of a circle with a radius of 90 feet.

13d. Put the compass point on *C*. Move the compass pencil to make the new radius on the goat's path directly below *C*. Draw a quarter-circle.

13e. How long is the radius of this quarter-circle? __40__ ft

13f. Put the compass point on *A* and move the compass pencil to the new radius on the goat's path. Draw the small quarter-circle.

13g. How long is the radius of this small quarter-circle? __15__ ft

13h. Shade each of the three regions with a different color or design.

14. Calculate the area of the three shaded regions. Use your calculator's memory to find the total area.

14a. Area of three-quarter circle __19,085.175__ ft²
Copy window.

14b. Area of larger quarter-circle __1,256.6371__ ft²
Copy window.

14c. Area of smaller quarter-circle __176.71459__ ft²
Copy window.

14d. Total area | 2 | 0 | 5 | 1 | 8 | . | 5 | 2 | 7 | ft²

15a. Imagine a 150-foot tether is fastened at Point *B*. First extend the sides of the barn in the following sketch. Then use the scale line at the bottom of the page to set your compass for 150 feet. On the scale line, put the compass point on the 0-foot mark and the pencil on the 150-foot mark.

15b. Draw the large three-quarter circle at Point *B*. Draw the two quarter-circles at Corners *A* and *C* and label each radius.

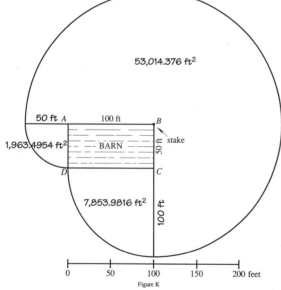

53,014.376 ft²

50 ft *A*   100 ft   *B*
1,963.4954 ft²   BARN   50 ft stake
             D   *C*

7,853.9816 ft²   100 ft

```
|----|----|----|----|----|
0    50   100  150  200 feet
          Figure K
```

15c. Use your calculator's memory to find the grazing area. Label the picture with the area of each piece.

15d. What is the total grazing area? | 6 | 2 | 8 | 3 | 1 | . | 8 | 5 | 3 | ft²

---

*16a. Now there is a 50-foot fence connected to the barn. The tether is still 150 feet and is fastened at Point *B*. Extend *AB* and *CE*. Draw the region that Billy can graze at Point *B*, Point *A*, and Point *E*. Hint: One of the grazing areas is a semicircle.

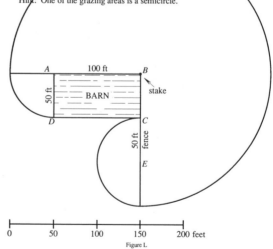

A   100 ft   *B*
                     stake
50 ft   BARN
D   *C*
            50 ft
            fence
            E

```
|----|----|----|----|----|
0    50   100  150  200 feet
          Figure L
```

16b. Do you think Billy will reach more or less grass than in Problem 15?

Answer __Less__
More or Less

Tell why you think so. __His tether will get caught on the fence.__
__He won't be able to reach as much grass.__

16c. Calculate the total grazing area. Use the calculator's memory.

Total area | 5 | 8 | 9 | 0 | 4 | . | 9 | ft²
R to the nearest tenth.
Compare with Problem 15d.

---

17. The following picture shows a field at the Guzzling Goat Estate. An old, abandoned log cabin sits in the middle of the field. Each dot on the map represents an oak tree. A fence protects the garden from the goat.

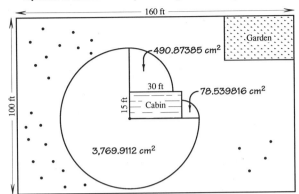

490.87385 cm²

78.539816 cm²

3,769.9112 cm²

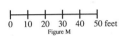

0 10 20 30 40 50 feet
Figure M

17a. A farmer wants to attach his goat to a corner of the cabin with a 40-foot rope. Decide which corner gives the goat the most grazing area. Draw a dot at that corner.

17b. Draw the region the goat can graze.

17c. How much area can the goat graze? Show your work on the sketch.

Area __4,339.3249__ ft²
Copy window.

18a. The square barn in the following sketch has a side length of 100 feet. A goat is fastened to a stake with a 200-foot tether. Draw the region that the goat can graze and label the radius of each region. Extend all the sides of the barn.

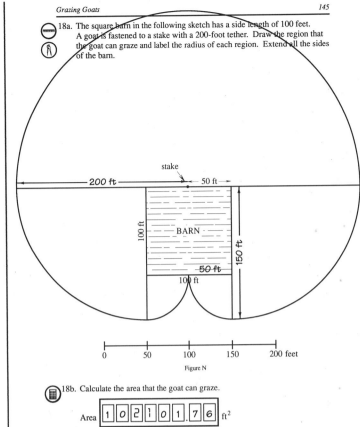

stake

200 ft   50 ft

100 ft   BARN   150 ft

50 ft
100 ft

0   50   100   150   200 feet
Figure N

18b. Calculate the area that the goat can graze.

Area [1][0][2][1][0][1][.][7][6] ft²

19a. A 50-foot fence and a 40-foot fence meet at a right angle. A goat is fastened to a stake where the fences meet. If the goat's tether is 60 feet long, what is the area of grass he can reach? Draw the area.

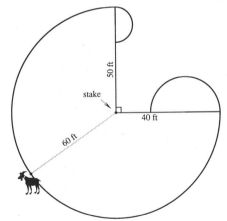

50 ft
stake
40 ft
60 ft

Figure P

19b. Calculate the area of the region the goat grazes.

Area [9][2][6][7][.][6][9][8][3] ft²

* 20. Calculate the perimeter of the region the goat grazes.

Perimeter [3][7][6][.][9][9][1][1][2] ft If fences are included, 436.99112 ft

21a. A 50-foot fence and a 40-foot fence meet at a right angle. A goat is fastened where the fences meet. If the goat's tether is 61.890377 feet long, what is the area of grass he can reach? Draw the area.

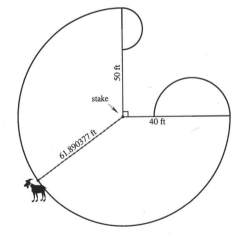

50 ft
stake
40 ft
61.890377 ft

Figure Q

61.890377	x²	×	π	÷	4	×	3	=	STO
61.890377	−	50	=	x²	×	π	÷	2	=	SUM
61.890377	−	40	=	x²	×	π	÷	2	=	SUM
									EXC

21b. Calculate the area. Show your work.

Area __10,000__ ft²
You'll know.

22. A goat is tethered to a triangular-shaped fence in the following sketch. Draw and shade the regi~~~~~~at is able to graze. Remember to extend the sides of~~~~~~essary.

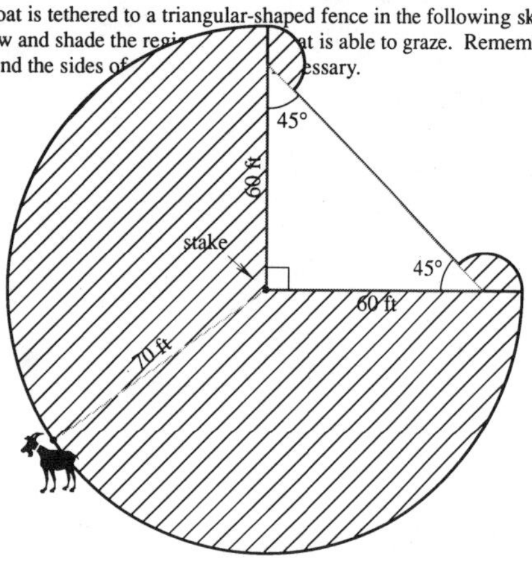

Figure R

23. The area that the goat grazes includes a three-quarter circle and two small sectors. Use the following steps to calculate the area that the goat is able to graze.

23a. Area of three-quarter circle __11,545.353__ ft^2
       Copy window.

23b. Radius of small sector _____10_____ ft

23c. The central angle of the small sector and the 45° angle form a straight line. Find the degree measure of the small sector.

     Degree measure _____135_____ °

23d. Area of one small sector __117.80972__ ft^2
       Copy window.

23e. Grazing area | 1 | 1 | 7 | 8 | 0 | . | 9 | 7 | 2 | ft^2